Human-Centric Machine Vision

Human-Centric Machine Vision

Editor

Asa Bensten

scitus
academics

Human-Centric Machine Vision
Edited by **Asa Bensten**

ISBN: 978-1-68117-265-1
Library of Congress Control Number: 2016937433

SCITUS Academics LLC,
www.scitusacademics.com
Box No. 4766, 616 Corporate Way,
Suite 2, Valley Cottage,
NY 10989

Notice

Printed in United States of America on Acid Free Paper

Preface

Machine vision (MV) is the technology and methods used to automatically inspect and analyze images for applications such as automatic inspection, process control and industry robot guidance. Machine vision is the ability of a computer to "see." A machine vision system uses one or more video cameras, digital analog conversion and digital signals processing. The resulting data is sent to the robot or computer controller. The complexity of the machine vision is similar to the recognition of voices. The machine's vision is wide. It has to do with computer vision, but it is different from computer vision. Machine vision methods are defined both as the process for the definition and creation of a MV solution and as the technical process during the solution process. Algorithms for the processing of visual information have recently evolved considerably, offering efficient and effective solutions to the variability and complexity of real world environments. These achievements lead to the development of machine vision systems that overwhelmed the distinctive industrial requirements, in which environments are controlled and tasks are very precise, in order to use state-of-the-art solutions to meet people's everyday needs.

This book, Human-Centric Machine Vision, can help solve the problems posed by the needs of our society, such as safety and security, health, medical imaging and the human machine interface. Changing, impulsive and multifaceted situations and the presence of people need to be addressed in suchtype of solicitations.

Table of Contents

1
CHAPTER
DESIGN OF OMNI-DIRECTIONAL TILT SENSOR BASED ON MACHINE VISION

Yiping Tang[1], Caiguo Chen[2]

[1]*College of Information Engineering, Zhejiang University of Technology, Hangzhou, China*

[2]*College of Computer Science, Zhejiang University of Technology, Hangzhou, China*

ABSTRACT

This paper presents a new Omni-Directional Tilt Sensor (ODTS), which consists of the LED light, transparent cone-shaped closed container, mercury, camera, embedded systems and so on. The volume of the mercury in the container is equal to half of the container's. When the detected surface is horizontal, the shape of mercury in the image captured by the camera is a black disc since the mercury is lightproof. When the detected surface tilts, the mercury flows and the mercury surface always maintains horizontally due to the gravity force of the earth. At this time, some area of the transparent cone-shaped closed container is not shaded by mercury and the border of the mercury's shape in the captured image is a half circle and a half ellipse. Thus there is a translucent crescent-shaped area in the image. With analyzing this area by the specific algorithm based on machine vision, the tilt angle and directional angle can be obtained. The experimental results show that the ODTS proposed has some advantages, such as simple maintenance, high precision, wide range, low cost, real-time, reliability and high visualization.

Keywords: ODTS, Machine Vision, Digital Image Processing, Embedded System, Tilt Angle and Tilt Directional Angle

1. INTRODUCTION

Tilt sensor is mainly applied to measuring the horizontality of a system and widely used in construction of bridges, laying of railway, civil engineering, oil drilling, aviation and maritime, industrial automation, intelligent platform, machining and other important fields. There are several kinds of commercial sensor for tilt angle measurement, which are available in the market. It mainly can be divided into three kinds solid pendulum [1,2], liquid pendulum [3] and gas pendulum [4] based on different working principles. They all have their advantages and disadvantages in terms of their working principles. In the gravitational field, the sensitive medium of solid pendulum is the weight of pendulum, while liquid pendulum's is electrolyte and gas pendulum's is gas. With a lot number of applications, the research of tile sensors of solid pendulum has been quite mature, but it is easy to be interfered by the external factors, such as the vibration caused by mechanical shock. The tilt sensor of liquid pendulum, however, has many advantages, such as high sensitivity, corrosion and moisture resistance, etc. But its fatal weakness is that its working performance is easily affected by the change of temperature and this fatal weakness limits its development and applications. The tilt sensor of gas pendulum has a simple structure, strong resistance to vibration and shock, but it can be greatly affected by environmental temperature and is low in measuring precision. In addition, some experts proposed a method to detect tilt angle according to the images [5]. However, it can only get the one-dimensional tilt angle because only the position of bubbles is detected.

The literature [6] has proposed a vertical-pendulumbased fiber Bragg Grating tilt sensor, which can detect the magnitude as well as the direction of the inclination from the horizontal direction. Fiber Bragg Grating (FBG) sensors is based on the modulation of the reflection wavelength of FBGs in response to temperature and strain. Compared to other types of fiber-optic sensors, FBG sensors have advantages of being inherently self-referencing and the capability in multiplexing a large number of FBG sensing elements. The sensor encodes the tilt angle with the wavelength separation between two FBGs to overcome the problem of temperature cross-sensitivity. Also it has high accuracy and accuracy of 0.1°and resolution of better than 0.007°can be achieved. But it is hard in maintenance and is not an optical system. Thus it can't give us direct visual results.

The literature [7] has proposed an optical sensor including an opto-electronic sensor with laser, optical components and image sensor. Its working principle is based on optical interferometry. And it has high measurement accuracy and is insensitive to magnetic environment. Also it can measure two axes at the same time. But because the liquid medium is oil and it can wet the glass, the quality of captured image may be affected thus lead to the measurement error.

Here we propose the Omni-Directional Tilt Sensor (ODTS) based on machine vision. In terms of tilt perception, it belongs to the tilt sensor of liquid pendulum. Different from existing tilt sensor of liquid pendulum, the liquid medium of ODTS is mercury whose advantages include avoiding wetting the glass and plastic, light-proof, good conductivity, etc. It minimizes the temperature interferences to the ODTS and can be used in the environment of large temperature range. Also the energy saving design is added to the sensor using the conductivity of mercury. The tilt angle and tilt directional angle is obtained by analyzing the image formed by the mercury in the container in the way of digital image processing. Thus it avoids some indirect measurement segments that may result in unnecessary measurement error. A prototype sensor is designed and experimental results show the tilt angle relative to the sea level can be detected at the accuracy of 1°and at the resolution of 0.01°

2. DESIGN OF THE ODTS

The ODTS based on machine vision consists of shell of the ODTS, LED light, transparent cone-shaped closed container, mercury , camera , embedded systems, power supply and compass, showed in **Figure 1** ("1" is the shell of the ODTS, "2" is the LED light, "3" is the transparent cone-shaped closed container, "4" is mercury, "5" is the camera, "6" is the embedded system, "7" is the power supply, "8" is the compass). The power supply provides the LED light and the embedded systems electricity. Then the embedded systems offer electricity to the camera through USB interface. And the transparent coneshaped closed container is composed of two cones with the same size and shape in the way back to back. It is fixed in the middle of the shell of ODTS and is always parallel with the detected surface, above of the container is the LED light and below is the camera. The LED light, facing right down to the transparent cone-shaped closed container, projects the white light. The camera captures pictures of the transparent cone-shaped container. At the same time, the embedded system reads the data of pictures from the camera through the USB.

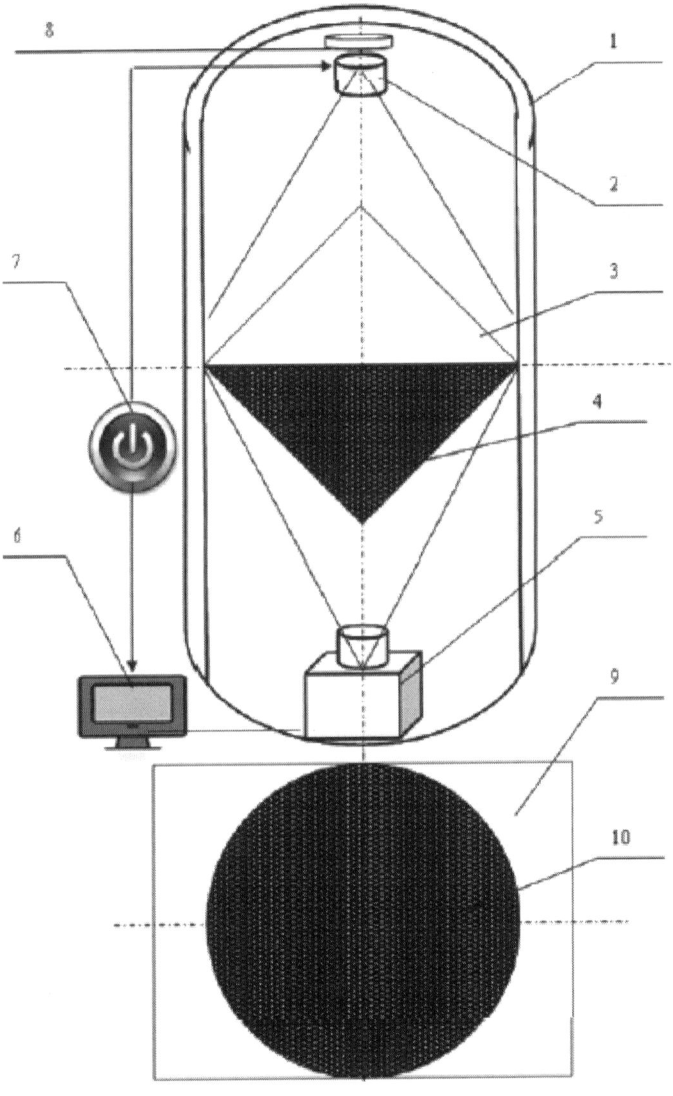

Figure 1. Structure of ODTS.

2.1. Design of the Transparent Cone-Shaped Container

When assembling the transparent con-shaped container, the mercury is poured into it and the volume of mercury is half of the container's. According to physical principle, when the ODTS is in the level state, because the light is shaded by the mercury in the transparent cone-shaped container, the camera can't catch the transmitted light penetrating the container from the LED light, showed in **Figure 1** ("9" is the captured image by camera, "10" is the image of the transparent cone-shaped closed container). When the surface to be detected tilts, the mercury flows and the mercury surface always maintains horizontally due to the gravity force of the earth. Because the transparent cone-shaped container is composed of two cones with the same size and shape, the volume of mercury flowing out of one cone is equal to the volume of mercury flowing into the other one and the level surface always passes the central point of the transparent coneshaped container. In other words, the level surface of mercury in the state of tilt rotates around Y axis. Thus some area of the transparent cone-shaped container between the LED light and the camera is in the state of non-shelter, showed in the **Figure 2**. From the capturing angle of camera, the shape of mercury is a disc in the projection image if the tilt condition doesn't happen, however, it would be a half-circle and a half-ellipse if the tilt condition happens. The major axis of ellipse is equal to the radius of disc and the tilt angle has functional relationship with length of the minor axis of ellipse. The smaller the minor axis of ellipse is, the bigger the tilt angle is. And the tilt directional angle is in the negative direction of ellipse's minor axis.

The resolution of the tilt angle is related to the radius R and the cone angle α of the transparent cone-shaped container. The equation of their relation is below.

$$\theta = ctg^{-1}\left[\left(R/\delta - 1\right) \times ctg\left(a\right)\right]. \quad (1)$$

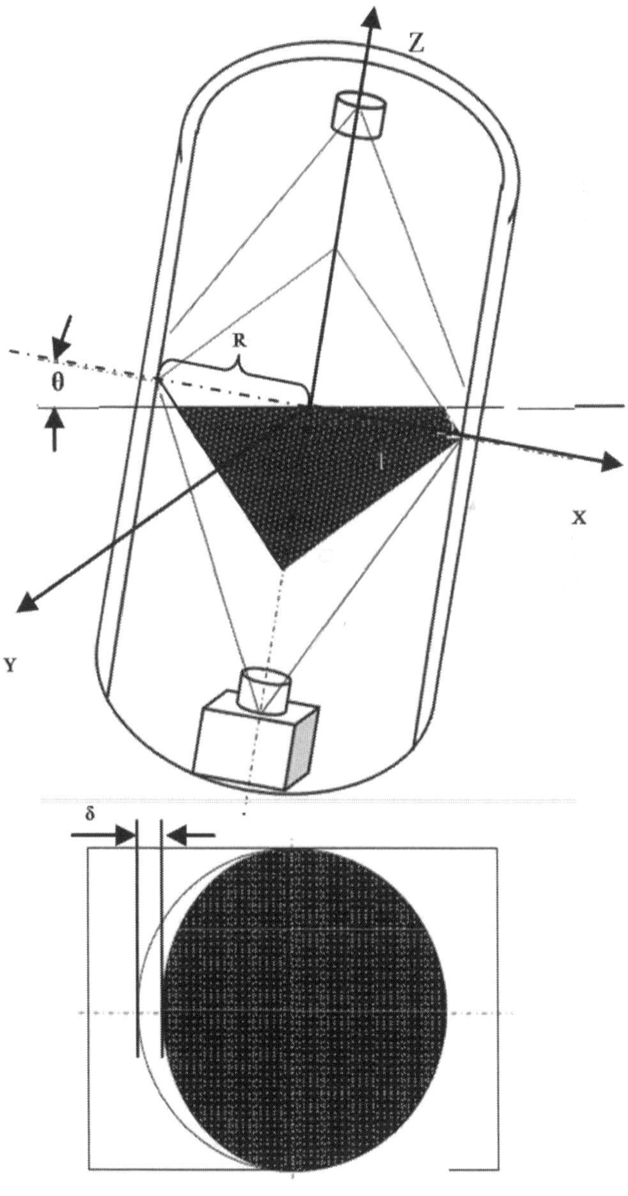

Figure 2. Image in state of tilt.

In the equation, R is the radius of the transparent coneshaped container, α is the cone angle of it, δ is the middle width of the crescent-shaped translucent part, θ is the tilt angle.

According to the Equation (1), the longer the radius R of the transparent cone-shaped container is, the higher the resolution of tilt angle θ is, and the resolution of tilt angle θ has functional relationship with the cone angle α. Generally speaking, the pixels of the transparent coneshaped container's radius R in the captured image is up to the vision range of camera and in this paper, the radius R of the transparent cone-shaped container is 38 mm and possesses 188 pixels in the captured image. Also the cone angle α is determined by the actual level measurement range. The top of **Figure 3** is several cones with different angles, the bottom of it is the curve diagram of the relationship between the middle width δ of the crescent-shaped translucent part and the tilt angle θ under the condition that the radius R of the transparent cone-shaped container is 38mm and the cone angle α is 15°, 30°, 45°, 60° and 75°. **Figure 3** shows that the small tilt angle θ has high resolution when the cone angle α is 15°. Therefor the choosing or design of the cone angle α of transparent cone-shaped container is determined by the actual measurement precision.

2.2. Liquid Medium for ODTS

Mercury is suitable to be the liquid medium in the ODTS with the advantages of not wetting the glass and plastic, light-proof, good conductivity, etc. Because mercury keeps liquid state in a large temperature range (–38~ + 356.66°C), the ODTS with mercury as the liquid medium has great adaptability of the environmental temperature. Besides, it can avoid the interference to the tilt measurement caused by the vibration in the vertical direction with the strong surface tension and large proportion of mercury and is able to makes the ODTS get the tilt angle and directional angle accurately using the light-proof of mercury. Besides, the electrode is connected when the tilt sensor leans to one side with the good conductivity of mercury, which can be applied to power saving. That means it activates the embedded system and connects the power supply for camera and LED light when the tilt condition happens. And the power supply is off and the embedded system is in dormant mode when the tilt condition doesn't happen. It is known the thermal expansion coefficient of mercury is 1.8×10^{-4} °C, in other words, if the temperature changes one degree, the volume of mercury changes 1/5556. According to the volume calculating equation of the cone, we calculate the derivative of temperature varying for the volume and get the Equation (2).

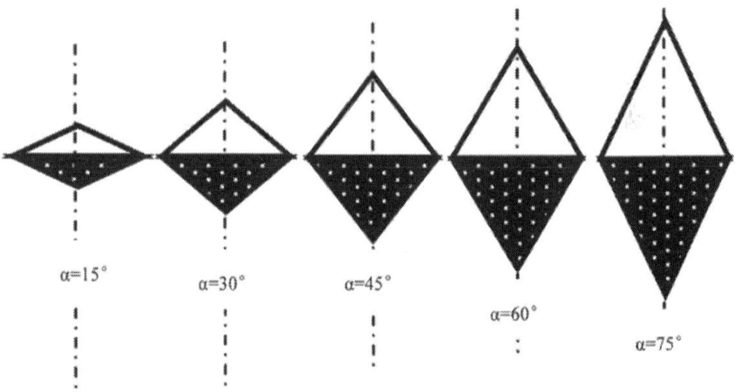

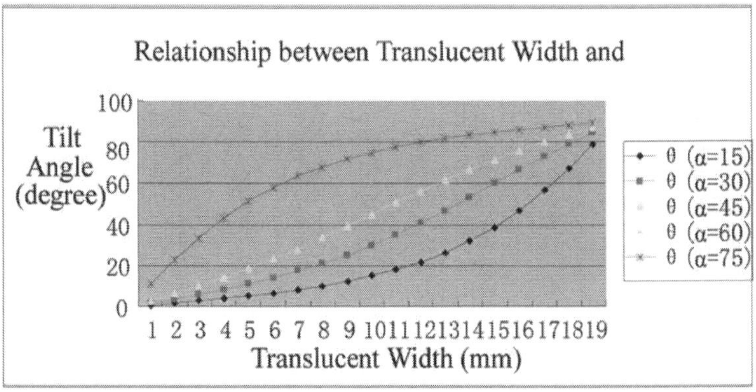

Figure 3. The curve between the cone angle α and the resolution of tilt measurement.

$$dV/dT = \pi R^2 \tan(\alpha) dR/dT. \quad (2)$$

In the equation, dV/dT is the thermal expansion coefficient of mercury. Combining with the Equation (1) and calculating the derivative, the change of tilt angle θ caused by temperature's change would be attained. According to the tilt detecting method in this paper, the measurement error caused by the temperature change can be controlled in within the scope of 1/1000.

2.3. Software Design for ODTS

The calculating part of the ODTS includes the embedded hardware and embedded software including system software and user software. Because of the paper's length limit, only the user software will be discussed in the paper. The user software consists of image obtaining unit, tilt angle and tilt directional angle detecting unit, system data storing unit, detecting data storing unit, displaying unit of the detecting result. And the overall block diagram of system software is showed in **Figure 4**. The image obtaining unit, including system initialization module and image reading module, is mainly used to read the video data from camera. The initialization module of the system is used to read some system constant which are stored in system data memory unit such as the radius R and the cone angle α of the transparent cone-shaped container, initial directional angle β0, resolution of the camera, the calculating table of tilt angle θ and the width δ of the translucent part, etc. And the image reading module is mainly used to read the video data from camera and save them in the dynamic memory unit. The tilt angle and tilt directional angel detecting unit is used to detect and calculate the tilt angle θ and tilt directional angle β of the detected object, including tilt directional β detecting module, tilt angle θ detecting module, the calculating module of the change rate of tilt angle θ and tilt directional angle β.

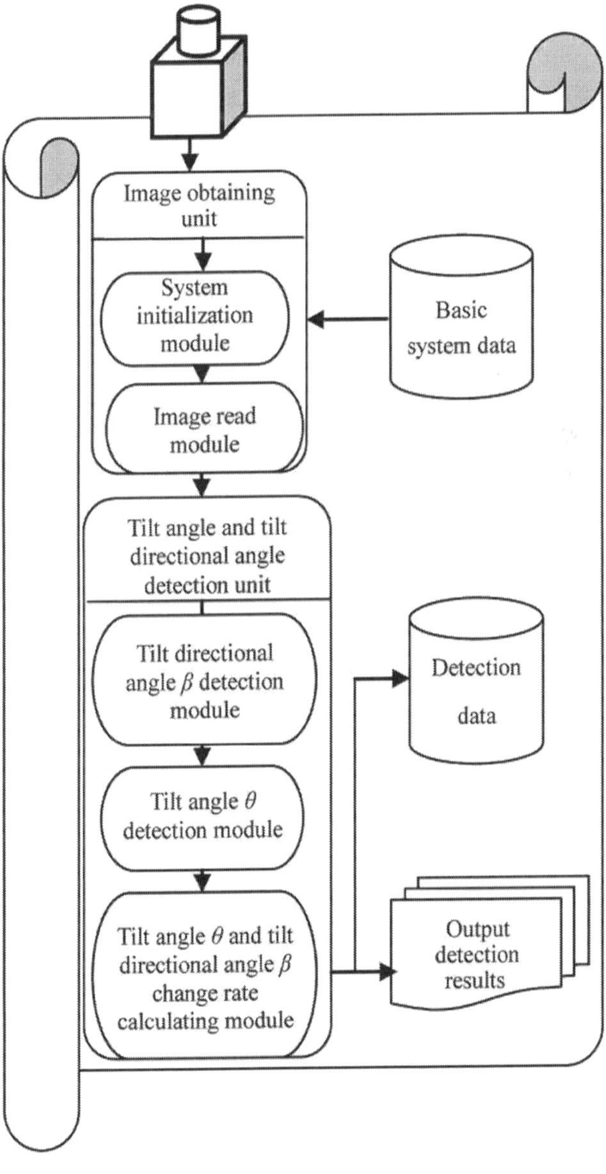

Figure 4. Overall block diagram of system software.

2.4. Detecting Algorithm for the Directional Angle β of ODTS

The definition of tilt directional angel expressed in angle β in this paper is a clockwise angle started from north direction. The tilt directional angle detected in the image is clockwise from the X positive axis, and it is expressed as angle βx, showed in **Figure 5**. Thus there is a following relationship between tilt directional angle β and detected tilt directional angle βx, showed in Equation (3).

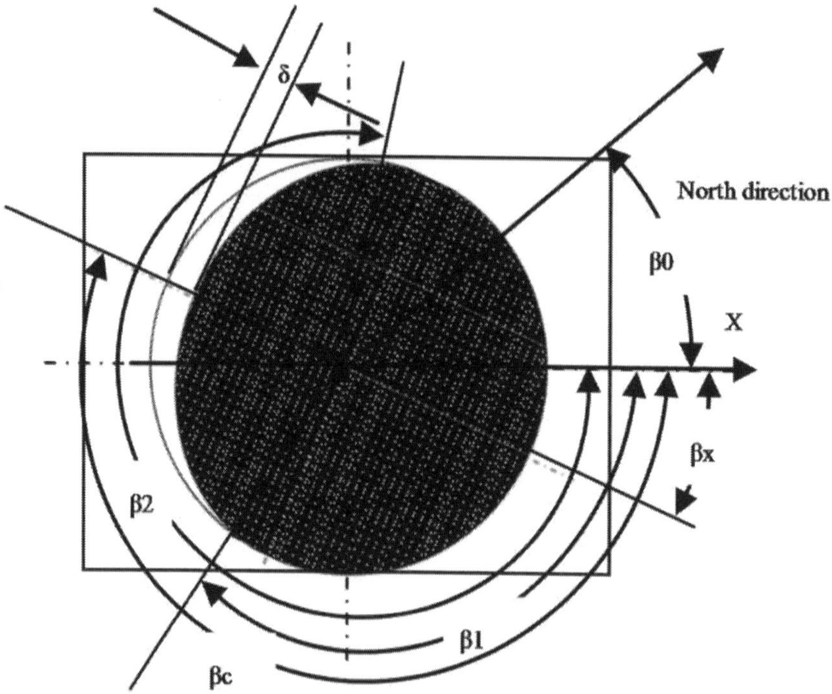

Figure 5. Detecting algorithm of tilt angle and tilt directional angle.

$$\beta = \beta x + \beta 0. \quad (3)$$

In this equation, β is the tilt directional angle, βx is detected tilt directional angle, $\beta 0$ is initial directional angle.

The initial directional angle $\beta 0$ is determined by the angle between the line of the cylindrical outer wall and the X axis's direction of obtained video image during the ODTS's calibration test, and it is written into the system data memory unit. The detected tilt directional angle βx is calculated based on the geometry of translucent part in the captured image, shown in **Figure 5**. It is known that the tilt directional angle is in the negative direction of ellipse's minor axis mentioned above. And the location of the minor axis would be in the middle of the crescentshaped's part. The detecting algorithm is showed as follows:

Step 1: generate a line in X axis's positive direction and search around the center point of the image in clockwise direction, if there is no bright pixel in X axis's positive direction, then search in the way mentioned above, if there is, skip to the step 3, if the circular outer pixel which the rotating line meets is bright pixel, the angle between the rotating line and the X axis's positive direction is $\beta 1$.

Step 2: continue searching around the center point in clockwise direction, if the circular outer pixel which the rotating line meets is not bright pixel, the angle between the rotating line of last bright pixel and the X axis's positive direction is $\beta 2$, then skip to step 5.

Step 3: continue searching around the center point in clockwise direction, if the circular outer pixel which the rotating line meets is not bright pixel, the angle between the rotating line of last bright pixel and the X axis's positive direction is $\beta 2$.

Step 4: continue searching around the center point in clockwise direction, if the circular outer pixel which the rotating line meets is not bright pixel, the angle between the rotating line of last bright pixel and the X axis's positive direction is $\beta 1$.

Step 5: use Equation (4) to calculate the angle βc of the ellipse's minor axis;

$$\beta c = (\beta 1 + \beta 2)/2 \tag{4}$$

And the detected tilt directional angle βx must be in the negative direction of ellipse's minor axis, therefor the detected tilt directional angle βx can be expressed in Equation (5),

$$\beta x = \beta c - \pi \tag{5}$$

2.5. Detecting Algorithm for the Tilt Angle θ of ODTS

The tilt angle is calculated with the Equation (1), and the parameters such as the radius R of the transparent coneshaped container, the cone angle α of the transparent cone-shaped container and so on, are attained from system data memory units as system constant. The width δ of the translucent crescent-shaped's middle part is calculated with the analysis algorithm of the image, specific algorithm is followed:

The pixel number of the translucent crescent-shaped's middle part is calculated according to the angle βc of the ellipse's minor axis resulting from the Equation (4) and the translucent crescent-shaped area which is formed by the transmitted light. If the resolution of the camera is 640 × 480, and the radius R of the transparent cone-shaped container is 200 mm, every pixel represents 0.83 mm. If the calculated pixel number of the translucent crescentshaped's middle part is five pixels, the width δ of the translucent crescent-shaped's middle part is 4.15 mm.

3. REALIZATION OF THE ODTS

According to the above-mentioned design thought, the prototype of the ODTS in this paper is designed, shown in **Figure 6**. To avoid the detecting interference from the environmental light, the transparent cone-shaped container, camera, and LED are fixed in a closed cylinder so that the ODTS can be used even in the harsh environment.

The transparent cone-shaped container filled with mercury whose volume equals to half of the container's is composed of two opposite faced cones with the cone angle of 15° showed in **Figure 6**(a).

According to the software block diagram showed in **Figure 4**, we have developed the application-oriented software of the ODTS, showed in **Figure 7**. With the aim to confirm the feasibility of the prototype and the application-oriented software, we had experimental study for the prototype on the platform of Windows XP/2000, JAVA (JDK1.5 version) system development language, Java Media Framework 2.1.1e video multimedia-based software.

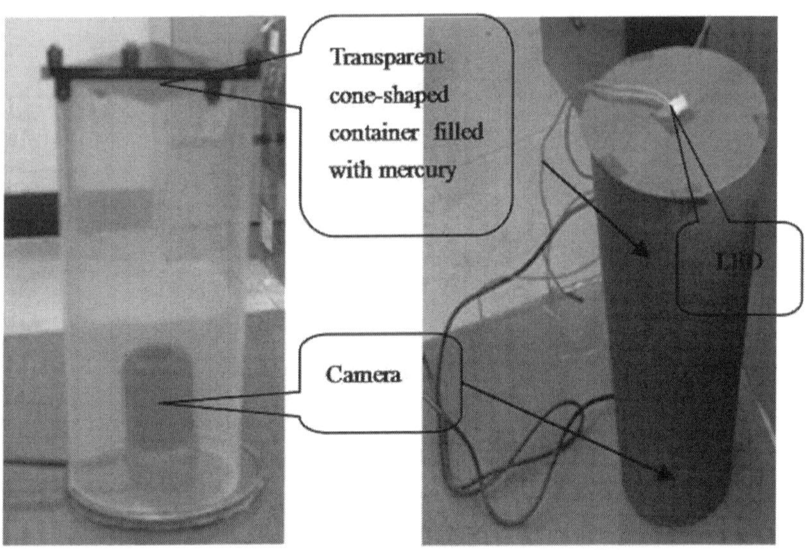

(a) (b)

Figure 6. Prototype of ODTS.

In order to make the software versatile and more userfriendly in various environments for users, the system is designed to have four custom-designed windows: 1) custom-designed window of video data source; 2) customdesigned window of system parameter; 3) custom-designed window of control parameter; 4) custom-designed window of detection area.

The custom-designed window of video data source is used to determine the obtaining devices of the tilt image video data, considering there are many interfaces of image sensor, such as USB video data interface, IP video net interface, simulation video interface, and AVI video data. The custom-designed window of system parameter is used to determine the radius R and cone angle α of the transparent cone-shaped container and to make the software more flexible. The custom-designed window of control parameter allows the users to carefully observe the detecting process of the tilt and provide real-time detection data for artificial leveling. The custom-designed window of detection area is used to customize the video source detection area. Because the body part of the disc of the image captured by camera is not in the center of image for sure, customizing the detection circle manually is needed to eliminate all kinds of errors in the process of assembling the ODTS.

4. EXPERIMENTAL RESULTS AND DISCUSSION

The ODTS is placed on the detected surface and is parallel with the detected surface. When the ODTS is horizontal, the shape of mercury in the image captured by the camera is a black disc and the RGB value of pixel is (0, 0, 0) which means black. At the same time, the RGB value of remaining pixels in the image is (255, 255, 255) which means white showed in **Figure 8**. The captured image is 640 × 480 pixels. With the Hough circle detecting algorithm based on diameter [8], the detected center of the black disc in the image was (331,267), and the radius of which possessed 188 pixels. The experimental research for the prototype showed in the**Figure 6** was done under the condition that the cone angle α of transparent coneshaped container was 15°, the actual radius R of the transparent cone-shaped container was 38mm, the light source was a white LED, and the resolution of camera was 640 × 480 pixels. So every pixel in the image represented 38/188 mm.

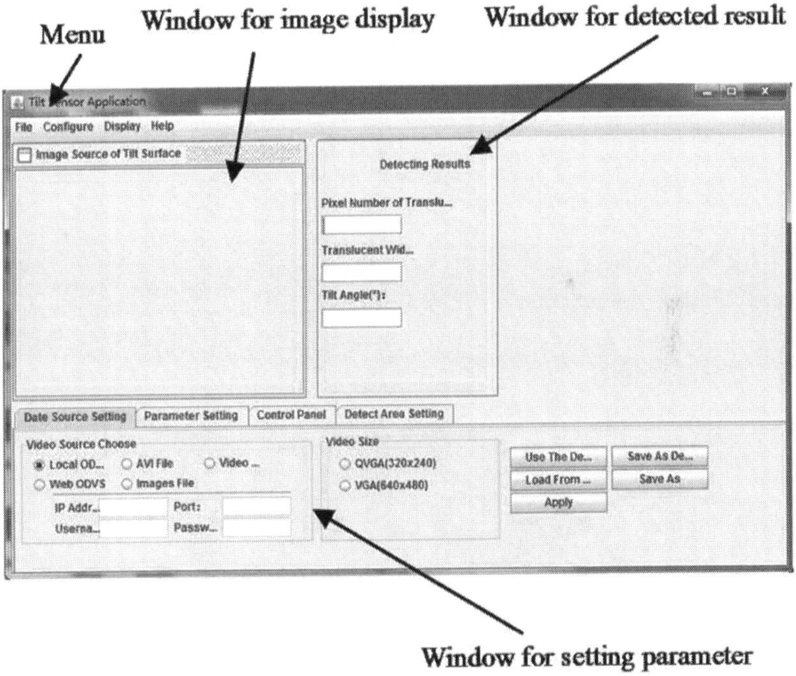

Figure 7. User interface of ODTS application software.

When the ODTS tilted 7° artificially, the formed shape of mercury in the image and the detected results are showed in **Figure 9**. With the detecting algorithm of tilt directional angle, the angle βc of the ellipse's minor axis was obtained, then the pixel number of the translucent crescent-shaped's middle part was calculated and the number was 59. Because the width of each pixel in the image was known, so the middle width δ of the crescent-shaped translucent part was 11.9 mm. With the Equation (1) and the known parameters of R, α and δ, the detected tilt angle θ was 6.98°. Also we have done some experiments under the condition the ODTS tilted 9°, 12° and 15° artificially, and the detected results are showed in **Table 1**.

By analyzing the table, the detected error of each tilt angle is within ± 1°, and the relative error is within ±5%. The detected error is relatively small when detecting a small tilt angle. The reason for that is the resolution of the ODTS with a small cone angle reacts sensitively when detecting a small tilt angle. It is consistent with the earlier analysis above.

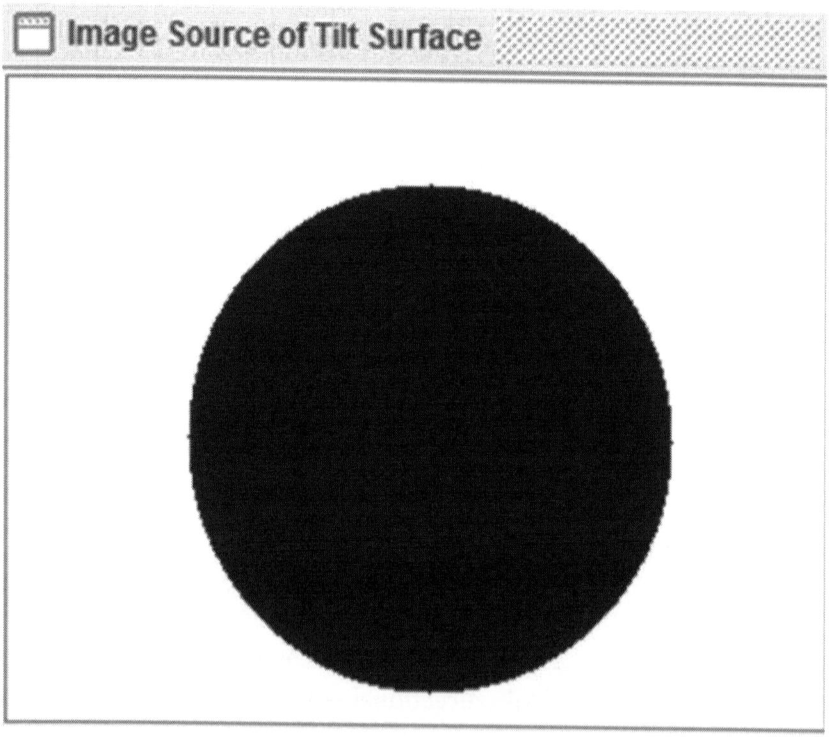

Figure 8. The image shape of mercury when ODTS is horizontal.

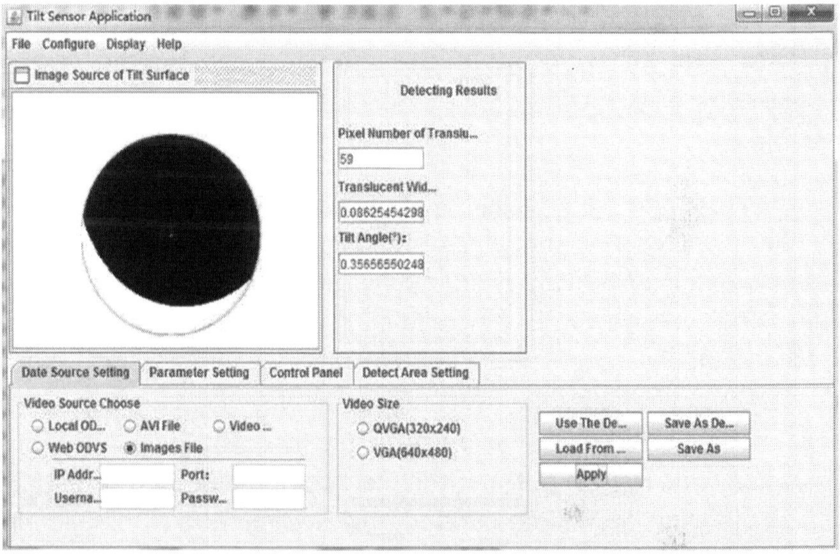

Figure 9. The image shape of mercury when ODTS tilts 7°.

Table 1. The detected results in different artificial tilt angle.

Tilt angle artificially (degree)	7	9	12	15
Pixel number of translucent middle part	59	68	81	92
Middle width of translucent part (mm)	11.9	13.7	16.3	18.5
Detected tilt angle (degree)	6.98	8.63	11.46	14.40
Error (degree)	–0.02	–0.37	–0.54	–0.6
Relative error (%)	–0.28	–4.1	–4.5	–4.0

The experimental results show that the detecting precision is relatively high. Moreover, because the detecting algorithm is mainly based on the analysis of the captured image, the detecting range can be very wide (0° ~ 90°). With the different video sources, all the images are processed one by one, thus the ODTS would has good realtime.

The ODTS in this paper includes a camera and an embedded system. It doesn't need the special power supply and the power of the camera and the LED light is offered by the embedded system. When the ODTS doesn't tilt, the embedded system is in dormant state, when it tilts, the mercury switch is connected and the embedded system is in working state (watchdog technology for saving energy). The fully sealed ODTS can work in harsh environment and the working temperature range of the mercury, camera, LED in the tilt sensor is wide. So we can conclude the designed ODTS has simple maintenance, low cost, reliability and high visualization.

Now the experiment for prototype is done on the computer. In the future, the embedded system seen as a central controller will be added into the ODTS and gives the signal to start capturing image when the detected surface tilts. At same time, the detected results will be displayed on the interface of the embedded system. The embedded system can also have internet interface to realize remote measurement easily. With remote accessing, we can see the video image of mercury as well as directly get the tilt angle, tilt directional angle and other information at remote computer when the ODTS tilts. Moreover, the embedded system equipped with platform automatic adjustment software would be seen as the upper computer of platform leveling to directly control the lower computer of anchor position servo system and to realize the automatic leveling. Two ways are available to get the access to the measurement data. Users can directly access the system database or also use the API interface provided by the system software. According to the special needs of users, the system can be equipped with wireless communication unit to support various wireless communication network accesses.

5. CONCLUSIONS AND FUTURE WORK

In this paper, we have proposed a novel tilt sensor (OmniDirectional Tilt Sensor) based on machine vision and presented a reliable detecting algorithm. A prototype has been built up and evaluated. The experimental results show that accuracy of 1° and resolution of 0.01° can be achieved. Compared with other tilt sensors, the ODTS has following main advantages: simple maintenance, high precision, wide range, low cost, real-time, reliability and high visualization.

The content of future study will focus on the applications of the ODTS, such as Car alarm electronics, dam safety monitoring, mudslides, landslides and other security monitoring area, offshore platforms, land surveying instrument automatic level school, swing control of ship, ship with chairs, ship bed, mouse, game input devices, civil engineering, water engineering, weapons platforms (tanks, mobile arms control plane), the radar antenna, bridge engineering, agricultural machinery (land leveling, combines, uenae machine and other tilt control.), earthquakes, volcanic detection, vehicle chassis, automatic leveling, automatic welding machines, automatic cutting machine, aviation, aerospace, mobile satellite antenna and other applications that requiring high real-timing. According to the different applications, different ODTSs all based on machine vision would be produced. The study of intelligent video analysis technology with the combination of machine vision to develop series of ODTS for the practical application should be furthered and the measurement precision should be improved further. With the further study, the ODTS that is simple in maintenance, adjustment and calibration, high in accuracy and visualization, wide in measurement range, low in cost, good in remote access, real-time, security and reliability, will be created and applied to important.

6. REFERENCES

1. C.-T. Wang, E.-H. Yang, J.-G. Zhang, Y.-X. Ma, B. Zhang, "The Omni-Directional Electronic Level Structure and Measuring Analysis Principle," Journal of Scientific Instrument, Vol. 27, No. 2, 2006, pp. 183-185.

2. J.-F. Liu and M.-Y. Li, "The Principle Analytics of Gravity Sensor Level Measuring Instrument," Sensors and Instrumentation, Vol. 24, No. 7, 2008, pp. 159-160.

3. Y. Wu, Y.-H. Song and W.-J. Su, "The Research of Liquid Pendulum Tilt Sensor," Coal Mine and Machinery, No. 6, 2004, pp. 31-32.

4. Y. Lin, L.-H. Pu and F.-X. Zhang, "The Structure Principle of the Omni-Directional Gas Pendulum Tilt Sensor," Electronic Components and Materials, Vol. 25, No. 5, 2006, pp. 19-22.

5. J.-H. Zhou, J.-Z. Wu and M.-Q. Xu, "The Micro Tilt Sensors of Image-Based Identification," Automation, Vol. 27, No. 11, 2006, pp. 39-44.

6. B.-O. Guan, H.-Y. Tam and S.-Y. Liu, "TemperatureIndependent Fiber Bragg Grating Tilt Sensor," IEEE Photonics Technology Letters, Vol. 16, No. 1, January 2004, pp. 244-226.

7. F. Hua, I. Reading and Z. P. Fang, "Novel Opical Sensor for Precise Tilt Angle Measurement," Control, Automation, Robotics and Vision, 2006.ICARCV'06. 9th International Conference, Singapore, 5-8 December 2006, pp. 1-4.

8. H.-Q. Liu, "Circle Detection Based on Hough Transform," Master's Thesis, Northeastern University, Shenyang, 2005, pp. 34-38.

2
CHAPTER

MACHINE VISION APPLICATION TO AUTOMATIC DETECTION OF LIVING CELLS/OBJECTS

Hernando Fernández-Canque

Glasgow Caledonian University, Scotland, UK

1. INTRODUCTION

The concept of Machine Vision (MV) originates in the early 1950's and practical MV applications appeared in the early 1980's. Early theoretical work suggested serious limitations in computational abilities as the main reason for inefficient use of MV. MV is a 'simple' processing system which receives and combines signals from cameras by manipulating images at the pixel level to extract information that can be used in a decision making activity to produce the output required. MV has several advantages over systems utilising conventional technologies. The attention span of human operators is relatively short (Butler, 1980). Camera images are detailed and therefore contain a large amount of information. This combined with the computer power available provides a huge potential for MV applications. The chapter will provide an overview on the developments and historical evolution of the concept of MV applications. This chapter will concentrate on MV application to automatic detection of objects with ill defined shape, size, and colour with high variability. Objects that change with time have no fixed structure; can present extra problems on application of automatic detection using MV. For this type of application, current manual detection requires highly specialised and highly trained operators. The application of MV will facilitate the detection of these objects with the advantage of fast response. It is easy to use, cost effective with consistent and reliable results. The detection of micro-organisms and the detection of suspicious activity in humans fall into this category. The first example examines development of an automatic system for microscopic examination of the recovered deposit for the detection and enumeration of the microorganism Cryptosporidium. The second example addresses the application of MV to the task of intruder monitoring within the context of visual security systems. The chapter will present these two applications to illustrate problems encountered in this type of detection.

In section 2, the chapter presents a general overview of MV applications and discusses some problems associated with the application of MV to objects of high variability. Section 3 will present software architecture of a MV application and its characteristics. Section4 will discuss MV application to variable objects. Section 5 concentrates on two problems associated with this type of application: focus control and error due to changes in illumination conditions. In section 6 AI implementation is discussed and in section 7 Two MV application examples of detection of highly variable objects as are presented.

2. AN OVERVIEW OF MV APPLICATIONS

Computer-based vision and automation tools are used in a wide variety of industrial and scientific applications, including electronics, automotive, semiconductor, pharmaceutical, and research applications. These systems perform process monitoring, information gathering, and "on-the-fly" feedback/control to correct manufacturing problems. Research and development into machine vision can be traced back for more than 30 years. The impact of new technologies in machine vision, as well as the historical evolution of this concept can be extracted from published papers in journal, conferences and industrial applications. This field is highly explored at the moment. Table 1 include a list where the generic terms identifying MV applications of more than 10 applications have been implemented; there is a vast potential for applications in variety of topics. A search in BIDS (BIDS 2011) database, using "MACHINE VISION" as keywords revealed 73,773 published articles covering the period 1952 to 2011. Of those 73,773 publications found not all present relevance to application of MV and most of them cover image processing in general term.

The early papers refer in general to the idea of image processing and pattern recognition in general terms. A more refined search in BIDS database, using "MACHINE VISION APPLICATIONS" as keywords revealed 1,042 published articles covering the period 1984 to 2010. Figure 1 shows a graph of the number of applications over a 5 years period between 1980 and 2010.

The graph shows a steady increase in the number of applications. In the first 5 years there was an increase from 12 applications in late 1980's to 83 applications in the early 1990's indicating a 7 fold increase. Since its introduction MV has seen an explosion in the number of applications. In the first 10 years the number of application had increased of about 30 times. In general the steady

Table 1. Subject areas with more than 10 MV applications

Acoustics	*Food science*	*Oceanography*	*Robotics*	*Dermatology*
Agriculture	*Forestry*	*Oncology*	*Sociology*	*Education*
Anatomy	*Internal medicine*	*Ophthalmology*	*Spectroscopy*	*Engineering*
Astronomy	*Genetics*	*Optics*	*Surgery*	*Media studies*
Biochemistry	*Geography*	*Pathology*	*Telecommunications*	*Gastroenterology*
Business	*Geology*	*Pharmacy*	*Toxicology*	*Geochemistry*
Cardiology	*Gerontology*	*Physiology*	*Transportation*	*Health care*
Chemistry	*Immunology*	*Plant science*	*Veterinary*	*Photography*
Communication	*Infections*	*Polymers*	*Zoology*	*Material science*
Biology	*Instrumentation*	*Psychology*	*Control systems*	*Mathematics*
Education	*Mechanics*	*Nuclear medicine*	*Behavioural science*	*Microscopy*
Electrochemistry	*Metallurgy*	*Rehabilitation*	*Biophysics*	*Management*
Energy & fuels	*Mining*	*Remote sensing*	*Microbiology*	*Evolutionary biology*
Entomology	*Neurology*	*Reproduction*	*Economics*	*Surgery*
environment	*dietetics*	*Respiratory system*	*Cell biology*	*Library science*

increase in the number of application is due to the increase in computing power, new and better image processing algorithms, better quality in acquisition of images (hardware) and reliability of Artificial Intelligent (AI) tools. To illustrate the problems of the detection of living/variable objects from the search in BIDS database the articles were classified according to the type of application algorithms/technology. This classification is presented in table 2. By sorting these articles according to the different algorithms/technology used, a general impression on the technology achievements can be approximated. This also provides information of expected development on the MV application.

Table 2. Research Statistics MV applications period 1980-2010

Field	*MV Applications*	*%*
General (theoretical) algorithms or technologies	158	15.16%
Industry related applications	259	24.85%
Control, Instrumentation	124	11.90%
Optics, Robotics, computer science	159	15.26%
Microorganisms, Living cells, variable shape objects	54	5.18%
Agriculture, Food Industry	135	12.96%
Flight Control, Car Control, Automatic Tracking, Traffic Safety	87	8.35%
Textile, Leather, Jewellery	66	6.33%

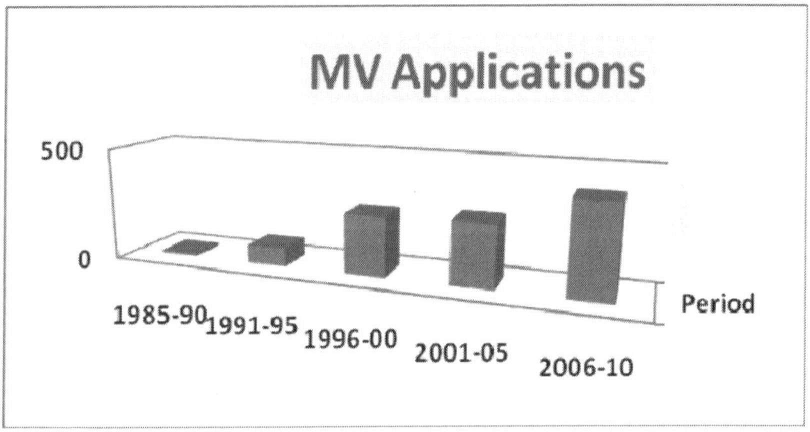

Figure 1. Number of MV applications between 1980 and 2010.

The vast majority of the research and application in the field of Machine Vision is found in the development of general algorithms. The needs of industry strongly influence the type of algorithms developed. The industry generally demands algorithms specialised in pattern recognition, especially algorithms tolerant to lighting variance and partial (dust) occlusion, and occasionally to changes in size (scaling). The industry's demand for gauging application encourages also the development of sophisticated edge detection algorithms, using subpixel accuracy (Hanks, 1998). This is also the main reason why powerful Vision Software development platforms such as IMAQ from National Instruments, Visilog from Norpix or PatMAX from Cognex Corporation, (these being just a few examples) appear on the market. The main benefit that these development environments have provided is that it is no longer necessary to spend long time developing routine algorithms for image processing. Algorithms such as threshold, image manipulation, spatial filtering, Binary Large Object (BLOB) analysing, edge detection, etc. are ready available. A vision engineer can concentrate on the development of the specific algorithms for each application. Also the management of Operating System related tasks are easier to handle and thus time saving. The movement of computer vision from the “experimental technology” category into industry-strength mainstream applications provides another benefit: the amount of research undertaken in the development of more powerful equipment for image acquisition is increasing, colour cameras with mega-pixel resolutions being widely available this days. The lighting system for machine vision is continuously evolving, different solutions being available with respect to the application demand (Braggins, 2000) e.g. Reflective Surfaces, Undulating Surfaces, Moving Parts. The fourth place in Machine Vision development of algorithms is taken by the agriculture and food industry (13%). The vast majority of these algorithms involve particle sorting e.g. Grain, Olives, Apples, etc or quality tests. This sorting is usually done using BLOB analysis, but advanced algorithms such as combining specific morphological and colour characteristics (Luo et al., 1999) can be found in this field and used for other applications. The algorithms involved in Flight Control, Car Control, Automatic Tracking, and Traffic Safety are usually highly specialized for these fields and are appearing with more frequency. This also applies for algorithms involving texture analysing, developed for textile and leather industry.

The research undertaken in the field of living cells/variable objects represents a total of only 5.18% of the total machine vision applications. The main reason for this low number of applications is the fact that the living cells are not size and shape invariant. On the contrary, the size, shape and sometimes even the colour vary during their life cycle. Hence a really large number of factors have to be taken into consideration when designing a machine vision application in this field. Also in terms of automatic classification the amount of artificial intelligence embedded in these applications is relatively complex and high. The "IfThen, "True-False" logic is usually not suitable, and a different, more advanced approach is needed e.g. Fuzzy Logic, Neural Networks. The intelligence embedded in these applications is relatively high; however the results can be impressive. The application of machine vision to detect this type of objects presents the problems associated with the physical variance of living cells and requires the development of specialized algorithms.

3. MACHINE VISION SOFTWARE ARCHITECTURE

A proposed architecture may include a block to control the camera/microscope and a block to control the image acquisition required to control the hardware. Ideally all controls should be done automatically. The system requires an image processing block with the required image processing algorithms to manipulate and analyse images according to the application. The algorithms will extract information required to provide an output for decision from the system. In many cases the MV should take a decision without human intervention but with the aid of an AI application section. The AI block will add computer capability to the MV system that exceeds human performance in some cases. A MV's software architecture should include all the elements presented in block diagram in figure 2. The MV should provide a way of informing users of the results. The communications block allows information to be provided in various forms/formats including remotely to any place required.

All blocks are accessed and organised by the Application Layer (AL), the MV incorporates a Graphical User Interface, providing access to an operator or expert to analyze/confirm results if required.

The MV system presented in figure 2 includes all the features and control algorithms required by a MV application. The AI decision section is tailored to a particular application.

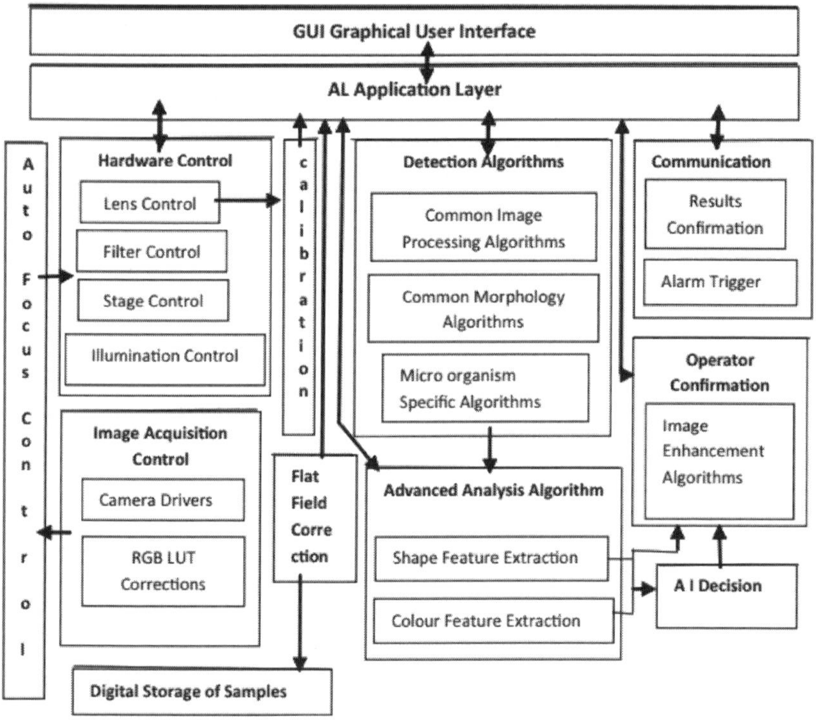

Figure 2. Machine Vision Software Architecture

4. MV APPLICATION TO VARIABLE OBJECTS

To establish a MV application to variable objects it is necessary to consider the general characteristics of the environment in which the MV will operate.

- in which hierarchy the MV will be used (decision making, alarm, identification...).
- application type. It can range from very complex systems with a lot of different information required to be extracted from images to simple applications with easy application.

- frequency of application (mass samples, batch or single analysis).
- level of MV automation (manual, semi automatic, automatic, mixed system).

Depending on the application an MV topology, architecture and algorithms can be planned. Subsequently the relevant outputs variables required for the AI application should be selected. It requires experience to find the best combination of outputs variables. Usually it is required to work with several algorithms at the same time in order to select the ones that perform best. Once the appropriate algorithms are selected they may require to be optimised to increase efficiency of the application.

5. PROBLEMS ASSOCIATED WITH AUTOMATIC DETECTION OF LIVING 'OBJECTS'

For both image analysis and image processing, attention has to be paid to errors occurring during the image formation and acquisition, as it is far more difficult if not impossible to eliminate these errors later using image post processing algorithms. There are limitations with respect to the accuracy of the object representation by an acquired image. Both the optics which forms the image of the object on the sensor and the digitisation process introduce errors (Ellenberger & Young, 2000). There are several phenomena which directly influence the acquired image therefore awareness is necessary (Ellenberger & Young, 2000). Living objects have high variability over their life cycle. They can change shape, size, colour or biological structure. In order to detect these objects advance algorithms need to be applied. The success of the advance algorithms application will depend on the elimination or reduction of variability of image due to the acquisition of frames. In this context the variation of image due to change in illumination and change of focus needs to be reduced. Some general problems in image processing affect the detection of objects. In the case of living cells, extraction of information to be input to artificial intelligence for the analysis requires minimizing these problems, in particular the problem with autofocus and problem with illumination. Some solutions are presented in this chapter.

5.1 Problems associated with autofocus control

In order for any image processing algorithms to be effective, the quality of the acquired image must be optimal. In microscopy one of the most important factors is the focus quality, as the even smallest focus deviation produces a blur effect on the acquired image. Therefore the focus control must be automated and performed as often as possible. Under these circumstances an autofocus algorithm must be employed. The autofocus algorithm must be relatively fast, involving the minimum computational effort possible. The image is brought to focus on the camera controlling the tuning of focus lenses stage using a stage controller. Auto-focus could be achieved by developing a feedback focus controller as exemplified in figure 3. This is possible if a measure of the focus quality in a numeric form is extracted (focus score). The hill climbing algorithm (Russell & Norvig, 2002) can be iterated with focus scores until the best focus is found.

The focus quality of an image can be linked with the perceived "sharpness" of the acquired image, therefore the number and the strength of edges in it. The number of edges can be determined using an edge-extraction algorithm. One of the fastest algorithms to extract edges in any direction is the Laplacian Edge Detection as it involves only one convolution. One problem associated with edge detection algorithms is the noise influence; therefore noise reduction algorithms are necessary. A good choice could be a median filter, as it has a minimal influence over continuous edges.

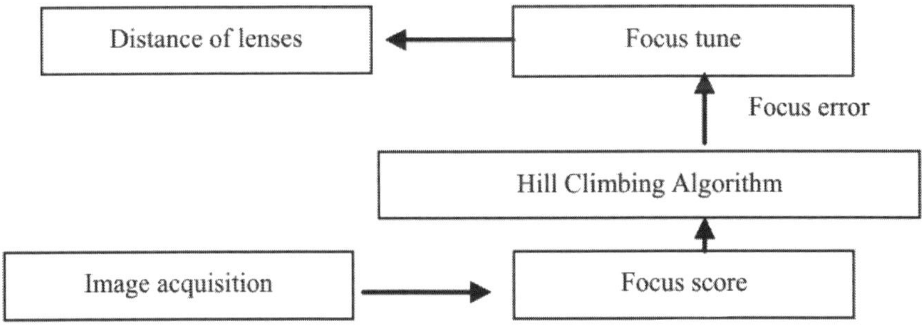

Figure 3. Autofocus control

5.2 Autofocus control implementation

A series of images of a test pattern are acquired using the minimal resolution possible and greyscale representation to minimise the computational effort. These images are shown in figure 4, in the acquisition order, with the first 2 being completely out of focus, and the other being close to optimal focus:

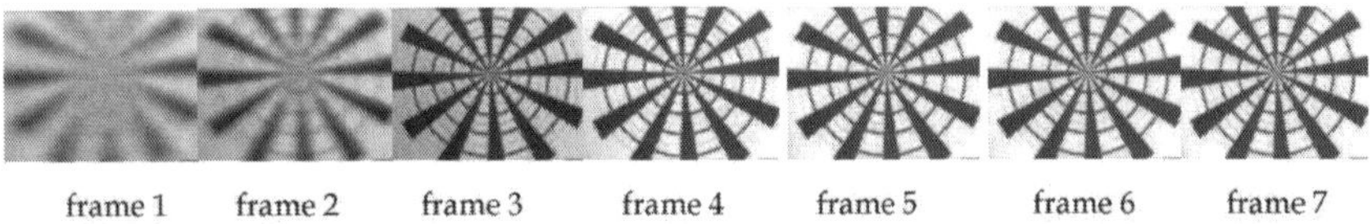

Figure 4. Focus test frame 1 to 7

From each image the light plane is extracted and a Laplacian Edge Extraction algorithm is applied. The kernel used in this case was

$$\begin{pmatrix} -1 & -1 & -1 \\ -1 & 8 & -1 \\ -1 & -1 & -1 \end{pmatrix}. \tag{1}$$

One of the resulting images is presented in figure 5(a).

(a) Test frame Edge information

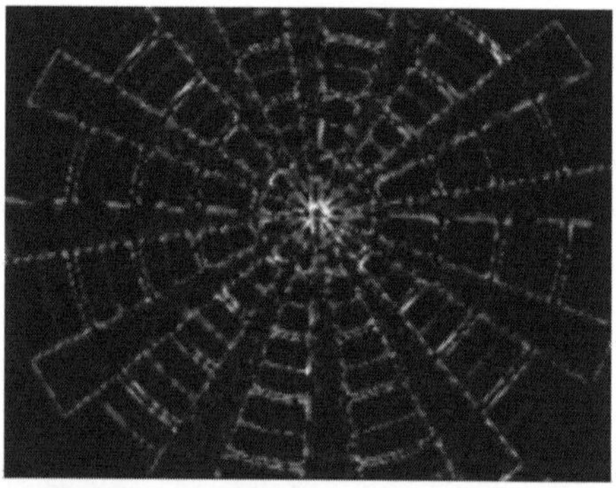

(b) Median filter applied

Figure 5. Edge extraction

A median filter defined on a small neighbourhood is applied to minimise the noise effect on the final focus score. The result is shown in figure 5(b). Although the extracted edges are slightly affected, all continuous edges are still present while most of the background noise has been eliminated. A larger neighbourhood may be considered to improve accuracy, but a significant increase in computational time has to be expected. A sum of all pixel values is then performed, the result being a single numerical value. By applying this algorithm on 10 test images the results presented in Table 3 are obtained. By comparing the focus score with the test images, it can be seen that they are closely tied up.

Table 3. Focus Measure Results

Image	*Focus Score*	*Image*	*Focus Score*
Frame 1	1317531	Frame 6	5765586
Frame 2	1374433	Frame 7	5873043
Frame 3	5374843	Frame 8	5879743
Frame 4	5902432	Frame 9	5868048
Frame 5	5756735	Frame 10	5868667

On the first two images, the score is relatively low, as they are completely out of focus. On the last seven the focus score is comparable, with the 4th image obtaining the best result. When comparing some of these frames the human eye will have difficulties detecting the optimal focus. The focus score will differentiate the best focus in frames that appear to have the same focus. The algorithms presented here have the advantage of high processing speed in reaching the best focus, in the order of milliseconds in an average PC system. Real time software controlled autofocus is possible.

5.3 Problems associated with illumination

It is possible to combine several light sources that illuminate the specimen in different ways. The monochromatic or narrow band light sources emit light at a single wavelength or a very narrow band (e.g. Laser, which is also coherent). Halogen and mercury lamps are broad band incoherent light sources. Such an incoherent light source can be converted to quasi coherent by closing the aperture to a pinhole (Pawley, 1995). Acquiring images using coherent illumination has some advantages and also some disadvantages: a sharp edge will show ringing effects and the edge will be shifted into the bright area. Also the images look granular (speckle effect), and any aberration or dust on the lens can produce disturbance in the image. However, the most important advantage is that resolution achievable can be better than with incoherent illumination (Goodman, 1996). One of the most important advantages of incoherent illumination is that the image brightness is not changed with modifications of the focal position, a very important consideration when auto-focus algorithms are employed. Another significant aspect for a Machine Vision System is the Image Representation. Colour images can be represented in several different formats (also called Colour Spaces).

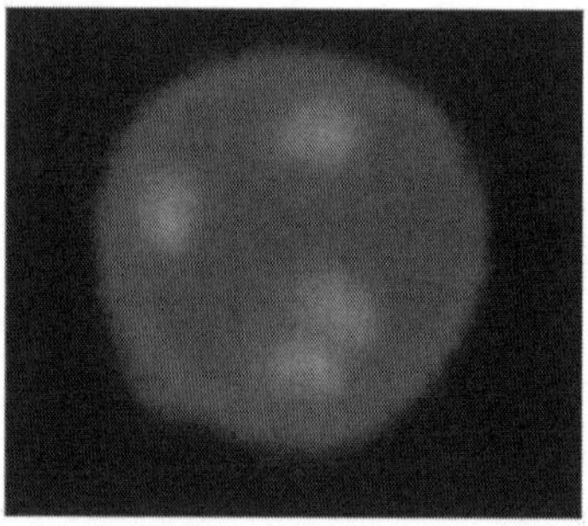

(a) Oocyst under normal illumination

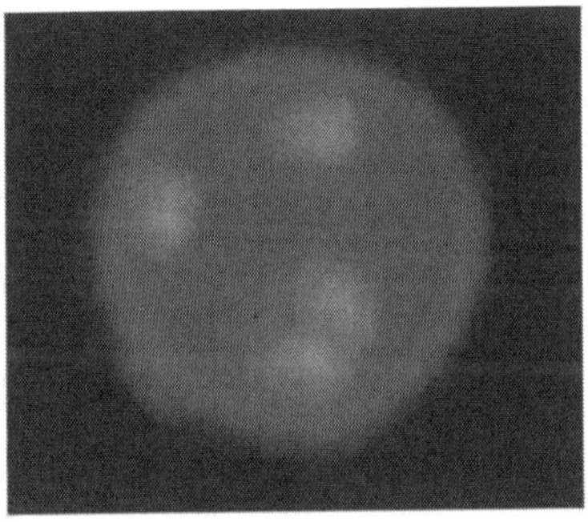

(b) Same image 10% brighter

Figure 6. Cryptosporidium oocyst with 10% change in illumination.

The most common representation of colours is the RGB colour space, as most image sensors provide data according to this model. RGB colour plane is suitable for image capture and reproduction, but can be very inconvenient for feature extraction. Problems are noticed when minor changes in the lighting conditions occur. Figure 6 shows a sample of a microorganism oocyst common in drinking water known as cryptosporidium. In figure 6 the illumination has been increased by 10% in capturing the image of this cryptosporidium oocyst. Figure 7 presents the histogram of the same cryptosporidium oocyst image with 10% difference in lighting conditions. The histograms are very different and make it difficult to separate the object of interest and its background.

One solution to overcome this problem is the use of a linear transform from the RGB colour space into an alternative model such as HSL – Hue, Saturation and Lightness, or HSI – Hue, Saturation and Intensity. Hue refers to the perceived colour (viewed technically as the dominant wavelength), saturation refers to the dilution of the colour by white light, and the lightness (or value) refers to the sensation of brightness relative to a white reference. The advantages of HSL over the RGB colour space are illustrated in figure 8 where the same 10% change in lighting condition is applied to the same cryptosporidium oocyst object of the previous histograms.

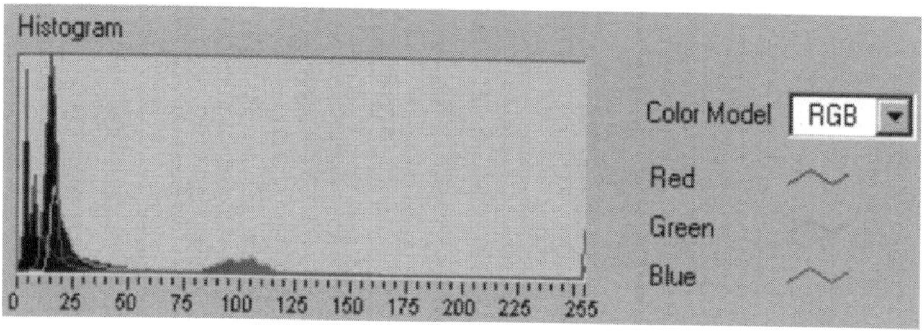

(a) Image normal illumination

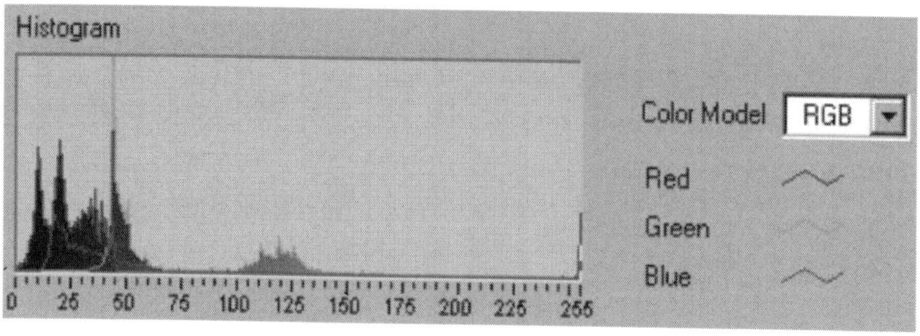

(b) Same image with 10% change in illumination

Figure 7. RGB histograms

The results of the histograms indicate that the Saturation plane is slightly affected and the Hue plane is relatively unaffected. The HSL space will make it possible to isolate the object of interest from the background. The RGB-HSL conversions are computational intensive and hardware conversions are preferred.

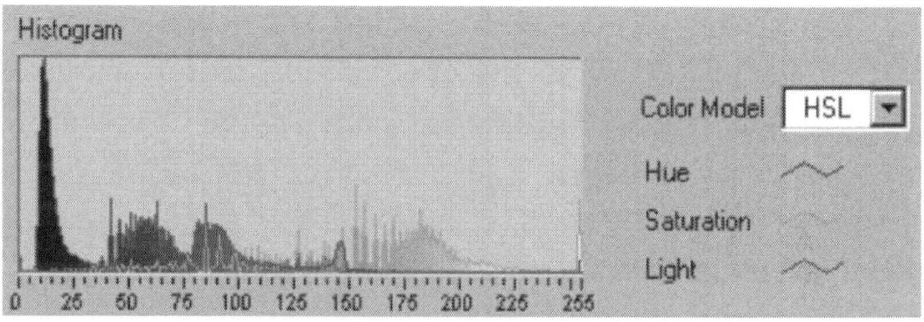

(a) Image normal illumination

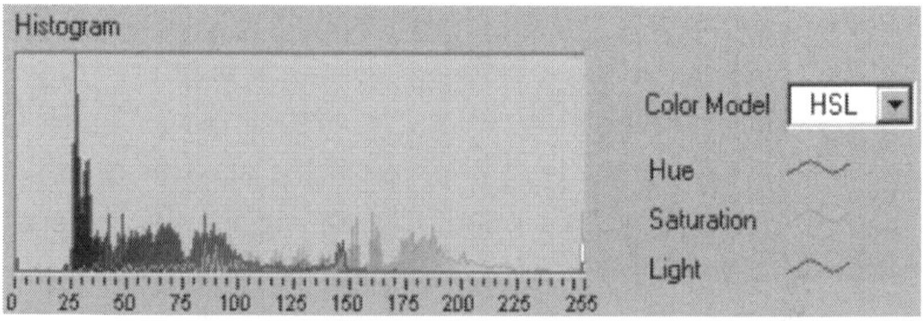

(b) Same image with 10% change in illumination

Figure 8. HSL histograms

6. ARTIFICIAL INTELLIGENCE APPLIED TO MV

In many cases the MV should take a decision without human intervention but with the aid of an artificial intelligent (AI) application section. The AI application will depend on:

- the type of application.
- the outputs from the vision algorithms.
- the testing/training samples available.
- availability of training vectors statically independent.

Computers already emulate some of the simpler activities of the human mind. They can perform mathematical calculations, manipulate numbers and letters, make simple decisions, and perform various storage and retrieval functions. In these applications, the computer is exceptional and usually exceeds the human mind in performance. Artificial intelligence gives computers added computing capability, allowing them to exhibit more intelligent behaviour. The most common types of artificial intelligence system are Expert Systems, Fuzzy Logic and Artificial Neural Networks (ANN). Providing a set of parameters that would completely and undoubtedly describe highly variable objects is extremely difficult. Choosing to implement the classification process by means of an ANN seems optimal, as all it should achieve is to provide a suitable training set to a carefully chosen neural network. Because of the variability of the objects in some cases problems are encountered with this type of AI in that there are not sufficient numbers of training samples to train the ANN. Under this circumstance confident training cannot be performed successfully. For this type of application a more flexible approach is needed to take into account different variation of the objects. Fuzzy logic system can in some cases successfully address this issue, as it logically implements degrees of membership based on likelihood. Therefore a fuzzy logic inference engine is in many cases the preferred AI decision tool in this type of applications.

7. EXAMPLES OF APPLICATION TO VARIABLES OBJECTS

Two examples of MV application to objects that are highly variable are presented in this section. The first example detects the existence of Cryptosporidium in water and the second example detects suspicious activity of humans using Closed Circuit Television (CCTV).

7.1 Example 1. detection of cryptosporidium in water

Cryptosporidium has been widely recognized as a serious cause for concern, with a very large number of waterborne infections caused by its oocysts. In its transmissive stage – the oocyst - is a frequent inhabitant of raw water sources used for the abstraction of potable water. Its importance is heightened because, coupled with its low infection dose, conventional water treatment process, including chemical disinfection, cannot guarantee to remove or destroy oocysts completely. Waterborne transmission is well documented (Smith & Rose, 1990, 1998), and can affect a large number of individuals. More than an estimated 427,000 have been affected in 19 documented waterborne outbreaks (Smith & Rose, 1998). Transmission is via an environmentally robust oocyst excreted in the faeces of the infected host (Smith & Rose, 1998). At least 21 species of Cryptosporidium have been named (Frazen & Muller, 1999). Cryptosporidium parvum is the major species responsible for clinical disease in human and domestic animals (Current, 1988; Currents & Gracia, 1991).The laboratory diagnosis of Cryptosporidium is dependent upon demonstrating oocysts in the sample by microscopy. Here, oocysts must be distinguished from other, similarly shaped, contaminating bodies present in the sample, and the microscopic identification of oocysts is dependent upon morphometry (the accurate measurement of size) and morphology. The current manual is expensive, labour intensive, time consuming and unreliable. Cryptosporidium is difficult to identify because of its size and morphology. Regulatory bodies from all over the world acknowledge the continuous monitoring of water sources for Cryptosporidium as imperative. Many requirements, rules and regulations are in place to attempt to address the control of Cryptosporidium which threatens the safety of drinking water. As an example the EEC produced a drinking water directive (EEC, 1998). The example presented here complies with this directive. The cryptosporidium structure in a computer generated model is shown in figure 9. Samples are stained and dried onto microscope slides and micro-organisms are detected using fluorescence microscopy. The drying process causes oocysts to collapse which in some cases leads to shape distortion and the physical release of sporozoites. This made the manual detection difficult.

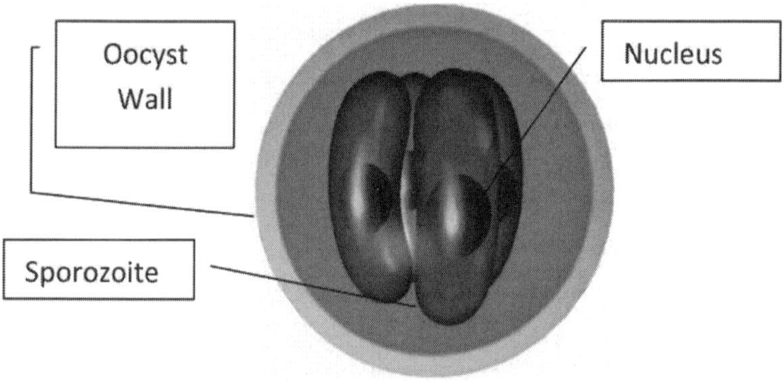

Figure 9. Computer generated model of Cryptosporidium

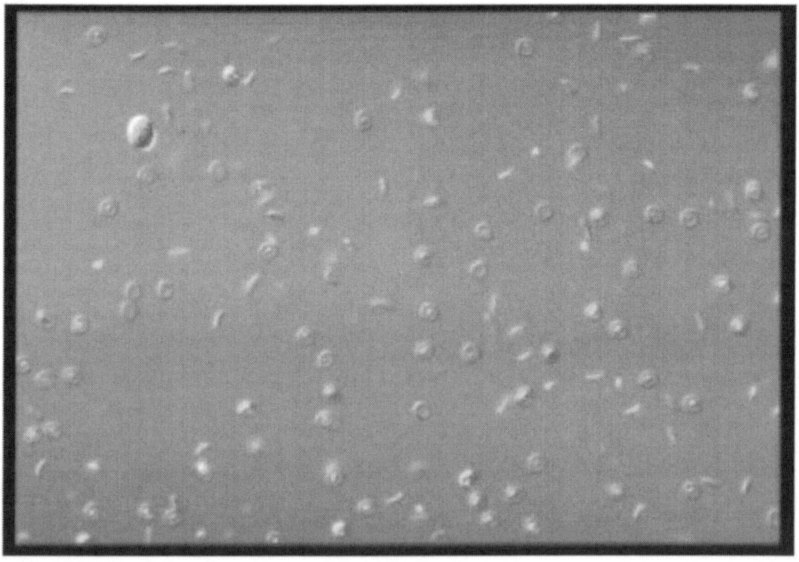

Figure 10. Water sample containing cryptosporidium oocysts

The acquired image of a slide containing Cryptosporidium, viewed under Differential Interference Contrast (DIC) is presented in figure 10. Figure 10 shows a sample containing cryptosporidium oocysts.

Significant contrast is achieved using a highlight details filter and elimination or reduction of noise. The binary noise present is efficiently eliminated using the following algorithm: (Fernandez-Canque et al, 2008, 2000).

i. A buffer copy of the image to be cleaned up is generated.

ii. Two successive erode functions are applied on the original image.

iii. All pixels from the buffer copy 8-connected to the non-zero pixels from the image are added to the image

iv. Step (iii) is repeated until no pixel is added.

Figure 11 (a) shows part of the sample with the noise eliminated and with the missing pixel reinserted.

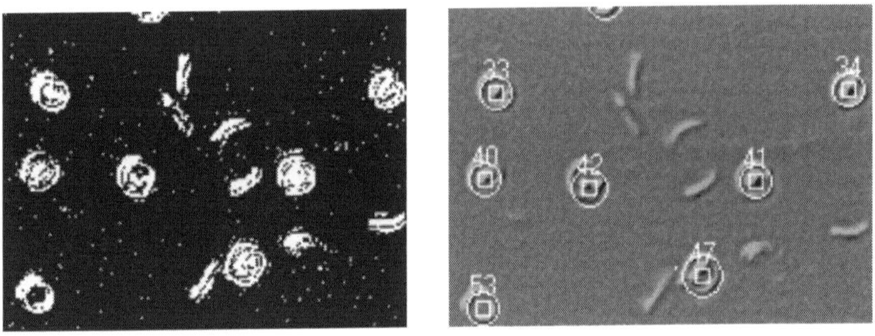

(a) (b)

Figure 11. (**a**) Sample with threshold images combined (**b**) Sample final result oocysts identified

The next step is to reinsert the missing pixels within the objects boundaries (FernandezCanque et al, 2000). A closing algorithm is performed, using a kernel size of 5. A NOT function is performed, followed by a labelling function. The result is an image which has a value of 0 associated with all objects, a value of 1 associated with the background and a value greater than 1 for every hole in the objects. By replacing the values greater than 1 with 0 and negating the image again we achieve holes filling. All objects too small to be a Cryptosporidium are eliminated. This is achieved using the same algorithm as for binary noise removal, but with 7 erosion functions applied. Then a distance function is applied, and a circle detection algorithm (Danielsson, 1980) is used for Cryptosporidium detection. The result is presented in Figure 11(b).An advance analysis algorithm can use different colour planes to allow the determination the existence of the 4 nucleus in an oocyst. On the green plane, both the wall and the nucleons of the Cryptosporidium are detected. Figure 12(a) show the wall and nucleons of a cryptosporidium oocyst after noise is reduced and objects of interest are separated from background.

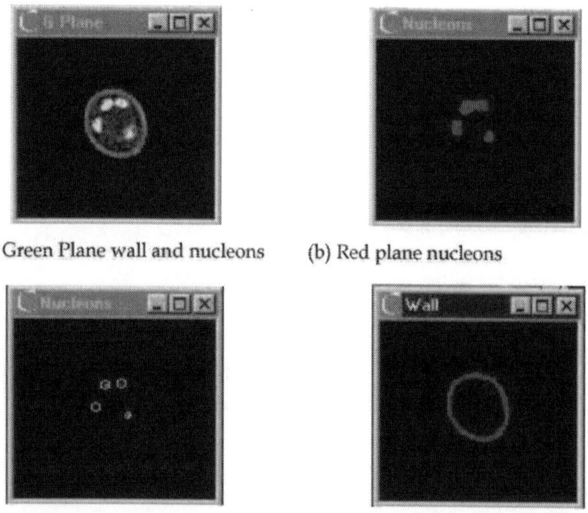

(a) Green Plane wall and nucleons (b) Red plane nucleons

(c) Red Plane noise reduced (d) Wall: subtraction of green and red plane

Figure 12. Green and Red plane

On the red plane, only the nucleons are detected. This gave an easy method of separation. Figure 12(b) shows the red plane after the image is cleaned of noise. On the red plane a lookup table function was applied. Finally, threshold and binarisation was used, followed by noise removal and BLOB closing. Figure 12(c) shows clearly the 4 nucleons to identify cryptosporidium. By subtracting the nucleons from the green plane in binary format the wall was obtained and measurements were done, this is shown in figure 12(d). The morphological characteristics of cryptosporidium can be extracted unequivocally. Image processing allows the manipulation of these figures at the pixel level to analyse details of very small dimensions. As Cryptosporidium have a diameter in the range of 4 to 6 microns, a human operator would find difficult to identify this micro-organism under the microscope. This provides a method of identification of cryptosporidium. After the completion of the Advanced Analysis the system goes into the next stage – A I Decision Making. Expert Systems have problems with flexibility for this application and ANN encounter problems with training. It was found that the use of Fuzzy Logic suits this application by mimicking human knowledge based decision making. The classification is based on the features extracted by the Advanced Analysis Algorithm and a customisable rule base. The proposed approach allows a reliable detection of waterborne microorganisms in large quantities of water and outperforms the current manual detection in term of cost, time of results, accuracy and reliability (Fernandez-Canque et al., 2009).

7.2 Example 2: Detection of suspicious activity

In recent years, the use of surveillance cameras has increased in popularity. This is partially due to reduction in cost and technological advances. CCTV systems have become very popular in observing public places. Current technology makes provision for an operator to examine live surveillance footage from remote locations as they can be transmitted over the internet, cables or wireless mediums. In this example the MV application detects suspicious activity automatically by studying human posture and observing full trajectories of people (Fernandez-Canque et al., 2009). In this study, work has been carried out with the aim of achieving fully automatic detection of intruders using a static camera and in real time. CCTV has the advantage that relatively large areas can be monitored and intruders can be seen as compared to other detection methods. The main use of CCTV is based on reaction to a past incident by revising image recorded; the aim of this work is to make the use of CCTV more efficient by assessing suspicious activity in an active manner and alert operators to an intrusion. By achieving an automatic detection some problems associated with this type of surveillance can be avoided. It is known that the span of concentration of any operator is very short (Saarinen & Julesz, 1991; Goolkasian, 1991), and there is unreliability due to operator's fatigue and poor detection due to large number of irrelevant images known as Eriksen effect(Eriksen & Murphy, 1982; Eriksen & Hoffman, 1972).

7.2.1 Intruder detection

To detect an intruder, the background with no intruders present is recorded while the camera transmits the video to the computer, and each frame is analyzed. After reduction of noise and distortion, frames are compared to the original image of the plain background with no intruder present. This process results in accruing the pixels of the object of interest. Pixels in this object are counted, large numbers these pixels reflect a significant background change, thus an intruder is likely present. If no intruder is detected, the background image is replaced with the current frame of the video, which is compared against the next video frame as the program repeats this cycle once. A pixel count is then applied to confirm if an object has been detected, and finally the parameters can be

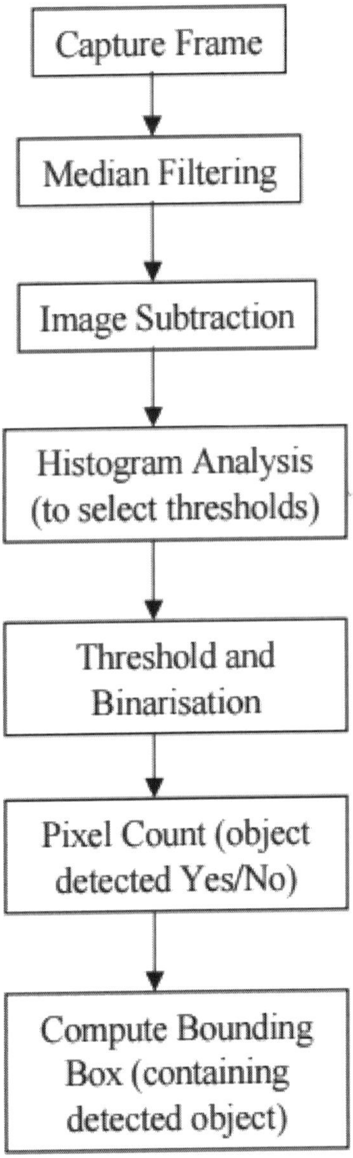

Figure 13. Block diagram object detection.

computed for a bounding box. This sequence of steps will encapsulate any detected objects in its bounding box, maintaining the original grey-levels of the object. This sequence of actions is illustrated as block diagram in figure 13.

The bounding box contains the coordinates of the intruder. This object of interest within this bounding box can be used for further analysis in the detection of suspicious activity. This simple process will allow the detection of an intruder. The comparison of frames can be efficiently implemented after noise is eliminate or reduced as indicated in the previous section.

7.2.2 Motion analysis

A particle analysis is performed on the binary image produced after thresholding. This analysis calculates two measures for each detected object or pixel cluster within the binary image. A pixel cluster is a grouping of connected pixels. The measures calculated are pixel area (size) and shape factor.

Pixel area is the number of pixels of intensity value 1 (white) in a given cluster. X is the cluster containing all pixels in the object of interest. The area of an object can be calculated as a relative measure with respect to the entire image area. In the discrete case, it is approximated by the number of pixels in the object of interest.

$$A(X) = \sum_{i,j} g(x_i, y_j) \tag{2}$$

Where $A(X)$ is the area of the object X, $g(x_i, y_j) = 1$ if the pixel lies within the object X *and* $g(x_i, y_j) = 0$ otherwise

The *area* measure can be used given a binary image to obtain the relative size of the object. This measure can give an indication of whether the object is sufficiently large (in relative terms) to warrant further analysis. It can also be weighted by a size factor which characterises the area of a single pixel. In that case, the measure is physically homogeneous to an area. A shape cannot be characterised by a single measure, or even a simple set of measures. Several quantities have been defined to account for specific shape characteristics.

The *shape factor, $F_{c'}$* is defined as:-

$$F_C = \frac{L(X)^2}{4\pi . A(X)} \tag{3}$$

Where *A*(*X*) is the area of the object *X* and *L*(*X*) is the perimeter of the object, defined below.

The perimeter designates the length of the object boundary. In the discrete case, the perimeter can be simply estimated as the number of points which lie on the object boundary. The shape factor measure is invariant to rotation, reflection and scaling. It has no dimension and is equal to 1 for a disk. It measures the elongation of an object. An elongated set has a higher shape factor. This measure, with its ability to distinguish the elongated form of a human figure, is particularly useful in the object detection process. The area and shape factor for all pixel clusters (which are potential objects of interest) within the binary image is calculated. A fixed threshold for each measure is used to select objects for further analysis. Any small differences in pixel intensity between the captured frame and the previously acquired frame will be effectively removed during the area and shape factor thresholding operation. Small differences do not indicate the presence of an object in the frame, but can often be attributed to small changes in illumination between successive frame captures. The threshold chosen for each measure is scene dependent. Once the approximate size of objects of interest is known relative to the size of the entire image, thresholds can be calculated to ensure only object areas greater than the threshold are retained for further analysis. After thresholding, the resulting binary image will contain the pixel clusters corresponding to objects meeting the selection criteria. The object detection algorithm is performed on each frame acquisition. Detected objects that have met the size, shape and Si factor (as defined in equation (7) Fernandez-Canque et al, 2009) criteria are tracked in terms of their position within camera images. The tracking algorithms require each object to be represented by a single pixel co-ordinate position within the image. The barycentre of detected objects is used to provide the single co-ordinate. The barycentre of an object is similar to its centre of gravity. The resultant co-ordinate position for each object gives a uniform positional locator between successive frame captures which is independent of object size and shape. The inertia moments define some global characteristics of the object but it is the first order moments of inertia which define the barycentre. They are defined in the discrete case as:-

$$M_{1x} = \frac{1}{A(X)} \sum_{X} x_i \tag{4}$$

$$M_{1y} = \frac{1}{A(X)} \sum_{X} y_j \tag{5}$$

Where M_{1x} is the first moment of inertia in the x plane.

M_{1y} is the first moment of inertia in the y plane

$A(X)$ is the area of the object X

(x_i, y_j) is a point in the object

The barycentre of each detected object is passed to the tracking algorithm after every frame acquisition. The positional locator of each object is passed to the tracking algorithm. Subsequent frame acquisitions provide a new positional locator for each detected object. The tracking algorithm computes the linear distance from every initially detected object to every object detected in the subsequent frame acquisition. The shortest distance between each initially detected object and subsequently detected objects is selected and the object which lies the shortest distance from the initial object is then determined to be the same object as in the previous frame. The process is repeated for each frame acquisition thus allowing objects to be tracked. The distance, L, between 2 co-ordinate positions is calculated as follows:-

$$L = \sqrt{(X_1 - X_0)^2 + (Y_1 - Y_0)^2} \quad (6)$$

Where (X_0, Y_0) is the co-ordinate position of the first point

(X_1, Y_1) is the co-ordinate position of the second point

Objects detected between consecutive frames are selected for Si factor analysis. Each object pair cannot always be assumed to be the same object between consecutive frame acquisitions. The Si factor provides one method for determining that tracked objects between successive frame captures are the same object within the images. The Si factor can be calculated as follows:-

$$Si = \frac{\frac{|(A(X_{nI1}) - (A(X_{nI2}) -|}{A(X_{nI1})} \times 100 + \frac{|(F_c(X_{nI1}) - (F_c(X_{nI2})|}{F_c(X_{nI1})} \times 100}{2} \quad (7)$$

Where $A\ (X_{nI1})$ is the area of object X_n in Image 1

$A\ (X_{nI2})$ is the area of object X_n in Image 2

$F_c(X_{nI1})$ is the shape factor of object X_n in Image 1

$F_c(X_{nI2})$ is the shape factor of object X_n in Image 2

The Si factor is calculated for all n objects detected and provides a confidence measure to determine that objects tracked between images are the same object. The lower the Si factor, the more the object detected in the subsequently acquired frame conforms to the size and shape characteristics of the object in the previously acquired frame. Thresholds may be set for the allowable values of Si factor. The value of such thresholds will vary depending on the scene being viewed and the natural variations of objects in the same class that are to be detected. Objects detected between successive frames that have a Si factor which lies above the threshold can be assumed to be different objects. This provides the capability for the tracking algorithm to detect when an object has been lost rather than tracking the incorrect object. The Barycentre of each detected object is passed to the tracking algorithm after every frame acquisition. Subsequent frame acquisitions provide a new position for each detected object. The tracking algorithm computes the linear distance from every initially detected object to every object detected in the subsequent frame acquisition. For the external scene, a sufficiently large area is covered by the camera to allow object tracking to be verified. The object detection algorithm is applied to capture sequential frames to determine initially if an object has been detected, then to track any such object.

Given the small size of objects in the external scene, the additional processing steps are carried out. These steps include the analysis of detected clusters yielding data on object size and shape characteristics. Such analysis is not required for an internal scene because any detected objects would be sufficiently large in comparison to the total area of the scene that errors due to noise could effectively be eliminated by setting large thresholds. However, in the external scene, any detected object will yield a small pixel area so setting high thresholds would likely cause even objects of interest to be thresholded out. The size and shape characteristics can be used to assist in not only detecting objects, but also to subsequently track them. Kalman filter (Kalman, 1960) can provide a good way of tracking an object of interest, in the case of identifying the object the use of the Si factor may be more useful. Especially when objects of similar characteristics are physically close the Si factor can distinguish between objects. A summary in block diagram for the additional series of processing steps for the external scene to track an object of interest are specified in figure 14. The following example details the application of the outlined algorithms to the external scene and also to the task of object tracking.

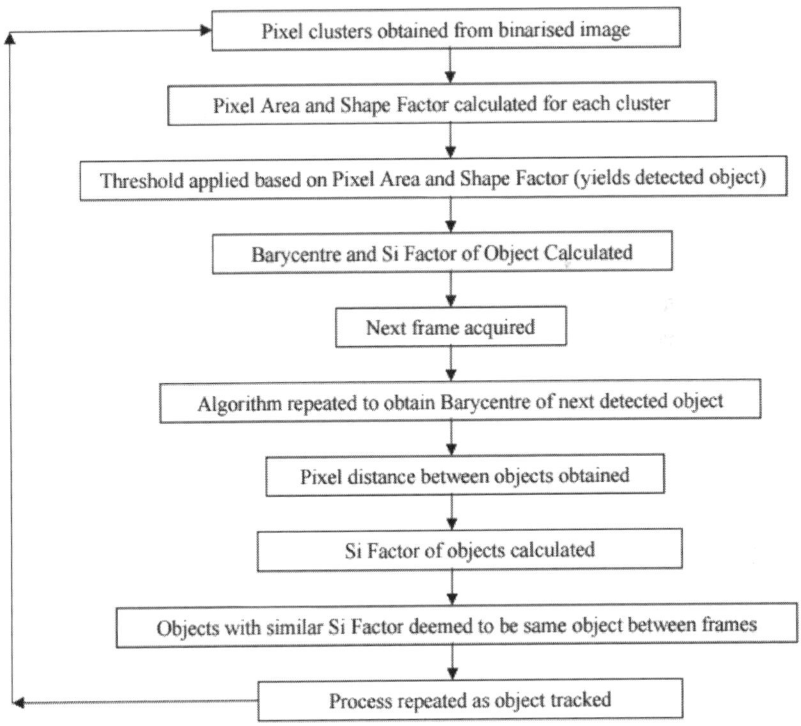

Figure 14. Block diagram. Object tracking.

The captured image in figure 15 is a car park area, and also contained a pedestrian footpath. Figure 15 shows captured frames containing one person.

Figure 15. Frame car park area containing one object of interest: one person

Figure 16 shows two frames used in the detection of suspicious activity. The example uses a sequence of these frames to track a person in this car park. Cluster will appear for objects of no interest such as birds, movements of branches, etc. After the detection and elimination of unwanted noise, figure 16(c) shows the detected person of the two scenes superimposed.

Figure 16. Two consecutive scenes (a) and (b) of a captured sequence of frames from a car park scene. In (c) the object of interest is shown for the 2 scenes after detection algorithms have been applied.

For the first frame of figure 16 the object detection algorithm is applied to this image producing the thresholded and binarised image for this frame. This frame contains 44 pixel clusters. The area and shape factor for each cluster is calculated.

Table 4 shows the analysis of the detected clusters. The minimum and maximum values for area and shape factor show the range of these measures across the 44 detected clusters.

Threshold selection is determined for a given scene based on the pixel size of the object type to be detected.

This thresholding operation yielded one detected object of area 211 (the largest cluster area), shape factor 3.11 and barycentre 102,137.

Table 4. Analysis of Clusters detected

	Area	Shape Factor	Barycentre
Minimum	1	0.47	n/a
Maximum	211	3.21	n/a
Threshold	150	2.5	n/a
Object	211	3.11	102.137

The pixel clusters which have been filtered out are caused by changes in the image between subsequent frame acquisitions. These clusters can be attributed to the movement of the tree branches in the wind. The analysis of each detected cluster and subsequent selection operation successfully removes these unwanted particles to leave only the desired object. The modified object detection algorithm can now be applied to 2 consecutive frame acquisitions. The object tracking algorithm is iteratively applied to each detected object in the initially acquired frame. The first order moments of inertia in the x and y plane are calculated for all detected clusters in each frame acquisition, and used as a positional reference by the tracking algorithm. The completion criteria for this algorithm is met when the nearest neighbouring cluster to each object in the initially acquired frame is found in the subsequently acquired frame. The object detection algorithm, when using the Si factor, is more immune to noise.

A sequence of images is captured from an external scene, figure 17 shows a test scene used. To determine suspicious activity the car park image is divided into four distinct areas, as shown in figure 17. The scene has four distinct areas: Area 1 pathways, Area 2 car park, Area 3 exit/entrances, Area 4 perimeter area. Risk Index takes values between 0 and 1, where 0 represent the lowest risk. For this exercise the areas were given the following risk indices: Area 1 risk 0.2, area 2 risk 0.6, Area 3 risk 0.7, and area 4 risk 0.8. The risk indices are determined based on the knowledge of the scene and the threat associated with human movement within that area. In the image presented, the Risk Indices have been chosen such that the higher the Risk Index the greater the risk associated with human movement within that area.

In the experiment conducted, human movement is represented by crosshairs within the segmented images. The crosshairs on each segmented image represents the time-series motion of a human walker in the image. Figure 17 shows the movement of a person within the segmented areas of the scene analysed.

The aim of analysing the time series motion is to elucidate the information relevant to the task of ultimately identifying suspicious activity, and present this data in a format which the detection system can use. The aim of this experiment is to automatically determine if a given activity, identified by the time series motion of a human walker in conjunction with the segmented image data, can be interpreted as suspicious. The information used by the detection system should incorporate both the walker's positional data, as well as the Risk Index data.

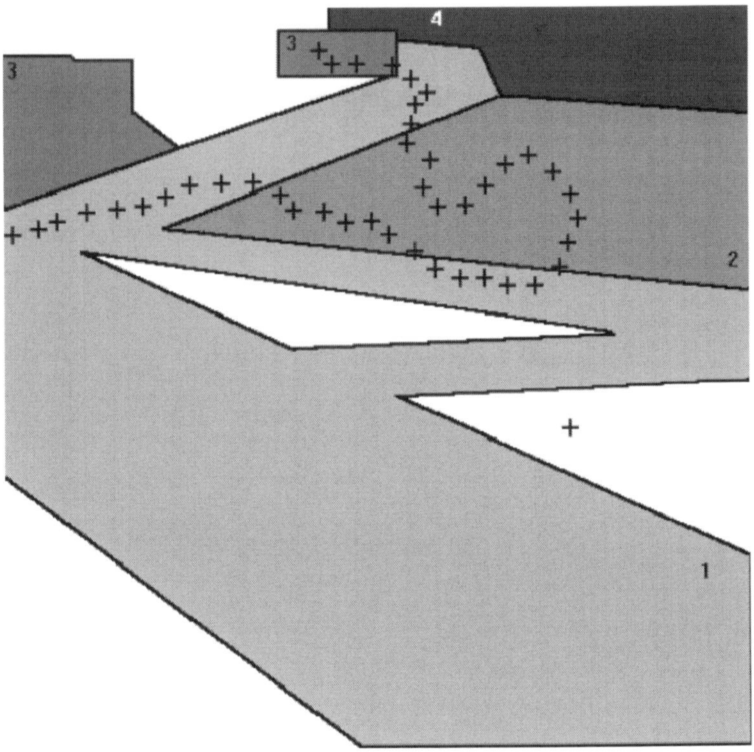

Figure 17. Trajectory of a human walker within a scene

From this tracking scene information of speed, direction and presence in any zone is extracted and presented to a trained ANN for determination of suspicious activity.

In this experiment, twenty five segmented images are presented, each identifying the path a human walker takes within the scene. Figure 18 shows the response of the ANN to the 25 path samples of people walking patterns in the different areas of the scene analysed indicating the degree of suspicious activity for each pattern.

The ANN results of suspicious activity show a good correlation with the human operator response within scenes. This provides a good forewarning role allowing further investigation by a human operator. The MV application presented here can provide an indication of suspicious activity as the output of the ANN. This ANN response is based on the direction of the intruder, the speed of movement, the position on the different risk areas and the pattern of movement within the scene.

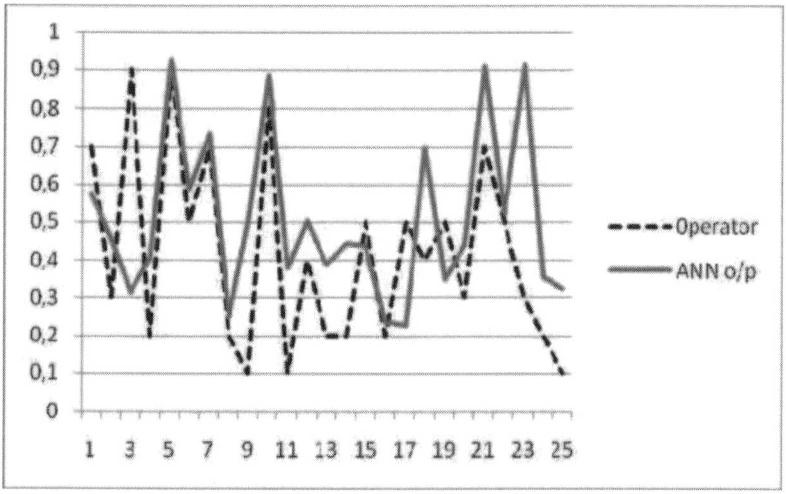

Figure 18. Response from the ANN and operator to 25 segmented image samples

7.2.3 Posture analysis

If the person is not moving in areas that are considered a risk, his or her posture may indicate suspicious activity. Each image is subjected to a reduction algorithm, producing a quantised image, followed by a 16 by 16 data array to be presented to the ANN.

The ANN used is trained to provide an output for waling, standing and crouching postures. Figures 19-21 shows results from a trained ANN to a set of 26 images containing humans in these positions.

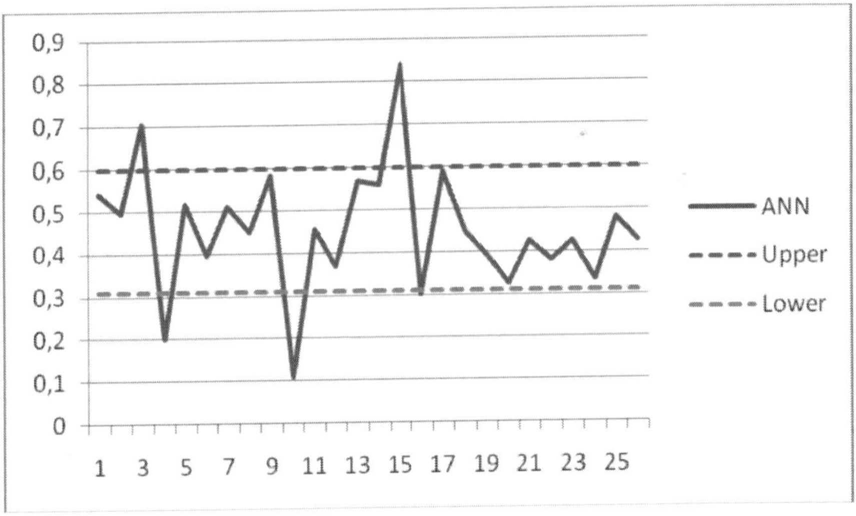

Figure 19. Classifier results from the ANN for walking postures

Figure 19 shows results for walking postures, Figure 20 for standing postures and Figures 21 for crouching postures. The ANN has been trained in such way that values on the y-axis between 0.3 and 0.6 indicate that a walking posture has been detected. Values between 0.52 and 0.81 indicate that a standing posture has been detected and values between 0.88 and 0.95 indicate detection of a crouching posture.

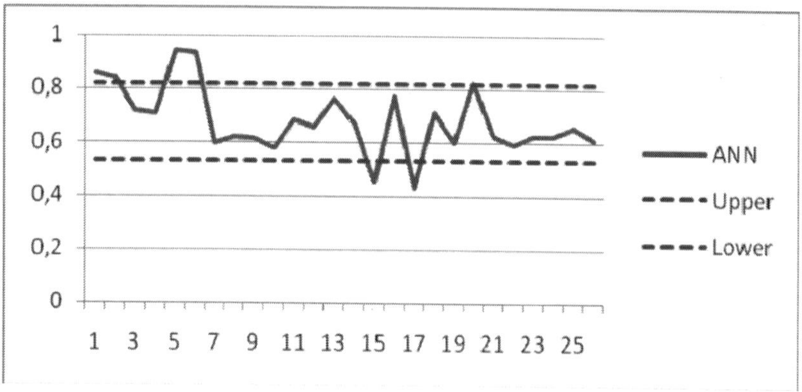

Figure 20. Classifier results from the ANN for standing postures

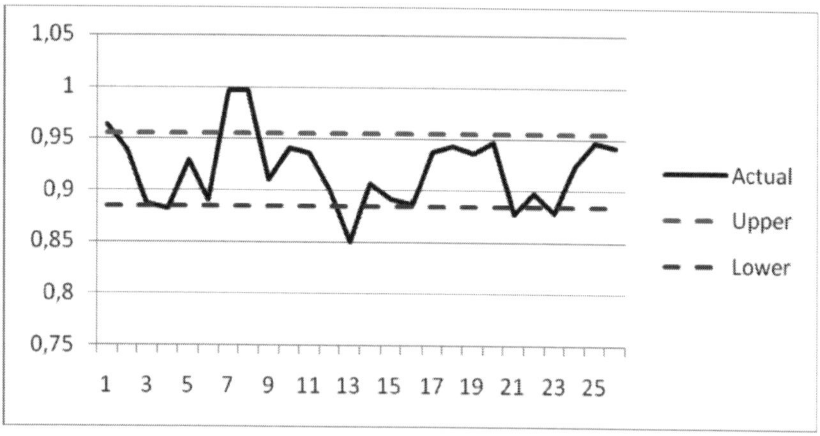

Figure 21. Neural Network response for crouching postures.

On the basis of the results obtained for each newly analysed posture, upper and lower limits (shown by chain lines) have been set which provide a range of values within which lies a high probability that a given posture has been detected. The walking posture test images included various viewing orientations. In the case of a person walking directly towards or away from the camera, difficulties are encountered in determining if the person is standing or walking. These walking postures are very similar in appearance to standing postures when presented as a two-dimensional camera image. This similarity, and consequent classification difficulty, was predicted for a two-dimensional image system. A number of the images in the walking posture data set show a higher than expected value although only 15% lie outside the upper and lower limits. The higher values obtained tend towards the values expected for a standing posture. The results produced for the crouching postures show values which are consistently very close to the expected values. The error in the crouching posture data was smaller and more uniform than for the other two posture types. The apparent similarity between a few walking and standing postures caused the classifier some difficulties. A crouching posture is easier to identify from a two-dimensional image. Since crouching could be interpreted as potentially the most suspicious posture, the system developed shows higher performance at detecting the postures of more relevance to the task in hand.

The results are close to the expected response. This can also be used as a warning role as the MV can determine whether suspicious activity is present in an open scene under CCTV surveillance

8. CONCLUSIONS

MV application trend indicates that the advance of computation power and hardware developments allows the number and type of application to increase substantially in particular in the last 15 years.

The application of MV to variable objects requires the consideration of various factors to be accurate. Algorithms are required to obtain clear and detailed morphology including advance process using advance algorithms. In this type of application where information obtained in different planes it is useful to eliminate problems produced by variation of illumination. A good focus control based on a focus score allows the MV application to manipulate objects of small dimensions to gather more details of the characteristics of the object to be analysed.

The Machine Vision example presented in this chapter can perform automated analysis to determine whether or not micro-organism oocysts are present in treated water. The system can reliably determine the presence of micro-organisms and enable samples to be accurately and efficiently reviewed by an operator if required. The proposed approach allows a reliable detection of waterborne micro-organisms in large quantities of water. This provides an industrial system to monitor micro-organisms in the water industry. The implemented algorithm complies with the standard operating protocol provided by the water authorities in UK and satisfies the EU directive on drinking water quality

The MV second example presented in this chapter can improve the performance of automated analysis to determine whether suspicious activity is present in an open scene under CCTV surveillance. The system can determine the presence and movements of a person and provide indications of suspicious activity based on pathway taken, speed, direction; the system can also provide indication of suspicious activity based on human posture analysis. These enable efficient monitoring and accurate review of scenes by an operator. The system proposed can provide a warning role to reduce the problem of human operator's fatigue and shortened attention span. This greatly increases the ability to carry out properly the task of constant and distant monitoring.

ACKNOWLEDGMENT

The author wishes to thank the Scottish Parasitic Laboratory for providing samples of micro-organisms in water. Also I would like to thank my wife Vicky Grandon for her continual support and comprehension. Special thanks to my students Sorin Bota and John Freer.

REFERENCES

1. BIDS (2011) Bath Information and Data Services, available from http:// www.bids.ac.uk

2. Braggins, D. (2000). Illumination for machine vision. Sensor Review, Volume 20, No1, pp 20- 30.

3. Butler, B. E. (1980). Selective Attention and Stimulus Localization in Visual Perception. Canadian Journal of Psychology, Vol. 34, 1980 pp 119-133

4. Current, W.L. (1988). The biology of Cryptosporidium. Am. Soc. Microbiology News, 54 / 1988, pp. 605-611

5. Current, W.L. And Gracia. (1991). Cryptosporidiosis. Clinical Microbiology Review, 4/1991, pp. 325-358

6. Danielsson, P. (1980). Euclidean distance mapping. Computer Graphics and Image Processing, 14/1980, pp.227-248

7. EEC (1998). Council Directive 98/83/EC of 3 November 1998 on the quality of water intended for human consumption, Official Journal L 330 , 05/12/1998 pp. 0032 - 005

8. Ellenberger, S. & Ian T. Young, I. (2000). Microscope image acquisition, Image Processing and Analysis, Oxford University Press, pp.1-35

9. Eriksen, C. W., Murphy, T. D. (1987). Movement of attentional focus across the visual field: A critical look at the evidence., Perception & Psychophysics, Vol. 42, 1987 pp 229-305.

10. Eriksen, C. W., Hoffman, J. E. (1972). Temporal and spatial characteristics of selective encoding from visual displays, Perception & Psychophysics, Vol. 12, 1972 pp 201- 204.

11. Fernandez- Canque, H. L.; Bota, S.; Beggs, B.; Smith, E.; Hintea, S. and Smith, H. V. (2000). Detection and Classification System for Water-Borne Micro-organisms Using Machine Vision. Journal TABEMED 2000 Acta electrotehnica napocensis. Romania. June 2000 ISSN 1224-2497 pp 105-111

12. Fernandez-Canque, H. L.; Hintea, S.; Csipkes, G.; Bota, S. and Smith, H. (2009). Machine Vision Application to the Detection of Water-Borne Micro-Organisms. Intelligent Decision Technologies an International Journal. IOS Press, ISSN 18724981,2009 Vol 3, Number 2. pp 93-100.

13. Fernandez-Canque, H. L.; Hintea, S.; Freer, J. And Ahmadinia, A. (2009). Machine Vision Application to Automatic Intruder Detection using CCTV. Proceeding 13th International Conference, KES2009 Knowledge-Based Intelligent Information and Engineering Systems. ISBN 13978364204594, Santiago, Chile September 2009. pp. 498-505.

14. Frazen, C and Muller, A. (1999). Cryptosporidia and Microsporidia – Waterborne Diseases in the Immunocompromised Host. Diagn Microbiol Infect Dis, 1999, 34: 245-262

15. Hanks, J. (1998). Using Edge Detection in Machine Vision Gauging Application. , National Instruments - 1998. Application Note 125.

16. Goodman, J.W. (1996). Introduction to Fourier optics, 2nd edition, McGraw-Hill, San Francisco, USA.

17. Goolkasian, P., (1991) Processing Visual-stimuli Inside and Outside the Focus of Attention. Bulletin of the Psychonomic Society. 1991 Vol. 29, No. 6, p 510.

18. Kalman, R.E. (1960). A new approach to linear filtering and prediction problems. Journal of Basic Engineering 82 (1): pp 35–45.

19. Luo, X., Jayas, D.S. and Symons, S. J.(1999) Identification of Damaged Kernels in Wheat using a Colour Machine Vision System, Journal of Cereal Science. 1999. 30 pp 49- 59.

20. Pawley, J.B. (1995). Handbook of biological confocal microscopy, 2nd edition, Plenum Press, New York.

21. Russell, S. J.; Norvig, P. (2003), Artificial Intelligence: A Modern Approach 2nd ed., Upper Saddle River, New Jersey: Prentice Hall, pp. 111–114, ISBN 0-13-790395-2

22. Saarinen, J., Julesz, B. (1991) The Speed of Attentional Shifts in the Visual field. Proceedings of the National Academy of Sciences of the United States of America, Vol. 88, No. 5, pp 1812-1814.

23. Smith, H.V. and Rose, LB. (1990). Waterborne Cryptosporidiosis. Parasitol Today 1990. 6, pp. 8-12.

24. Smith, H.V. and Rose, LB. (1998). Waterborne cryptosporidiosis: Current status. Parasitol Today. 1998. 14, pp.14-22.

3

CHAPTER

RESEARCH ON WORKPIECE SORTING SYSTEM BASED ON MACHINE VISION MECHANISM

Juan Yan, Huibin Yang

College of Mechanical Engineering, Shanghai University of Engineering Science, Shanghai, China

ABSTRACT

This paper describes industrial sorting system, which is based on robot vision technology, intro- duces main image processing methodology used during development, and simulates algorithm with Matlab. Besides, we set up image processing algorithm library via C# program and realize recognition and location for regular geometry workpiece. Furthermore, we analyze camera model in vision algorithm library, calibrate the camera, process the image series, and resolve the identify problem for regular geometry workpiece with different colours.

Keywords: Machine Vision, Industrial Robot, Target Recognition, Image Processing

1. INTRODUCTION

With the development of society, enterprises have become increasingly demanding on production automation, so that more and more industrial robots have been used in automated production lines. For example, in order to enhance operational efficiency in modern logistics distribution centers and to improve the efficiency of large- scale centralized distribution to reduce operating costs, as the core equipment distribution center and the main operating procedures, sorting systems and sorting operation efficiency and technology are increasingly by theorists and engineering concern. Another example is the tool change robot in the machining center. Compared to ma- nual tool change method, this tool works more quickly and more accurately, greatly reduces tool change time and increases production efficiency. In the automotive industry, due to the auto parts more complex vehicle bodies, in many cases on the body cannot use manual welding. Currently, automobile manufacturers utilize a lot of body welding robots to improve product quality and to reduce the labor intensity. Visibly, doing the work on the production line with industrial robots is an inevitable trend.

Machine vision technology uses cameras and computers to simulate human vision features, which are widely used in electronics, aerospace, automotive and automotive parts manufacturing industry, the pharmaceutical industry and electronics fields [1]. In the traditional production line, sorting artifacts with industrial robots usually uses teaching methods or offline programming operations. All the actions and placements, etc. should be strictly preset. Once the working environment or condition changes, it will affect the efficiency and accuracy of crawling robot, unable to meet the high-speed production of large quantities. Introduction of machine vision in industrial production can greatly improve productivity and reduce costs. Industrial machine vision technology based on sorting system with high detection speed, high reliability, and high real-time, compared to traditional mechanical sorting, is more intelligent, more efficient and has other irreplaceable advantages.

This paper researches the sorting system based on the machine vision and the methods of camera calibration. The straight linear method is used and the system is simulated by Matlab. It also studied the correlation of image processing algorithms, combined thresholding proposed centroid location method to solve the different colors of regular geometric shape of the workpiece recognition problem. Threshold segmentation and edge detection method can lock the workpiece area; centroid location can accurately locate the geometric center of the workpiece. And this integrated approach can effectively solve the regular geometric shape of the workpiece sorting problem.

2. SORTING SYSTEM BASED ON MACHINE VISION HARDWARE ARCHITECTURE ARTIFACTS

In this paper, the mechanical axis motion platform, is built on the work of sorting machine vision systems. Overall system structure is shown in Figure 1.

The hardware platform consists of mechanical three-axis motion platform, camera platforms, PC and motion control unit, four major components. Hardware platform package sorting system is shown in Figure 2.

Mechanical three-axis motion platform: Using screw-nut mechanism, while the linear guide linear motion needs as a guide and support.

The system uses a servo motor drive: although the control unit is complex, the high repeat accuracy, no step phenomenon and no cumulative error [2].

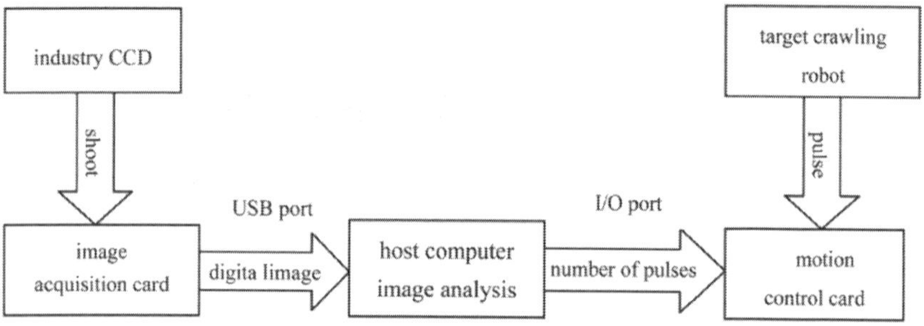

Figure 1. Piece sorting system structure based on machine vision.

Figure 2. Workpiece sorting system based on machine vision hardware platform.

Camera Platform: Camera platform unit is mainly constructed by MV-2000UC camera and light source com- ponents. Hanging bracket role monocular camera is to obtain the experimental stage of the video image of the workpiece. White LED surface light source provides light for digital cameras captured images. The light will be fixed at the top of the workpiece in order to eliminate the shadow of the workpiece itself.

PC: Using existing laboratories as a PC, since the development environment is good, fast, easy to operate and low cost. At that time with respect to the IPC, its anti-interference ability and stability is poor, such as teaching or laboratory for stable work environment occasions. PC camera platform receives the experimental stage to obtain a video image of the workpiece using the vision system to identify the target species, the centroid of the workpiece is then calculated, and finally the image according to the relationship between the coordinate system and the object coordinate system, the calculated position of the target relative and direction, and then passes the information parameter to the control unit.

Motion Control unit: mainly control the composition of the cabinet and robots. It is responsible for the para- meters analyzing, then the robot-related operations and finally the completion of the target workpiece sorting grab and place.

3. CAMERA CALIBRATION

Camera calibration is one of the important parts in machine vision [3] . Calibration includes calibration camera and visual systems. First of all based model of the camera, and then to establish the relationship between the coordinate system, and finally through the calibration can establish the correspondence between image pixels and the spatial three-dimensional coordinates [4]. Workpiece sorting system is based on machine vision. The camera calibration as a key link to other related work is a prerequisite for the smooth conduct of the direct impact on subsequent sorting processes. Camera calibration process is based on the model of the camera imag- ing process to solve internal and external camera parameters, and these parameters determine the correspon- dence between the image pixel point and three-dimensional coordinate space.

There are many ways in camera calibration, the current methods commonly used in machine vision are direct linear method, perspective projection matrix method, Zhang Zhengyou France, the two-step camera calibration method. For the facts of relatively stable laboratory and low interference environment, this paper chooses the direct linear method, which is characterized by convenient computing but less accuracy. It is difficult to be pre- cise shooting environment complex self-correcting. DLT method called direct linear method, by Abdel-Aziz and Karara and was first proposed in 1971 [5] . This method does not consider the non-linear distortion of the camera, getting the relevant parameters of the camera by directly solving a set of linear equations. It acquires pinhole imaging model for the study, ignoring specific intermediate imaging process and using a 3 × 4 order matrix to represent a direct correspondence between the point and the two-dimensional space object image point. The linear transformation matrix is with only a difference of a perspective matrix scale factor. Providing space point (X,Y,Z) P coordinates in the camera coordinate system of (x,y,z), the camera will capture the image on the CCD imaging plane, which is provided for the image point coordinates (x,y) corresponding to the image pixel coordinates (u,v).

By the world coordinate system to the camera coordinate system, using the following formula rotation—trans- lation conversion formula described:

$$\begin{bmatrix} x \\ y \\ z \\ 1 \end{bmatrix} = \begin{bmatrix} R & T \\ 0 & 1 \end{bmatrix} \begin{bmatrix} X \\ Y \\ Z \\ 1 \end{bmatrix} \tag{1}$$

where in R is a rotation matrix, T is the translation matrix. In the case where distortion is not considered (i.e., an ideal perspective projection), the image coordinates of the camera coordinate system is described by the following formula:

$$s \begin{bmatrix} X \\ Y \\ 1 \end{bmatrix} = \begin{bmatrix} f & 0 & 0 \\ 0 & f & 0 \\ 0 & 0 & 1 \end{bmatrix} \begin{bmatrix} x \\ y \\ z \end{bmatrix} \tag{2}$$

In the image processing, is often used in image coordinate of the pixel as a unit, so to convert the image coordinate system to the coordinate system of the pixel, i.e.

$$\begin{bmatrix} u \\ v \\ 1 \end{bmatrix} = \begin{bmatrix} \frac{1}{d_X} & 0 & 0 \\ 0 & \frac{1}{d_Y} & 0 \\ 0 & 0 & 1 \end{bmatrix} \begin{bmatrix} X \\ Y \\ 1 \end{bmatrix} \tag{3}$$

Without considering the various types of the imaging by the specific process, can be obtained:

$$s\begin{bmatrix} u \\ v \\ 1 \end{bmatrix} = \begin{bmatrix} r_{11} & r_{12} & r_{13} & r_{14} \\ r_{21} & r_{22} & r_{23} & r_{24} \\ r_{31} & r_{32} & r_{33} & r_{34} \end{bmatrix} \begin{bmatrix} X \\ Y \\ Z \\ 1 \end{bmatrix} \quad (4)$$

where, (X,Y,Z) of the three-dimensional world coordinate space points, (u,v) coordinates of the corres- ponding pixel, r_{ij} is a perspective view of elements of the transformation matrix. It contains three equations, finishing eliminates, obtain the following two linear equations on people r_{ij}:

$$r_{11}X + r_{12}Y + r_{13}Z + r_{34} - uXr_{31} - uYr_{32} - uZr_{33} = ur_{34} \quad (5)$$

$$r_{21}X + r_{22}Y + r_{23}Z + r_{24} - vXr_{31} - vYr_{32} - uZr_{33} = ur_{34} \quad (6)$$

This equation describes the relationship between the two three-dimensional world and the corresponding points between image points. If the three-dimensional world coordinates and the corresponding image coor- dinates are known, the transformation matrix regarded as unknown, then there will be a total of 12 unknowns. For two equations above each object point has, in general, can be set $r_{34} = 1$, then there will be a total of 11 unknowns. Taking six goals can get 12 points a overdetermined equation Using the least squares method des- cribed above can easily find solution of linear equations [6] . Using more points, we make much more than the number of equations number of unknowns, using the least squares method for solving can reduce the impact of errors caused by the perspective transformation matrix obtained after its decomposition can get cameras inside and outside the parameters.

Based on the direct linear method was calibrated to the camera. Put the calibration paper on a suitable position in the robot coordinate system, as shown in Figure 3. Cross figure crosshairs for the world coordinate system. Only a simple translation of the relationship is needed between it and the robot base coordinate system, i.e., calculating the target position in the world coordinate system, then subtracting a certain shift amount and finally obtaining the target based on the robot base in the standard position.

Figure 3. Camera calibration chart based DLT.

Corner extraction algorithm using corner point data is shown in Table 1.

On the Matlab model with a blue asterisk plotted coordinates of each point (real value), the table on each corner point coordinates a left multiplication result (calculated) M-1 obtained plotted with a green plus sign, as shown in Figure 4.

The verification result from Figure 4 is that, by using direct linear method in this system, the calibration results is accurate, easy to calculate and close to actual value. Besides, the calibration results are also good, which provides a reliable foundation for accurate positioning of the workpiece in a sorting system.

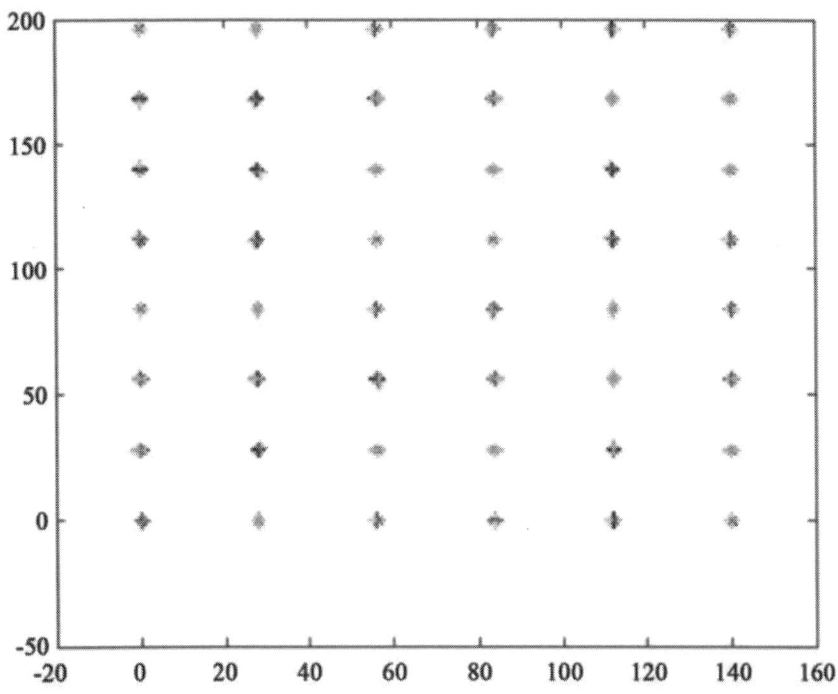

Figure 4. Camera calibration results based DLT.

Table 1. Angular point data table.

		Angular point data table		
(u,v)	Column 1	Column 2	Column 3	Column 4
Line 1	(234.5, 168)	(261.5, 166.5)	(289.5, 166.5)	(316.5, 166.5)
Line 2	(235.5, 194.5)	(262.5, 194.5)	(289.5, 193.6)	(316.5, 193.5)
Line 3	(235.5, 221.5)	(262.5, 221.5)	(289.5, 221.5)	(316.5, 220.5)
Line 4	(235.5, 248.5)	(262.5, 248.5)	(290, 248.5)	(316.5, 247.5)
Line 5	(236.5, 275.5)	(262.5, 275.5)	(290.5, 275.5)	(317, 275)
Line 6	(236.5, 302.5)	(263.5, 302.5)	(290.5, 302.5)	(317.5, 302.5)
(u,v)	Column 5	Column 6	Column 7	Column 8
Line 1	(344, 166)	(371, 166)	(397.5, 165.5)	(425, 165.5)
Line 2	(343, 193)	(370, 194)	(397.5, 192.5)	(425.5, 192.5)
Line 3	(343.5, 220.5)	(370.5, 220.5)	(398.5, 220.5)	(425.5, 219.5)
Line 4	(344, 247.5)	(371, 247.5)	(398.5, 247.5)	(425.5, 247.5)
Line 5	(344.5, 247.5)	(371.5, 274.5)	(398.5, 274.5)	(425.5, 274.5)
Line 6	(344, 301.5)	(371.5, 301.5)	(398.5, 301.5)	(398.5, 301.5)

4. THRESHOLDING SEGMENTATION

This design uses machine vision technology, the different colors of the workpiece intelligent sorting rules. When the camera calibration is completed, after the pixel coordinates to the scenecoordinate correspondence to obtain the target, will be on the video image is processed by computer.

First, the camera image acquired in the target workpiece is detected. Target detection is extracted from the image portion of interest, i.e., the image segmentation; the image processing to the image analysis is a key step. At present, a lot of image segmentation methods, such as thresholding method, edge detection and region extraction method. In this paper, we use the thresholding method and edge detection method to detect the target workpiece.

Thresholding as the most common color distinction is a region-based image segmentation technique. Briefly, image segmentation threshold is transformed to a color image to grayscale, the first grayscale range of an image to determine the gray value threshold, then the image of the gray value of each pixel with this threshold value, and are classified according to the size of the result of the comparison, based on the threshold values of all the pixels in the image is divided into two areas.

A pair of the original image $f(x,y)$ is taken to define a single threshold value T of the divided

$$\text{image is} : g(x,y)=\begin{cases}1 & f(x,y)>T \\ 0 & f(x,y)\leq T\end{cases} \tag{7}$$

In the actual case, the difference between the image of the target workpiece and background brightness is small, so the threshold needs to be adjusted manually. Figure 5 shows the use of maximum between-class va- riance method combined with manual adjustment method in Matlab to finalize the process threshold.

From the segmentation results can be seen, when the threshold of T is 100, it's the best segmentation, can accurate segmentation of the target range of workpiece, which proves Ostu method combined with manual adjust- ment is the most suitable way for this system.

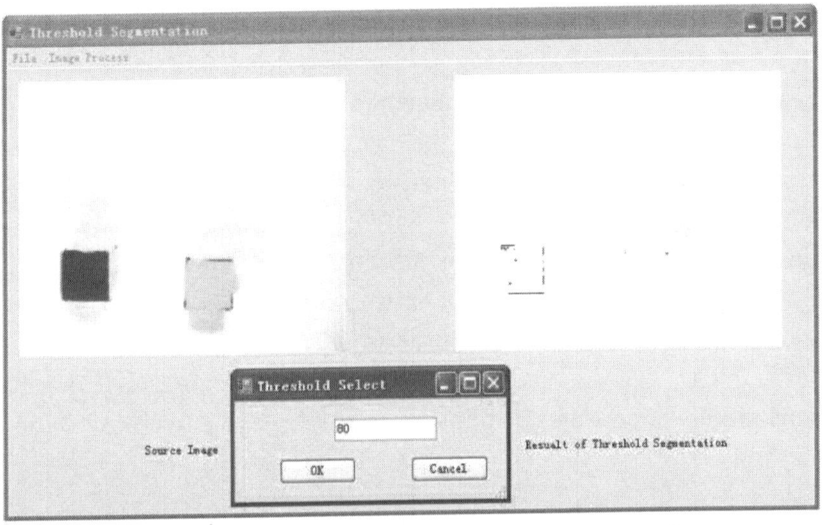

(a)

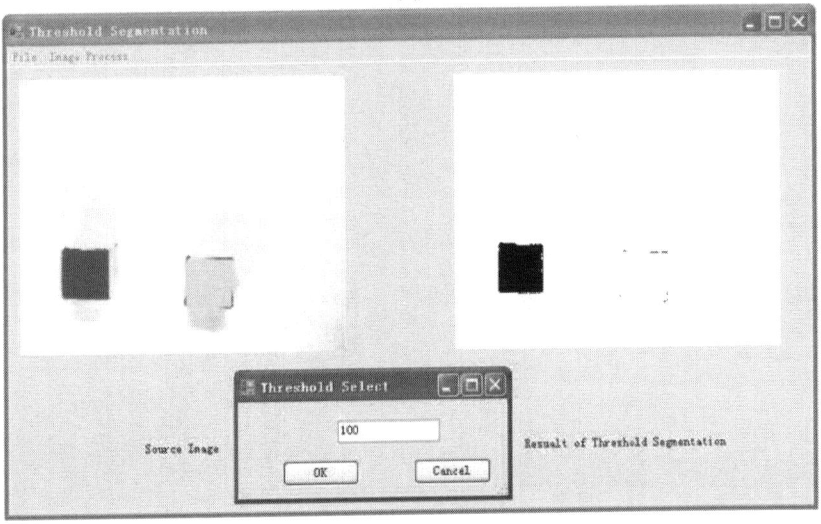

(b)

Figure 5. Threshold segmentation results. (a) When the threshold T to 80 threshold segmentation results; (b) When the threshold T to 100 threshold segmentation results.

5. DETERMINE THE CENTROID

In the sorting operation of the workpiece, the workpiece needs to be identified for positioning, the general centroid coordinates describing the location information of the workpiece. But the calculation method for multi- target centroid such as starting algorithms geometric center of the target group, the calculation is more com- plicated; through rows of pixels accumulating and averaging roughly centroid location, can not meet the precise positioning. According to the characteristics identified herein workpiece shape rules proposed rule graphics centroid location method [7] .

When the function is applied to shape analysis, suppose there are binary function:

$$m_{pq} = \int_{-\infty}^{+\infty}\int_{-\infty}^{+\infty} x^p x^q f(x,y)\,\mathrm{d}x\mathrm{d}y \quad p,\ q \in N_0 = \{0,1,\cdots\} \tag{9}$$

Take $(p+q)$ as the moment of order. The moment for $M \times N$ digital image $f(i,j)$, $(p+q)$ is defined as:

$$m_{pq} = \sum_{i=0}^{M-1}\sum_{j=0}^{N-1} i^p i^q f(i,j) \tag{10}$$

0-order moment is the area of the sum of the image gray, m_{00} values represent object binary image, if used to standardize an order moments m_{10} and m_{01}, we get the coordinates of the object's center of gravity (i,j).

$$\begin{cases} \bar{i} = m_{10}/m_{00} = \sum_{i=0}^{M-1}\sum_{j=0}^{N-1} if(i,j) \Big/ \sum_{i=0}^{M-1}\sum_{j=0}^{N-1} f(i,j) \\ \bar{j} = m_{01}/m_{00} = \sum_{i=0}^{M-1}\sum_{j=0}^{N-1} jf(i,j) \Big/ \sum_{i=0}^{M-1}\sum_{j=0}^{N-1} f(i,j) \end{cases} \quad (11)$$

For binary images, grayscale only 0 and 1, the focus is the centroid. Finally, the first moment m_{10} and m_{01} is divided by zero-order moments to get the coordinates of the center of mass of the object:

$$(\bar{i}, \bar{j}) = (M_{10}/M_{00}, M_{01}/M_{00}) \quad (12)$$

After tests it is proved that the algorithm is simple and effective and is suitable for any graphics.

In this paper, the workpiece has been recognized as a rectangular, triangular, circular or a regular shape of the workpiece. The program is written in C#, in an ideal environment, workpiece recognition results are shown in Figure 6.

The rule workpiece centroid recognition results of Figure 6 demonstrates that, it is simple and efficient to adopt rule centroid locolization algorithm and is suitable for any graphic. Besides, programming is simple, re- cognition is speedy and recognition results are accurate.

6. CONCLUSIONS

This paper describes the main algorithm in the industrial sorting machine vision technology used in the system, using thresholding to detect the target work area and describe the target workpiece position information com- bined centroid location method. The recognition algorithm is programmed in MATLAB environment to conduct a simulation algorithm and it is developed using C# rule artifacts recognition software. According to the results obtained, to identify the robot reaches the top of the target number of pulses required to send to the motion control card, by motion control card for controlling the motor and the drive to achieve sorting purposes.

The results show that the practical application of technical methods discussed in this article is simple and effective. The sorting system identifies the type of workpiece correct rate of 100%, error of the target location is less than 5 mm, and further validates the feasibility of the system for robot.

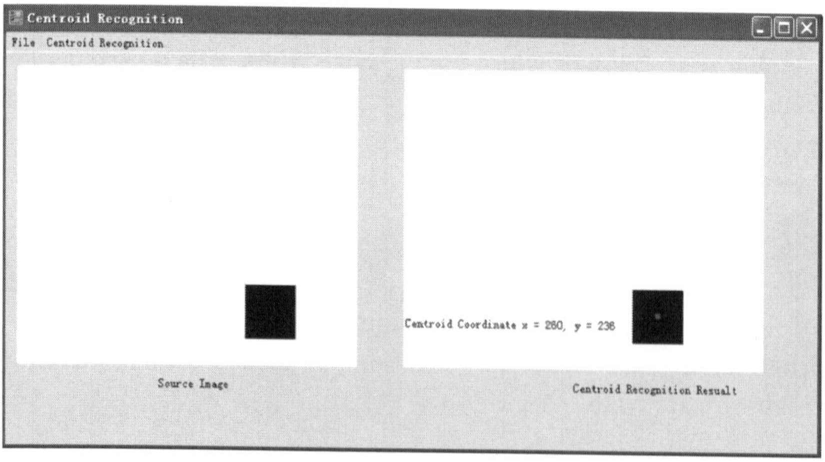

(a)

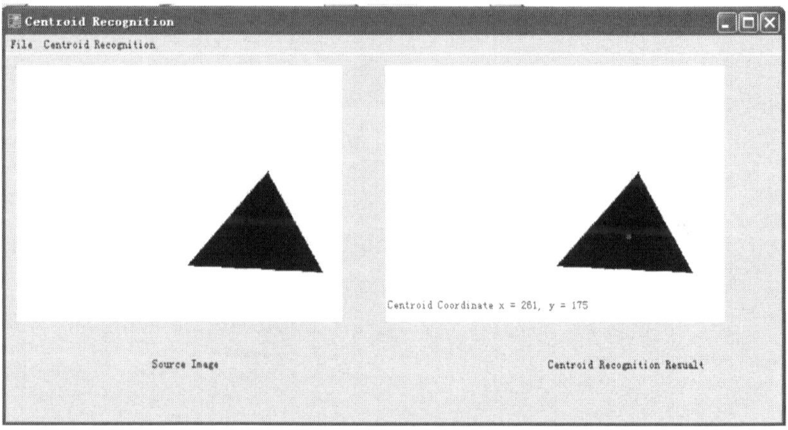

(b)

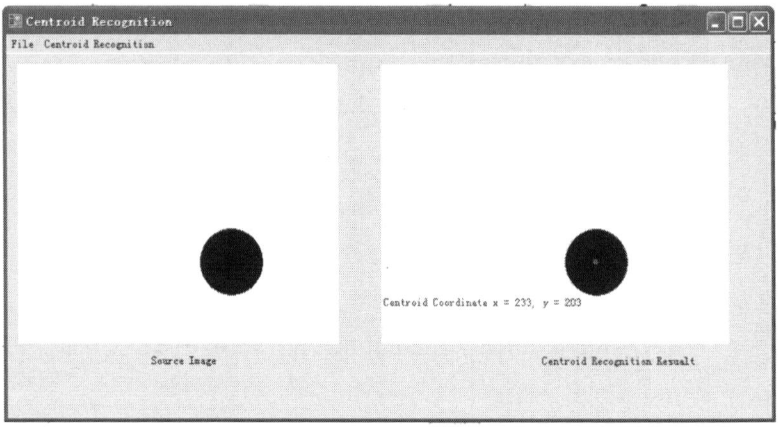

(c)

Figure 6. Rule workpiece centroid recognition results. (a) Rectangle centroid recognition results; (c) Triangle centroid recognition results; (c) Circular centroid recognition results.

REFERENCES

1. Zhuang, K.L., Wang, J.Z. and Zhou, J. (2011) Application of Machine Vision Technology in Terms of Angle Detection. Equipment Manufacturing Technology, 4, 9-11.

2. El Masry, G., Cubero, S. and Molto, E. (2012) In-Line Sourting of Irregular Potatoes by Using Automated Computer- Based Machine Vision System. Journal of Food Engineering, 112, 60-68.

3. Liu, Z.Y., Zhao, B. and Zou, F.S. (2012) Machine Vision Technology in the Sorting of the Workpiece. Computer Applications and Software, 29, 87-91.

4. Quan, H.H. and Zhang, L.P. (2007) Research on Machine Vision-Based Assembly Line Parts Recognition. Modular Machine Tool & Automatic Manufacturing Technique, 12, 58-60.

5. Forsyth, D.A. and Ponce, J. (2002) Computer Vision: A Modern Approach. Prentice Hall, New Jersey.

6. Shapiro, R. (1976) Direct Linear Transformation Method for Three-Dimensional Cinematography. Research Quar- terly, 49, 197-205.

7. Ou, X.Y., Hou, X.Z. and Zheng, K. (2012) Machine Vision Based Automatic Teaching System of Six DOF Robot. Manufacturing Automation, 34, 1-4.

4
CHAPTER

DOUBLE LIGHTING MACHINE VISION SYSTEM TO MONITOR HARVESTED PADDY GRAIN QUALITY DURING HEAD-FEEDING COMBINE HARVESTER OPERATION

Mahirah Jahari [1,2], Kazuya Yamamoto [1], Munenori Miyamoto[3], Naoshi Kondo[1], Yuichi Ogawa[1], Tetsuhito Suzuki[1], Harshana Habaragamuwa[1] and Usman Ahmad[4]

[1]*Graduate School of Agriculture, Kyoto University, Kitashirakawa-Oiwakecho, Sakyo-ku, Kyoto 606-8502, Japan*

[2]*Department of Biological and Agricultural Engineering, Faculty of Engineering, University Putra Malaysia, 43400 Serdang, Selangor, Malaysia*

[3]*Agricultural Research Center, Agricultural Operations Business, Yanmar Co., Ltd., 2481, Umegahara Maibara, Shiga 521-8511, Japan*

ABSTRACT

A machine vision system to evaluate harvested paddy grain quality during harvesting using double lighting was developed. The prototype consisted of a low-cost web camera and two lighting systems: a ring white LED for front lighting, and a flat dome white LED light for backlighting. Both lighting systems were arranged in a coaxial axis, making the system simple, compact and easy to handle. The aim of the system is to analyse the captured images and determine the amount of unwanted materials (rachis branch, grass and leaves, and stems) and damaged grain (brown and crack rice) present in the paddy as it is being harvested. In this paper, we introduce the first step in the development of the system: the design and selection of components to optimize the performance of the system to monitor harvested paddy grain quality. The idea would be to mount the system on top of the inlet channel of the grain tank of a combine harvester to provide real-time assessment of harvesting operational parameters.

Keywords: machine vision system; grain monitoring; combine harvester

1. INTRODUCTION

Paddy grain quality is an important parameter that is continually changing from field to consumption. More precisely, paddy grain quality can be defined in terms of the sum of all the attributes that lead to consumer product acceptability. Although this quality is often subjectively assessed by humans, including such attributes as appearance, smell, texture, and flavor, there are six main physical characteristics which objectively determine the material quality of paddy: moisture content level, grain maturity, varietal purity, present of dockage (such as straw, leaves and rachis branch), and present of discolored and cracked grains.

For these material paddy grain quality characteristics, most research has either focused on pre-harvest attributes or on post-harvest attributes, particularly the milling process. Research on pre-harvest attributes has demonstrated the significant within-field variability of paddy grain quality (protein and moisture content) [1,2,3], while in the post-harvest milling process, quality assessment has focused on physical characteristics, such as immature grain, varietal purity, and discolored grain (identification of damaged grain kernels) [4], inspecting and identifying rice varieties [5], degree of milling [6], yield prediction, and percentage of whole kernels [7], *etc*. To date, though, no research has been done on quality assessment of the material attributes of the paddy during harvesting. In this study, we focus on a methodology to assess, in real-time, the material quality attributes of the harvested paddy, such as dockage and cracked grain.

The rationale for this is that farmers need to monitor the harvested paddy grain and adjust their combine harvester operation settings (such as travelling speed, threshing depth, sieves, wind blower, *etc*.) to optimize grain yield, minimize grain damage and quality deterioration, and minimize dockage (see Table 1). Currently, in order to do this, though, they need to continually stop the harvester and inspect the harvested paddy grain in the grain tank during harvesting. Improper adjustment of operating parameters can lead to grain damage, increased grain loss, excessive unwanted material (straw, grass and *etc*.) and clogging [8,9]. Moreover, the farmers can only qualitatively assess the damaged grain and amount of dockage in the harvested grain, leading to inconsistent assessment, and an assessment that is highly dependent on the experience and expertise of the farmer.

Recent developments in precision and computer-assisted automated agriculture using sensors and machine vision [10] promise to help the farmer to make better management decisions. Besides the precision and efficiency offered, a machine vision system offers farmers the opportunity to build value-added characteristics and brand awareness of their product through consistency, minimizing the need for further downstream processing, and the robustness and ease of use of their product [11]. Such advantages could be obtained if the current time-consuming and inconsistent manual inspection of paddy grain quality during harvest could be replaced by a machine vision system that aids in real-time decision making for combine harvester operations.

In order to achieve this, we aim to develop a paddy grain monitoring system which can be mounted in the grain tank of a head-feeding combine harvester. The monitoring system can conduct real-time image analysis of harvested paddy when it enters the grain tank. The results of image analysis will then be used to inform the operator what parameters should be adjusted, or used as input parameters for automatic adjustment. This paper reports the first step in the development of a machine vision system to evaluate harvested paddy grain quality in a combine harvester grain tank.

Table 1. Harvesting grain conditions and necessary adjustment of the combine harvester parameters.

Type of Conditions	Harvesting Grain Condition	Necessary Adjustment of Combine Harvester Setting
Unwanted material	Many long rachis branches	Increased travelling speed
		Stronger wind blower
		Narrower opening sieve
		Narrower dust ejection
	Large amount of grass and leaves	Stronger wind blower
		Narrower opening sieve
		Shallower threshing depth
	Many stem	Narrower opening sieve
Damage Grain	Large amount of brown and cracked rice	Decreased travelling speed
		Weaker wind blower
		Wider opening sieve

To construct such a machine vision system it will be important, as a first step, to select an appropriate illumination system which optimizes the detection of damaged grain and unwanted material in the harvested grain. Moreover, the system will need to be simple, compact, and relatively low cost, as well as physically robust as it will be used in harsh field conditions. To date, most machine vision grading of agriculture products has used front lighting systems for color related information. Brosnan *et al.* (2004) reported that the quality of rice is based on variety of properties such as size, shape, color, chalkiness and number of broken rice kernels, color and chalkiness [11]. Shantaiya *et al.* (2010) used the morphological and color features to identify different varieties of rice using feed forward neural network [12]. Verma (2010) used the back propagation through time neural to sort the rice into chalky, sound, and broken kernels [13]. Yao *et al.* (2010) develop an inspection system of rice exterior quality (head rice rate, chalk rice, crackle rice) based on computer vision [14].

Novini (1990) reported that most illumination system arrangements could be grouped as one of the following: front lighting, back lighting, and structured lighting [15]. Normally front lighting and structured lighting gives color information, while back lighting generates instant contrast as it creates dark silhouettes against a bright background. By enhancing image contrast, a well-designed illumination system can improve accuracy and lead to successful image analysis [16]. Therefore, this paper focuses on the design and selection of lighting components, and the construction of a robust, prototype machine vision system to monitor harvested paddy grain quality with the expectation that the system will then need to be further developed to enable farmers to operate the combine harvester at full capacity and maximum efficiency through real-time measurement of and adjustments to harvesting operations.

2. THE PROPOSED MACHINE VISION SYSTEM FOR MONITORING HARVESTED GRAIN QUALITY

2.1. Design of Double Lighting System

In this study, a double lighting system was developed for monitoring harvested paddy grain: a frontlight system and a backlight system. Each will in turn be discussed.

2.1.1. Frontlight System

Selection of an appropriate illumination system is the most important component of the machine vision system. In terms of selection critieria, uniformity of light distribution brightness is of primary concern. The Ring-type white LED (Hayashi Watch-works Co., Ltd., type: HDR55W, Tokyo, Japan) and the Dome-type white LED (CCS Inc. Co., Ltd., type: HPD-100SW, with a temperature of 5500 K, Kyoto, Japan) illumination systems were compared using a whiteboard to evaluate their distribution brightness (Figure 1).

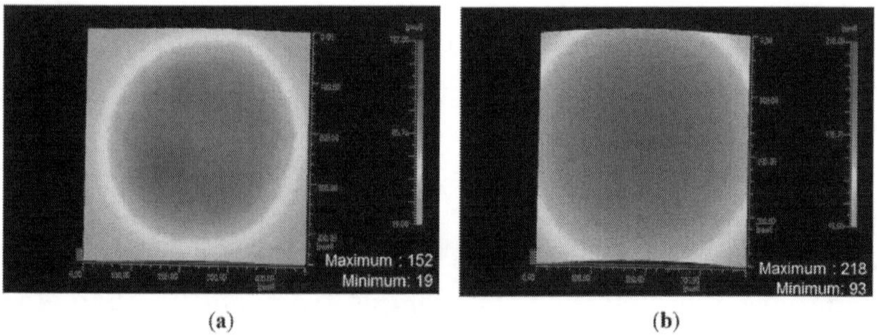

Figure 1. Brightness distribution by using whiteboard for different types of lighting system. (**a**) Ring light; (**b**) Dome light.

These figures show a distribution brightness in the range of 0 to 255 (from minimum to maximum pixel value) for the two lighting systems. For example, the Ring light has a maximum brightness of 152 and a minimum of 19 (Figure 1a), while the Dome light ranged from 218 to 93 (Figure 1b); there is not such a big difference between them. In order to make the light system compact and for ease of mounting in the grain tank, the Ring LED light was a better choice for the frontlight system. This is because the camera can be placed between the Ring lights and thus maintain a compact system. In addition, a Ring light is not as heavy as a Dome light.

These Ring lights are a white LED type (CCS Co., Ltd., type: LDR2-90-30SW with a temperature of 5500 K) with Polarizing (PL) filter. The Ring LED lights were set at an angle of 45° to the object plate to concentrate the light at the center of the target objects [17]. As the targeted illumination area was set at 50 mm × 50 mm, the Ring LED lights were set up at a distance of 47 mm in front of the object plate.

2.1.2. Backlight System

The distribution brightness on a whiteboard of a Flat dome light (CCS Inc. Co., Ltd., type: LFX2-100SW with a temperature of 6600 K) and a Coaxial light (CCS Inc. Co., Ltd., type: LFV-35SW with a temperature of 6500 K) were compared for use in a backlight system (Figure 2).

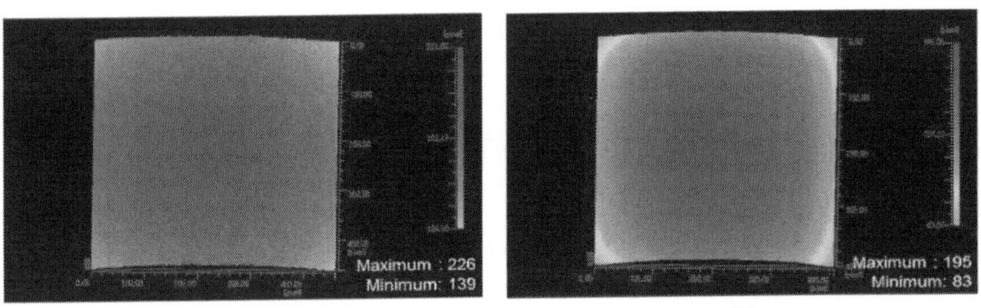

(a) (b)

Figure 2. Brightness distribution by using whiteboard for different types of lighting system. (**a**) Flat dome light; (**b**) Coaxial light.

These figures show the distribution brightness in the range of 0 to 255 (from minimum to maximum pixel value) for the two lighting systems. For example, the Flat dome light has a maximum brightness of 226 and a minimum of 139 (Figure 2a), a small variation in in brightness denoting a relatively uniform light distribution, while the Coaxil light ranged from 195 to 83 (Figure 2b). Therefore, we chose the Flat dome light, with its more uniform light distribution, to be used in the backlight system.

Normally, a critical problem for image acquisition when using both a front and back lighting set up on the same axis with conventional (diffusion plates) and LEDs (for example: CCS Co., Ltd., type: TH-63X60SW) is that the frontlight image of the objects will be poorly contrasted from the background color; making it difficult to distinguish between the target objects and the background.

In our system, we used a square white Flat dome light unit (CCS Co., Ltd., type: LFX2-75SW with a temperature of 6600 K) with a dotted pattern for indirect backlighting to resolve this problem during frontlit image acquisition. This Flat dome LED light has dots printed on the surface of the light diffusion plate (Figure 3). The dot pattern on the surface of the light diffusion plate controls illumination diffusion and transmission [18]. It can illuminate objects with a more uniform and diffused light. Besides that, when using this Flat dome light in the backlighting system, a PL filter does not need to be used in front of the backlight system.

As a result, the background of a frontlight image will be dark in color and thereby ease differentiation between target objects and the background. The conventional method for taking a frontlight image is to put the sample on a black plate for high contrast between the background and objects. However, this makes it difficult to take the backlight image with the same orientation and conditions.

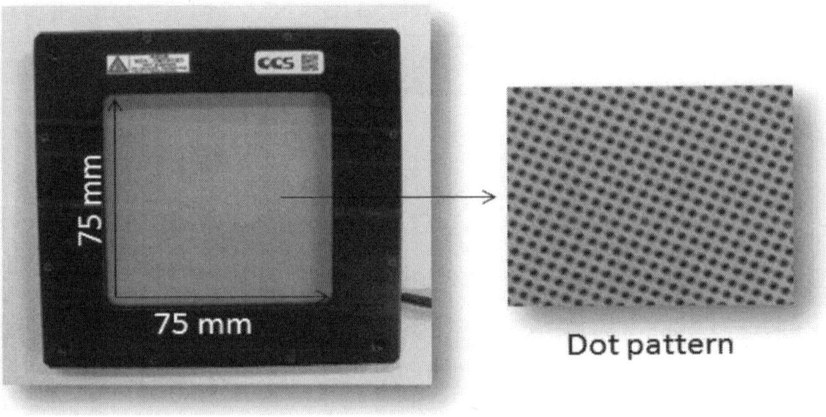

Figure 3. Flat dome light units (indirect lighting).

2.2. Overall Setup of Double Lighting System

2.2.1. Design of Whole System

A schematic of the proposed double lighting system is shown in Figure 4. The front and backlight systems were aligned along the same axis.

The advantage of using a double lighting system aligned along the same axis is that both frontlit and backlit images can be sequentially acquired simply by turning the backlighting off and on. Moreover the same orientation allows the system to be more compact and easily mounted in the a grain tank of a head-feeding combine harvester. This double lighting system has been patented in Japan (Patent No. 5780642) [19].

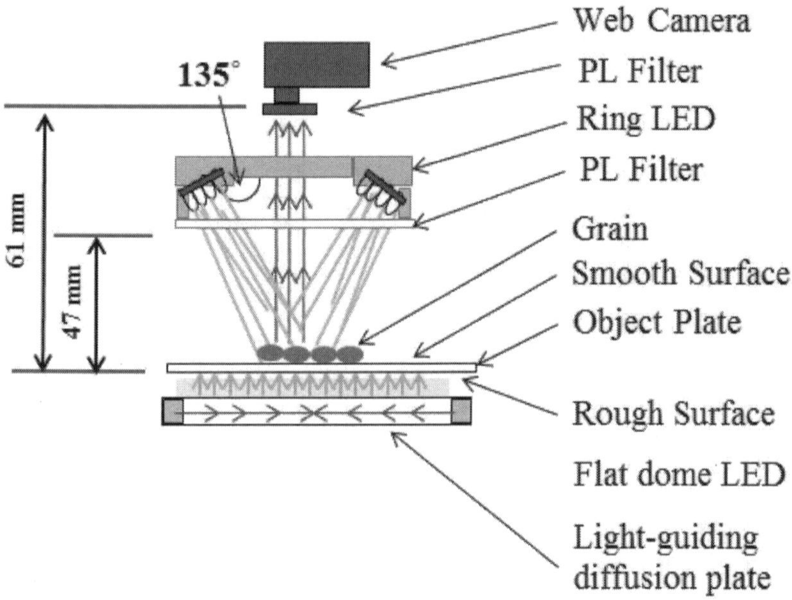

Figure 4. Layout of schematic diagram for double lighting system.

In order to acquire high-quality images, camera operating parameters were first optimized. Logicool Webcam Software version 1.1 (Logitech. Com., Romanel-sur-Morges, Switzerland) was used to adjust camera parameter settings and image capture specifications, including combinations of shutter speed and gain for ease of background removal and object classification. Once these camera parameters were optimized, images were captured at a resolution of 22 pixel/mm and a size of 1600 by 1200 pixels. The color images were 24-bit depth in the RGB color model. The data were stored in JPEG format on a computer. Control of brightness for both lighting systems was performed by a power unit (CCS Co., Ltd., type: PD2-3024-2).

The first experimental prototype was very simple and acquired sequential front- and backlight images via on-off control of the backlight source alone (Figure 5).

Figure 5. Appearance of the experimental equipment.

2.2.2. Object Plate

As shown in Figure 4, a glass plate: one side smooth and the other rough, was used as the object plate to produce a robust imaging system. The rough surface of the object plate performs the same function as a diffuser panel: distributing light uniformly. Samples were placed on the smooth surface of the object plate and the backlight LEDs attached to the rough surface side. Normally, after paddy grain has been removed from the sampling area, dust and water (for high moisture content grain) will remain on the surface of the object plate. By ensuring the surface of the sampling area on the object plate is smooth, the cleaning process should be easier and to lead to a rapid image capture of the next sample.

2.2.3. Camera

To maintain the compactness of the system and restrain costs, we used a WEB camera with a resolution of 2 megapixels (Logicool Co., Ltd., type: C905M, UXGA class) and PL filter.

3. MATERIALS AND METHOD

3.1. Target Materials

Paddy (*Kinuhikari*) harvested in mid-September 2011 in Shiga Prefecture, Japan was used as representative samples. Within this sample, 4 major objects will be detected: paddy with a long rachis branch (Figure 6a); grass (Figure 6b); stems (Figure 6c); and brown and cracked rice (Figure 6d).

Normally, the harvested grain will contain many paddy with a long rachis branch if the combine harvester is operated at too slow a travelling speed, the wind blower is too weak, the sieve opening is too wide, or dust ejection is set too wide during harvest. Too much grass in the harvested paddy grain reduces the quality of the harvested grain and can create problems later in storage. Excessive amounts of grass in the harvested paddy grain is caused by setting the wind blower too weak, the sieve opening too wide, or the threshing depth too deep during harvest. Setting the sieve opening too wide will also lead to the inclusion of too much stem material in the harvested paddy grain. Figure 6d shows the brown and crack rice. The presence of abundant brown or cracked rice indicates the combine harvester was being operated at too high a travelling speed, or the wind blower was set too strong or the sieve opening too narrow.

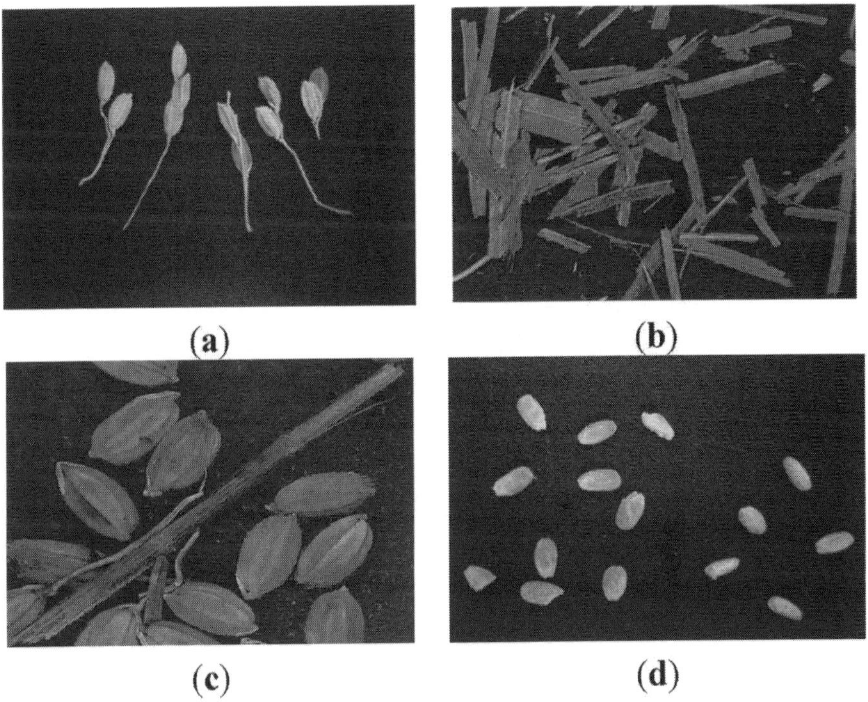

Figure 6. Object in harvested grains. (**a**) Long rachis branch; (**b**) grass; (**c**) stem; (**d**) brown and cracked rice.

3.2. Image Acquisition Method

3.2.1. Frontlight System Performance

Two frontlight images of the paddy, as well as the brown and cracked rice, were captured using the frontlight system (Ring LED lights) with two different backlight systems: the dot patterned Flat dome LED light or a conventional white Flat LED light (example: CCS Co., Ltd., type: TH-63X60SW). During frontlight image capture the backlight system was turned off. The images captured by these two systems were compared for the different object types (paddy and brown rice) and background lighting systems to evaluate the performance and efficiency of the frontlight system.

3.2.2. Comparison of Frontlight and Backlight Image Performance

From the harvested paddy grain, we obtained a sub-sample of roughly 100 g. The sampling area in our compact prototype system is small; therefore, to avoid the problems of too much overlapping and grains touching, only a 1 g sub-sample was used to acquire the image for each representative sample type: paddy, paddy with a long rachis branch, grass, stems, and brown and cracked rice. The images taken with the front and back lighting were then evaluated in terms of target material detection.

4. RESULTS AND DISCUSSION

4.1. Result of Frontlight System Performance

For images taken with our double lighting system, the background is blue-black as a result of the dot-patterned Flat dome light unit in the background, while the conventional system has a whitish background (Figure 7). As a consequence, the contrast between the target objects and background is lower in the conventional system. A clear boundary threshold between for the double lighting system using the saturation and hue distribution was found between the target objects (rough and brown rice) and the background compared to that for the conventional system (Figure 8). These results confirm that using the double lighting system makes it easier to distinguish between target objects and the background.

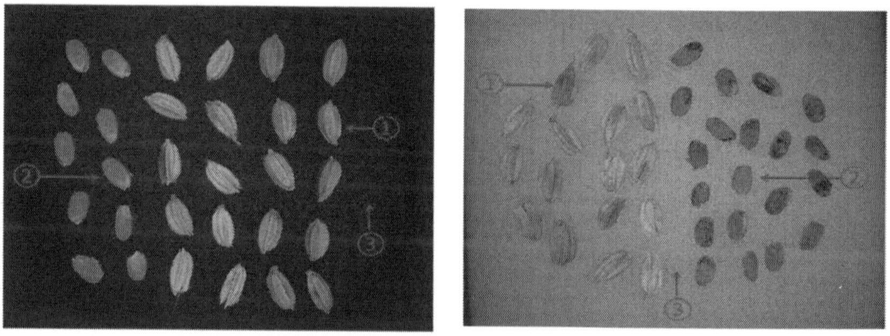

(a) (b)

Figure 7. Frontlight images. (**a**) Double lighting system; (**b**) conventional system.

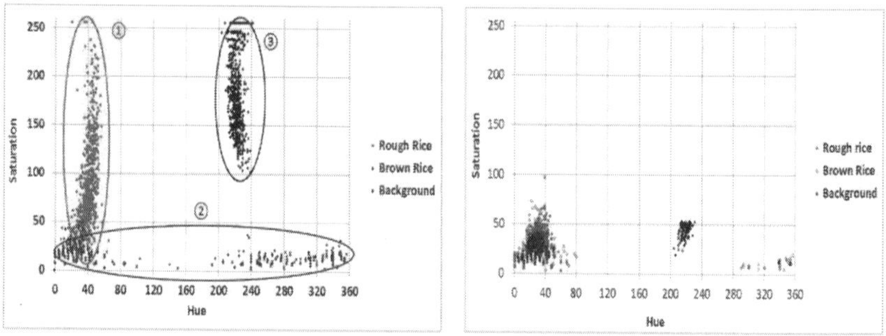

(a) (b)

Figure 8. Saturation and hue distribution from frontlight images captured with the (**a**) double lighting system and (**b**) conventional system.

4.2. Comparison of Frontlight and Backlight Image Performance

While color information can be used to establish a threshold for paddy, grass and stem detection, the use of color information (HSI) to distinguish brown rice is difficult (Figure 8a). This is because some HSI color components of brown rice overlap with those of paddy HSI color components. Figure 9b below shows a frontlight brown rice image with 2 types of brown rice: (1) brown rice that is almost white in color and easy to detect; and (2) brown rice color that is almost brown in color, the same color as paddy. However, by using backlight images (Figure 10b), both types of brown rice are easily detected. Therefore, for husked rice detection, it is best to use the backlight images for detection purposes.

(a) (b)

Figure 9. Image using frontlight images. (**a**) Long rachis branch, grass and stem; (**b**) 2 types of brown rice.

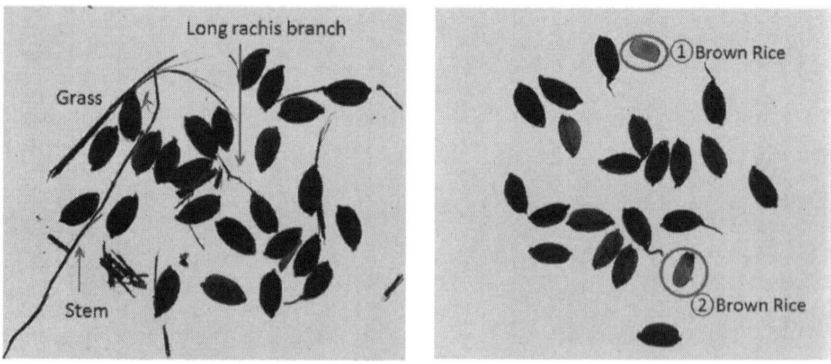

(a) (b)

Figure 10. Image using backlight images. (**a**) Long rachis branch, grass and stem; (**b**) 2 types of brown rice.

In many cases, agricultural product grading or detection needs only one lighting system, but in the case of harvested paddy, it has been shown that two lighting systems are necessary. For paddy, rachis branch, grass and stem detection, frontlight images are necessary, while backlight images and the dark silhouettes created on the bright background can detect paddy, long rachis branch, and brown rice.

5. CONCLUSIONS

In this study the principles of a new machine vision system approach to the monitoring of harvested paddy grain quality has been established. The system consists of a double lighting system (front and backlighting) set up along a coaxial axis. To maintain a compact and robust system capable of being mounted and operated in the harsh environment of a grain tank, Ring LED lights for frontlighting and Flat dome LED lights for backlighting were found to give the most uniform lighting distribution. Moreover, when using dot-patterned Flat dome LED lights for backlighting, having them turned off provides a higher-contrast background for frontlight images. Additionally, the rough surface of the botton of the object plate serves the same function as a diffuser panel, allowing for a more uniform light distribution, while the smooth front surface of the object plate aids in the cleaning process. Most importantly, this system can differentiate between four major target objects in freshly harvested paddy.

From a user and commercial perspective, the system is robust, compact, easy to assemble and low cost. As such, the proposed machine vision system shows great potential to be mounted in the grain tank of a head-feeding combine harvester for real-time monitoring of harvested paddy grain and decision support for combine harvester operations. Continued experimentation will be conducted to further enhance image processing and detection of target objects in the harvested paddy grain, such as damaged grain (husked and cracked rice) and unwanted materials (long rachis branch, grass and leaves, and stems).

ACKNOWLEDGMENTS

The authors would like to express their gratitude to Garry Piller for his editing and proofreading of this manuscript.

AUTHOR CONTRIBUTIONS

Naoshi Kondo (N.K) and Munenori Miyamoto (M.M) concept idea and discussion; Mahirah Jahari (M.J), Kazuya Yamamoto (K.Y), Munenori Miyamoto (M.M) and Naoshi Kondo (N.K) conceived and designed the experiments; Mahirah Jahari (M.J) and Kazuya Yamamoto (K.Z) performed the experiments; Mahirah Jahari (M.J), Kazuya Yamamoto (K.Z) and Harshana Habaragamuwa (H.H) analyzed the data; Munenori Miyamoto (M.M), Naoshi Kondo (N.K), Yuichi Ogawa (Y.O) and Tetsuhito Suzuki (T.S) contributed reagents/materials/analysis tools; Mahirah Jahari (M.J) and Usman Ahmad (U.A) wrote the paper.

REFERENCES

1. Reyns, P.; Spaepen, P.; de Baerdemaeker, J. Site-specific Relationship between Grain Quality and Yield.*Precis. Agric.* **2000**, *2*, 231–246.

2. Bramble, T.; Herrman, T.J.; Loughin, T.; Dowell, F. Single Kernel Protein Variance Structure in Commercial Wheat Fields in Western Kansas. *Crop Sci.* **2002**, *42*, 1488–1492.

3. Maertens, K.; Reyns, P.; de Baerdemaeker, J. On-line Measurement of Grain Quality with NIR Technology. *Trans. ASAE* **2004**, *47*, 1135–1140.

4. Paliwal, J.; Visen, N.S.; Jayas, D.S.; White, N.D.G. Cereal Grain and Dockage Identification Using Machine Vision. *Biosyst. Eng.* **2003**, *85*, 51–57.

5. Hobson, D.M.; Carter, R.M.; Yan, Y. Characterisation and Identification of Rice Grains through Digital Image Analysis. In Proceedings of the IEEE Instrumentation and Measurement Technology Conference, Warsaw, Poland, 1–3 May 2007; pp. 1–5.

6. Liu, W.; Tao, Y.; Siebenmorgen, T.J.; Chen, H. Digital Image Analysis Method for Rapid Measurement of Rice Degree of Milling. In *1997 ASAE Annual International Meeting Technical Papers*; Paper No. 973028; ASAE: St. Joseph, MI, USA, 1997.

7. Lloyd, B.J.; Cnossen, A.G.; Siebenmorgen, T.J. Evaluation of Two Methods for Separating Head Rice from Brokensfor Head Rice Yield Determination. In *2000 ASAE Annual International Meeting Technical Papers*; Paper No. 006074; ASAE: St. Joseph, MI, USA, 2000.

8. Matsui, M. Threshing Unit of Head Feeding Type Combine. *J. Jpn. Soc. Agric. Mach.* **1999**, *61*, 45–46.

9. Takahara, K.; Hayashi, S. Cleaner Control System for Head-feeding Combine Harvesters. *J. Jpn. Soc. Agric. Mach.* **1996**, *58*, 125–126.

10. Bebis, G.; Egbert, D.; Sham, M. Review of Computer Vision Education. *IEEE Trans. Educ.* **2003**, *46*, 2–21.

11. Brosnan, T.; Sun, D.W. Improving Quality Inspection of Food Products by Computer Vision—A Review. *J. Food Eng.* **2004**, *61*, 3–16.

12. Shantaiya, S.; Ansari, U. Identification of Food Grains and Its Quality Using Pattern Classification. In Proceedings of the 12th IEEE International Conference (ICCT-2010), Bhubaneswar, India, 3–5 December 2010; Volume 2.

13. Verma, B. Image Processing Techniques for Grading & Classification of Rice. In Proceedings of the 2010 International Conference on Computer & Communication Technology (ICCCT '10), Allahabad, India, 17–19 September 2010; pp. 220–223.

14. Yao, M.; Liu, M.; Zhen, H. Exterior Quality Inspection of Rice Based on Computer Vision. In Proceedings of the IEEE 2010 World Automation Congress (WAC), Kobe, Japan, 19–23 September 2010; pp. 369–374.

15. Novini, A. Fundamentals of Machine Vision Component Selection. In *Food Processing Automation II—Proceedings of the 1990 Conference Hyatt Regency*; ASAE: Lexington, KY, USA, 1990; p. 60.

16. Gunasekaran, S. Computer Vision Technology for Food Quality Assurance. *Trends Food Sci. Technol.* **1996**, *7*, 245–256.

17. CCS Inc. *Flat-Dome Lights LFXS2 Series Manual*; CCS Inc.: Kyoto, Japan, 2015; pp. 77–80.

18. CCS Inc. *Ring Lights LDR2 Series Manual*; CCS Inc.: Kyoto, Japan, 2015; pp. 9–12.

19. Miyamoto, M.; Kondo, N.; Ogawa, Y.; Yamamoto, K. Combine Harvester. Yanmar Co., Ltd; Kyoto University. Japan Patent No. 5,780,642, 24 July 2015.

5

CHAPTER

VISION-BASED HAND GESTURE SPOTTING AND RECOGNITION USING CRF AND SVM

Fayed F. M. Ghaleb[1], Ebrahim A. Youness[2], Mahmoud Elmezain[2], Fatma Sh. Dewdar[2]

[1]*Faculty of Science, Mathematatices Department, Ain Shams University, Cairo, Egypt*

[2]*Faculty of Science, Computer Science Division, Tanta University, Tanta, Egypt*

ABSTRACT

In this paper, a novel gesture spotting and recognition technique is proposed to handle hand gesture from continuous hand motion based on Conditional Random Fields in conjunction with Support Vector Machine. Firstly, YC_bC_r color space and 3D depth map are used to detect and segment the hand. The depth map is to neutralize complex background sense. Secondly, 3D spatio-temporal features for hand volume of dynamic affine-invariants like elliptic Fourier and Zernike moments are extracted, in addition to three orientations motion features. Finally, the hand gesture is spotted and recognized by using the discriminative Conditional Random Fields Model.

Accordingly, a Support Vector Machine verifies the hand shape at the start and the end point of meaningful gesture, which enforces vigorous view invariant task. Experiments demonstrate that the proposed method can successfully spot and recognize hand gesture from continuous hand motion data with 92.50% recognition rate.

Keywords: Human Computer Interaction, Conditional Random Fields, Support Vector Machine, Elliptic Fourier, Zernike Moments

1. INTRODUCTION

The task of locating the start and the end points that correspond to a gesture of interest is a challenging task in Human Computer Interaction. We define a gesture as the motion of the hand to communicate with a computer. The task of locating meaningful patterns from input signals is called pattern spotting [1] [2]. In gesture spotting, an instance of pattern spotting, it is required to locate the start point and the end point of a gesture. The gesture spotting has two major difficulties: segmentations [3] [4] and spatio-temporal variabilities [5] [6]. The segmentation problem is how to determine when a gesture starts and when it ends in a continuous hand trajectory. As the gesturer switches from one gesture to another, his hand makes an intermediate move linking the two gestures. A gesture recognizer may attempt to recognize this inevitable intermediate motion as a meaningful one. Without segmentation, the recognizer should try to match reference patterns with all possible segments of input signals. The other difficulties of gesture spotting are that the same gesture varies dynamically in shape and duration; even of the same gesturer. Therefore, the recognizer should consider both the spatial and the temporal variabilities simultaneously. An ideal recognizer will extract gesture segments from the input signal, and match them with reference patterns regardless of the spatio-temporal variabilities. Tracking methods that depend entirely on an image-plane representation of the hand have been worked on extensively. Typically such systems are computationally less expensive than those methods that use a 3D model. Moment invariants, as discriminative feature descriptors, have been used for shape representation for many years. The shape-based image invariants can be divided into two different categories: boundary based image invariants such as Fourier descriptors; region-based image invariants included various moment-based invariants such as Zernike moments. There are two types of shape-based image invariants: boundary-based and region-based. The boundary based image invariants focus on the properties contained in the image's contour while the region-based image invariants take the whole image area as the research object.

Boundary-based invariants such as Fourier descriptors explore only the contour information; they cannot capture the interior content of the shape. On the other hand, these methods cannot deal with disjoint shapes where single closed boundary may not be available; therefore, they have limited applications. For region-based invariants, all of the pixels of the image are taken into account to represent the shape. Because region-based invariants combine information of an entire image region rather than exploiting information just along the boundary pixels, they can capture more information from the image. The region-based invariants can also be employed to describe disjoint shapes.

Lee, H.-K. and Kim, J.H. [7] develope a new method by using the Hidden Markov Model based technique. To handle non-gesture patterns, they introduce the concept of a threshold model that calculates the likelihood threshold of an input pattern and provides a confirmation mechanism for the provisionally matched gesture patterns. Yang, H.-D., Sclaroff, S. and Lee, S.-W. [8] propose a novel method for designing threshold models in a conditional random field (CRF) model which performs an adaptive threshold for distinguishing between signs in a vocabulary and non-sign patterns.

These methods have the following consequent drawback to detect the reliable end point of a gesture and find the start point by back-tracking. Therefore, the delayed response may cause one to wonder whether one's gesture has been recognized correctly or not. For that reason, the systems in [7] [8] are not capable for real-time applications.

To face the mentioned challenges, CRF forward gesture spotting by using Circular Buffer method is proposed, which simultaneously handles the hand gesture spotting and recognition in stereo color image sequences without time delay. A hand appearance-based sign verification method using SVM is considered to further improve sign language spotting accuracy. Additionally, a depth image sequence is exploited to identify the Region of Interest (ROI) without processing the whole image, which consequently reduces the cost of ROI searching and increases the processing speed. Our experiments on own dataset, showed that the proposed approach is more robust and yields promising results when comparing favorably with those previously reported throughout the literature.

2. HAND GESTURE SPOTTING AND RECOGNITION APPROACH

An application of gesture-based interaction with Arabic numbers (0 - 9) is implemented to demonstrate the co- action of suggested components and the effectiveness of gesture spotting & recognition approach (Figure 1).

2.1. Preprocessing

Automatic segmentation and preprocessing is an important stage in our approach. The segmentation of the hand takes place using color information and 3D depth map. Firstly, the hand is segmented (i.e. Area of interest (AOI)) using Gaussian Mixture Model (GMM) over YC_bC_r color space, where Y channel represents brightness and (C_b, C_r)

channels refer to chrominance [9]. Channel Y is eliminated to reduce the effect of brightness variation and only the chrominance channels are employed that fully represent the color information. Accordingly, Image acquisition includes 2D image sequences and depth image sequences, which devised by an algorithm of passive stereo measuring based on mean absolute difference and the known calibration data of the cameras. The depth map is to neutralize complex senses background to increase the robustness of skin segmentation for AOI completely (Figure 2).

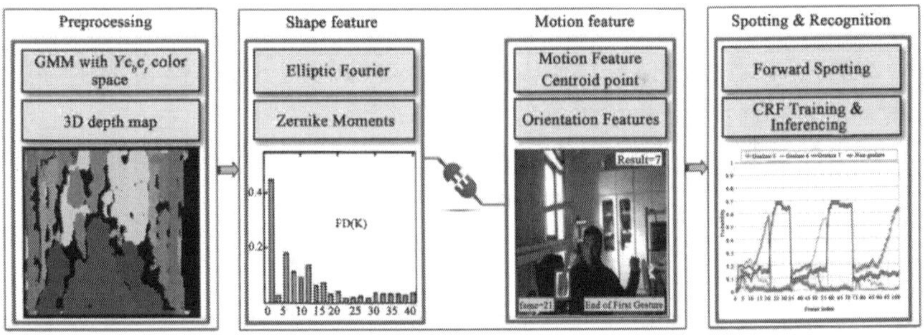

Figure 1. Hand gesture spotting and recognition concept.

2.2. Tracking and Feature Extraction

To retrieve the extracted features during occlusion, a robust method for hand tracking is considered using Mean- shift analysis in conjunction with depth map. The motivation behind mean shift analysis is to achieve accurate and robust hand tracking. Mean-shift analysis uses the gradient of Bhattacharyya coefficient [10] as a similarity function to derive the candidate of the hand which is mostly similar to a given hand target model. This structure correctly extracts a set of hand postures to track the hand motion. After that, two types of feature are employed to correctly spot and recognize hand gesture. The orientation features of hand image sequences are extracted by the trajectory of the hand motion centroid. Additionally, the shape features are considered with a variety of invariant descriptors such as elliptic Fourier's descriptors and invariant Zernike moments.

2.2.1. Orientation Features

The orientation gives the direction of the hand when traverses in space during the gesture making process. A gesture path is spatio-temporal pattern that consists of centroid points (xhand, yhand). Therefore, orientation feature is based on; the calculation of the hand displacement vector at every point which is represented by the orientation according to the centroid of gesture path (θ_{1t}), the orientation between two consecutive points (θ_{2t}) and the orientation between start and current gesture point (θ_{3t}).

$$\theta_{1t} = \tan^{-1}\left(\frac{y_{t+1}-c_y}{x_{t+1}-c_x}\right),\ \theta_{2t} = \tan^{-1}\left(\frac{y_{t+1}-y_t}{x_{t+1}-x_t}\right),\ \theta_{3t} = \tan^{-1}\left(\frac{y_{t+1}-y_1}{x_{t+1}-x_1}\right) \tag{2.1}$$

$$\left(c_x, c_y\right) = \frac{1}{n}\left(\sum_{t=1}^{n} x_t, \sum_{t=1}^{n} y_t\right) \tag{2.2}$$

where (c_x, c_y) refers to the centroid of gravity at n points, and T represents the length of hand gesture path such that $t = 1,2,\cdots,T-1$.

In this manner, gesture is represented as an ordered sequence of feature vectors, which are projected and clustered in space dimension to obtain discrete code words. This is done using k-means clustering algorithm [11], which classifies the gesture pattern into K clusters in the feature space.

2.2.2. SVM-Based Dynamic Affine-Invariants Features

The shape flow as the global flow of hand is characterized and stated by the elliptic Fourier descriptors and Zernike moments $G_i = \left[C_{xk}, C_{yk}, z_{00}, z_{11}, z_{22}\right]^{\mathrm{T}}$ that described as follows:

The elliptic Fourier descriptors for action silhouettes are obtained using a trigonometric form of the shape curve C_k.

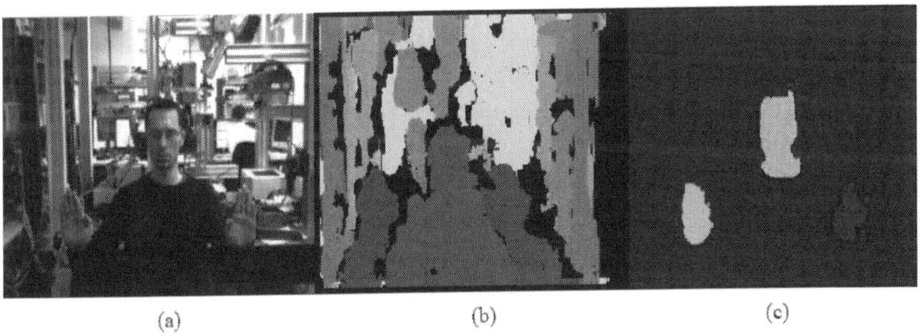

Figure 2. (a) Source image frame; (b) Depth value from the Bumblebee stereo camera system; (c) Skin color segmentation of hands.

$$C_k = C_{xk} + jC_{yk} \tag{2.3}$$

where

$$C_{xk} = \frac{1}{T}\int_0^T x(t)e^{-jk\omega t},\ C_{yk} = \frac{1}{T}\int_0^T y(t)e^{-jk\omega t} \tag{2.4}$$

ω defines the fundament frequency and is equal to T/2π. T referents the function period and k refers to a harmonic number. It can be verified that this choice of coefficients guarantees that the resulting curve descriptors are invariant to shape translation, rotation and scaling, and they are independent from the choice of starting point on a contour [12].

Invariance of hand image can be achieved by using Zernike moments, which give an orthogonal set of rotation-invariant moments. Additionally, scale and translation invariance can be implemented using moment normalization [13]. More simply, the complex Zernike moment (Z_{pq}) with an order p and repetition q of image intensity function f(ρ,θ) is:

$$Z_{pq} = \frac{p+1}{\delta_N} \sum_{x=0}^{N-1} \sum_{y=0}^{N-1} f\left(\frac{x}{a} + \bar{x}, \frac{y}{a} + \bar{y}, t\right) R_{pq}(\rho) e^{-jq\theta} \tag{2.5}$$

Here, δ_N is a normalization factor, p is a positive integer while q either negative or positive integer subject to the constraints p – |q| = even and |q| ≤ p. The function f is normalized with respect to scale and translation by

using the center of silhouette image $(\bar{x}, \bar{y})$ and the scale factored a. $R_{pq}(\rho)$ represents are dial polynomial [12] .

Thus, the Zernike moment features invariant along with geometric features to shape translation, rotation and scaling with remarkable similarity to the Hu invariant moments is assigned by $G_z = [z_{00}, z_{11}, z_{22}]$.

2.3. Spotting and Recognition

To spot meaningful gestures of numbers (0 - 9), which are embedded in the input video stream accurately, a two-layer CRF architecture is applied (Figure 3). In the first layer a stochastic method for designing a non-ges- ture model with CRF is proposed without training data. CRF is capable of modeling spatio-temporal time series of gestures effectively and can handle non-gesture patterns. The non-gesture model provides a confidence measure that is used as an adaptive threshold to find the start and the end point of meaningful gestures. As, a forward spotting technique in conjunction with a Differential Probability (DP) value and circular buffer is employed to discriminate between meaningful gestures and non-gesture patterns. In the second layer, CRF are used to find the maximal gesture, which having the largest value among all ten labels gestures. Finally, SVM decide the final decision based on the building dataset of hand shape with elliptic Fourier and Zernike moments.

2.3.1. Spotting with CRFs

CRFs are a framework based on conditional probability approaches for segmenting and labeling sequential data. CRFs use a single exponential distribution to model all labels of given observations. Therefore, there is a trade- off in the weights of each feature function, for each state. In our application, each state corresponds to segments of the number. In addition, each label in CRFs is employed as exponential model to conditional probabilities of the next label for a given current label.

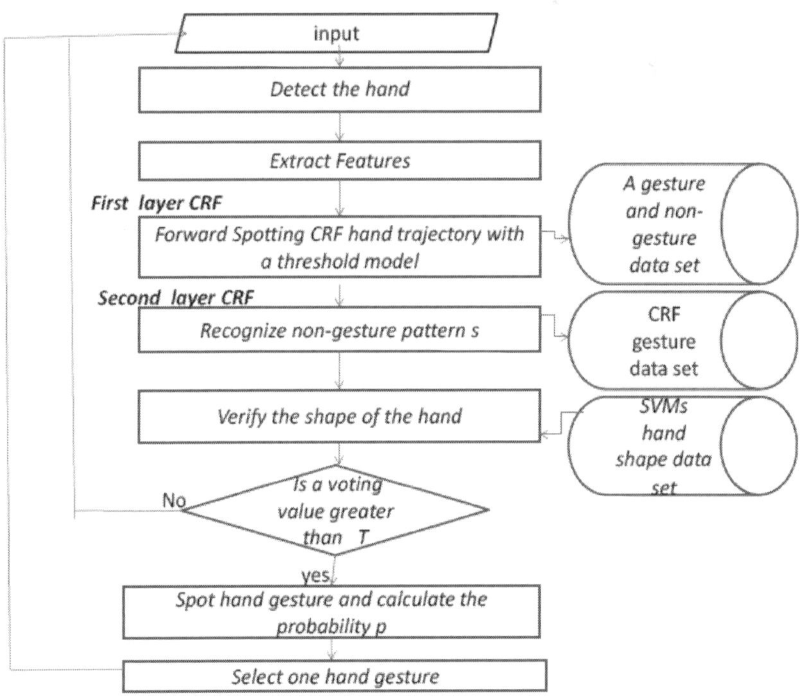

Figure 3. A two layer flow chart for spotting meaningful gestures based on CRFs and SVMs.

(1) Spotting with CRFs

Conditional Random Fields were developed for labeling sequential data (i.e. determining the probability of a given label sequence for a given input sequence) and are undirected graphical models (i.e. discriminative models). The structure of current label is design to form the chain with an edge between itself and previous label. Moreover, each label corresponds to a gesture number. The probability of label sequence y for a given observation sequence O is calculated as:

$$P(y|O,\theta)=\frac{1}{Z(O,\theta)}\cdot\exp\left(\sum_{i=1}^{n}F_\theta(y_{i-1},y_i,O,i)\right) \tag{2.6}$$

where parameter $\theta=(\lambda_1,\lambda_2,\cdots,\lambda_{N_f};\mu_1,\mu_2,\cdots,\mu_{N_g})$, the number of transition feature function represents by N_f, the number of state feature function represents by N_g and the length of observation sequence O is n.

F_θ is defined as:

$$F_\theta=\sum_f\lambda_f t_f(y_{i-1},y_i,O,i)+\sum_g\mu_g s_g(y_i,O,i) \tag{2.7}$$

where a transition feature function at position i and i − 1 is $t_f(y_{i-1},y_i,O,i)$ (i.e. represents the weight on the transition from label i to label i − 1 when the current observation is O). State feature function at position i is sg (y_i, O, i) (i.e. represents the weight on the label i when the current observation is O). λ_f and μ_g represent the weights of the transition and state feature functions, respectively. Z(O, θ) is the normalized factor and is calculated as follows:

$$Z(O,\theta)=\sum_{y}\exp\left(\sum_{i=1}^{n}F_{\theta}\left(y_{i-1},y_{i},O,i\right)\right) \tag{2.8}$$

The CRFs are initially built without label for non-gesture pattern; Because CRFs use a single model for the joint probability of the sequences p(y|O, θ).

Using gradient ascent with the BFGS optimization technique with 300 iterations is used for trained CRFs to achieve optimal convergence. Therefore, the labels of CRFs are $y=\{Y_0,Y_1,\cdots,Y_9\}$. To create the Non-gesture model (N-CRFs) using the weights of transition and state features function of initial CRFs all other patterns than

gesture patterns are modeled by adding a label (N) for non-gesture patterns. Moreover, $y_N=\{Y_0,Y_1,\cdots,Y_9,Y_N\}$

are the labels of N-CRFs. The proposed N-CRFs model does not need non-gesture patterns for training and also can better spot gestures and non-gesture patterns.

(2) N-CRFs Model Parameters

The label of non-gesture pattern is created, by using the weight of state and transition feature function of the initialized CRFs model. There are two main parameters of CRFs named state feature function and transition feature function as in Equation (2.7). From the idea of Dugad et al. [14] who propose an adaptive threshold model based on the mean and the variance of sample, the weight of state feature function is computed as:

$$\mu_g(N)=\overline{\mu_g}+T_N\sqrt{\sigma_g} \tag{2.9}$$

where $\overline{\mu_g}$ is the mean of state feature functions of the labels of initial CRFs from Y_0 to Y_9 and $\sigma_g$represent the variance of the gth state feature functions T_N reflects the width of state features function in some way. The optimal value of T_N is 0.7 and is determined by multiple experiments which have been conducted with a range of values on a training data set.

It is difficult to spot and recognize short gestures because short gestures have fewer samples than long gestures. A challenging problem is caused by the fact that there is a quite bit of variability in the same gesture even for the same person. A short gesture detector is added to avoid this problem, where the weights of self-transition feature functions are increased as follows:

$$\lambda_f(Y_l,Y_l)=\begin{cases}\lambda_f(Y_l,Y_l)+\Psi_f(y_l), & \text{if Cond 1}\\ \lambda_f(Y_l,Y_l), & \text{otherwise}\end{cases} \tag{2.10}$$

Such that:

$$\Psi_f(y_l)=\frac{\left(\bar{N}_{frame}-\sigma_{N_{frame}}\right)-N_{frame}(Y_l)}{\max_l N_{frame}(Y_l)} \tag{2.11}$$

and

$$\text{Cond 1}: N_{frame}(Y_l)<\left(\bar{N}_{frame}-\sigma_{N_{frame}}\right) \tag{2.12}$$

where $N_{frame}(Y_l)$ is the average frame number of a gesture Y_l, $\sigma_{N_{frame}}$ represents the average frame number of all gestures from Y_0 to Y_9 and $\sigma_{N_{frame}}$ is the variance of them. $\psi_f(y_l)$ is additional weight of the gesture Y_l notable in case of a short length gesture.

The weight of the self-transition feature function of the label of non-gesture patterns is approximately assigned with the maximum weight of transition feature functions to initialize CRFs as follows:

$$\lambda_f(Y_N, Y_N) = \max_l \lambda_f(Y_l, Y_l) + \frac{\sum_{i=1}^{l}\sum_{g=1}^{N_g}\mu_g(Y_l)}{\bar{N}_{state\_feature}} \tag{2.13}$$

where $\bar{N}_{state\_feature}$ is the average number of transition feature functions in which the weight is greater than zero.

As described above about the transition parameters of non-gesture model, a method is employed to compute the weights of transition feature functions between the labels of gesture models and the label of non-gesture patterns. Therefore, the weights of transition feature functions from the non-gesture label to other labels are computed by the following equation:

$$\lambda_f(Y_N, Y_i) = \frac{\lambda_f(Y_N, Y_N)}{l}, \quad \forall i \in \{1, 2, \cdots, l\} \tag{2.14}$$

Additionally, the weights of transition feature functions from the gesture labels to non-gesture label occurs by the given equation below:

$$\lambda_f(Y_i, Y_N) = \frac{\lambda_f(Y_i, Y_i)}{l}, \quad \forall i \in \{1, 2, \cdots, l\} \tag{2.15}$$

As a result, the N-CRFs model can better spot gestures and non-gesture patterns.

2.3.2. CRF Forward Spotting via Circular Buffer

Several samples of each gesture in the gesture vocabulary are stored in the database to be used in training the classifier. A gesture is stored as a sequence of (x, y, t) joint coordinates. In recognition mode, a circular buffer is used to temporarily store the real-time information. The circular buffer contains a number of sequential observations instead of a single observation. It is used to reduce the impact of observation changes for a short interval which are caused by incomplete feature extraction. The circular buffer is set to store 13 frames. The size of the circular buffer is chosen to be equal to the shortest gesture (i.e. gesture "1" represents a shortest gesture in our system). This ensures that at some stage during a continuous motion, the buffer will be completely filled with gesture data, and will not contain any transitional motion data. In addition, a maximum of one complete gesture can be stored in the buffer at one time.

Figure 4 illustrates the operation of the circular buffer in gesture segmentation. At $t = t_1$ the buffer contains transitional data and gesture data. At $t = t_2$, the buffer is filled entirely with data from Gesture 2, and contains no transitional motion data. The gesture recognition module is activated after detecting the start point from continuous image sequences. The main objective is to perform the recognition process accumulatively for the segmented parts until it receives the end signal of key gesture.

Assume that, the size of circular buffer is initialized with the input observation sequence with length T = 13 as in our system, $O=\{o_1,o_2,\cdots,o_T\}$. The DP value is equal to difference observation probability between the maximal gesture labels and the Non-gesture label.

When the value of DP(t) at time t is negative, the start point in this case is not detected and therefore the circular buffer is shifted on unit (i.e. $O_{t+1}=o_{t+1},o_{t+2},\cdots,o_{T+1}$). This process is repeated until DP value is positive. In the case of DP value is positive; assume that A1 represents the first partial key gesture segmented. Then, the observed key gesture segmented is represented by union of all possible partial gesture segments $A = \{A_1 \cup A_2 \cup \cdots\}$.

At each step, the gesture type of A is determined. When the value of DP becomes negative again or there is no gesture image, the final gesture label type of observed gesture segment A is determined. When there is more gesture images, the previous steps are repeated with re-initializing the circular buffer at the next time t. Therefore, a forward scheme has the ability to resolve the issues of time delay between gesture spotting and recognition.

2.3.3. SVMs-Based Gesture Verification

The main motivation behind using SVMs-based gesture verification to decide whether or not to accept a gesture spotted. This helps to discriminate gestures which may have similar hand motions but different hand shapes. SVMs are trained with a set of images of a gesture hand shape according to the extracted features via elliptic Fourier and Zernike moments. Therefore, the histograms of gradient features are extracted for training SVM from training samples [15] .

In our work, the hand shape at the start of the gesture is verified. Then the hand appearance is verified over a period of several frames. As a result, voting value over frames is used to consider whether to accept or reject the gesture. If voting value is greater than a specific threshold, which experimentally determined, then the candidate gesture is chosen be a meaningful gesture.

3. EXPERIMENTAL RESULTS

The input images were captured by Bumblebee stereo camera system which has 6 mm focal length at 15FPS with 240 × 320 pixels image resolution, Matlab implementation. Classification results are based on our database that contains 600 video samples for isolated gestures (i.e. 60 video samples for each gesture from 0 to 9) which are captured from three persons. Each isolated number from 0 to 9 was based on 42 videos for training CRF and SVMs. Additionally, the database contains 280 video samples of continuous hand motion for testing. Each video sample either contains one or more meaningful gestures.

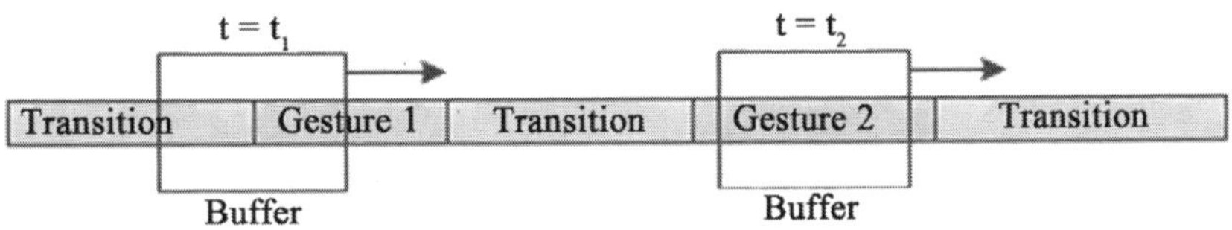

Figure 4. Gesture segmentation by circular buffer.

On a standard desktop PC, training process is more expensive for CRFs since the time which the model needs ranges from 20 minutes to several hours based on observation window. On the contrary, the inference (i.e. recognition) process is less costly and very fast for all models with sequences of several frames.

In automatic gesture spotting task, there are three types of errors called Insertion (I), Substitution (S) and Deletion (D). The insertion error is occurred when the spotter detects a nonexistent gesture. It is because the emission probability of the current state for a given observation sequence is equal to zero. A substitution error occurs when the key gesture is classified falsely (i.e. classifies the gesture as another gesture). This error is usually happened when the extracted features are falsely quantized to other code words. The deletion error happens when the spotter fails to detect a key gesture. In order to calculate the recognition ratio (Rec.) (Equation (3.2)), insertion errors are totally not considered. However, insertion errors are probably caused due to substitution and deletion errors because they are often considered as strong decision in determining the end point of gestures to eliminate all or part of the meaningful gestures from observation. Deletion errors directly affect the recognition ratio whereas insertion errors do not. However, the insertion errors affect the gesture spotting ratio directly. To take into consideration the effect of insertion errors, another performance measure called reliability (Rel.) is proposed by the following equation:

$$\text{Rel.} = \frac{\#\text{correctly recognized gestures}}{\#\text{test gestures} + \#\text{Inseration errors}} \times 100 \qquad (3.1)$$

The recognition ratio and the reliability are computed based on the number of spotting errors (Table 1).

$$\text{Rec.} = \frac{\#\text{recognized gestures}}{\#\text{test gestures}} \times 100 \qquad (3.2)$$

Experimental results of CRF show that the proposed method automatically recognizes meaningful gestures with 92.50% recognition (Table 1). It is noted that the proposed method achieved good recognition r ate due to a good election for the set of feature candidates to optimally discriminate among input patterns. In addition, A short gesture detector has the ability to efficiently alleviate spatio-temporal variability. Thus, this system is capable for real-time applications and resolves the issues of time delay between spotting and recognition tasks.

Lee, H.-K. and Kim, J.H. [7] developed a new method using the Hidden Markov Model based technique. To handle non-gesture patterns, they introduce the concept of a threshold model that calculates the likelihood threshold of an input pattern and provides a confirmation mechanism for the provisionally matched gesture patterns. For gesture segmentation, it detects the reliable end point of a gesture and finds the start point by back-tracking the Viterbi path from the end point (i.e. backward technique). The model performs gesture spotting with recognition rate 93.14%. However, the proposed method has a problem in that the system cannot report the detection of a gesture immediately after the system reaches its end point. It is because the endpoint detection process postpones the decision until the detection of the next gesture in order to avoid premature decision. The delayed response may cause one to wonder whether one's gesture has been recognized correctly or not. For that reason, their system is not capable for real-time applications.

Table 1. Meaningful gesture spotting results for gesture numbers from "0" to "9".

Gesture path	Train data	Meaningful gestures spotting results						
		Test	I	D	S	Correct	Rec. (%)	Rel. (%)
"0"	42	28	1	0	1	27	96.43	93.10
"1"	42	28	1	0	0	27	96.43	93.10
"2"	42	28	1	1	1	26	92.86	89.65
"3"	42	28	1	1	1	26	92.86	89.65
"4"	42	28	1	2	1	25	89.93	86.21
"5"	42	28	1	1	1	26	92.86	89.65
"6"	42	28	1	1	1	26	92.86	89.65
"7"	42	28	1	2	1	25	89.93	86.21
"8"	42	28	1	2	1	25	89.93	86.21
"9"	42	28	1	1	1	26	92.86	89.65
Total	420	280	10	11	9	259	92.50	89.31

Yang, H.-D., Sclaroff, S. and Lee, S.-W. [8] proposed a novel method for designing threshold models in a conditional random field (CRF) model which performs an adaptive threshold for distinguishing between signs in a vocabulary and non-sign patterns. A short-sign detector, a hand appearance-based sign verification method, and a sub-sign reasoning method are included to further improve sign language spotting accuracy. Their experiments demonstrate that their system can spot signs from continuous data with an 87.00% spotting rate. In order to spot signs from continuous data, a two-layer CRF architecture is applied with a sub-sign reasoning method, a short-sign detector, and an appearance-based shape verification method. In the first layer, in-vocabulary signs and non-sign patterns are discriminated by a threshold model with CRF. Spotted signs in the first layer are temporarily saved. Subsequent to detecting a sign sequence, the second layer CRF is applied to find sub-sign patterns. Sub-sign patterns within signs are modeled with a CRF. The input sequence of the second layer CRF includes more than one sign. The results of the second layer CRF are used to find the candidate label with the maximum probability. Finally, the appearance-based sign verification method is performed for the selected candidate sign. These steps are employed with end point detection technique that is not suitable for real-time applications.

Elmezain, M., Al-Hamadi, A. and Michaelis, B. [16] proposed a stochastic method for designing a non-gesture model with Hidden Markov Models (HMMs) versus Conditional Random Fields (CRFs). He used as an adaptive threshold to find the start and the end point of meaningful gestures, which are embedded in the input video stream. Also, he employed the forward spotting technique with sliding window with size ranging from 1 to 7 to empirically decide the optimal value. Their system was enhanced using relative entropy measure and increasing self-transition weight for HMMs and CRFs short gesture, respectively. The experiments of them could can successfully spot and recognize meaningful gestures with 93.31% and 90.49% reliability for HMMs and CRFs respectively.

In the light of this comparison (Table 2), it is being notice that the proposed approach performs competitively with another state-of-the-art method [7] [8] [16] in addition to carry out without sacrificing real-time performance. To assess the efficiency of the proposed method, the obtained results have been compared with those of other previously published studies in the literature, as shown in Table 2. From this comparison, it turns out that our approach performs competitively with other state-of-the-art approaches, and its results compared favorably with previously published results. Notably, all the methods that we compared our method with have used nearly similar experimental setups. Thus, the comparison is meaningful.

Table 2. Comparison with the state-of-the-art.

Method	Recognition rate
Our method	92.50%
Lee, H.-K. and Kim, J. H. [7]	93.14%
Yang, H.-D., Sclaroff, S. and Lee, S.-W. [8]	87.00%
Elmezain, M. Al-Hamadi, A. and Michaelis, B. [16]	90.49%

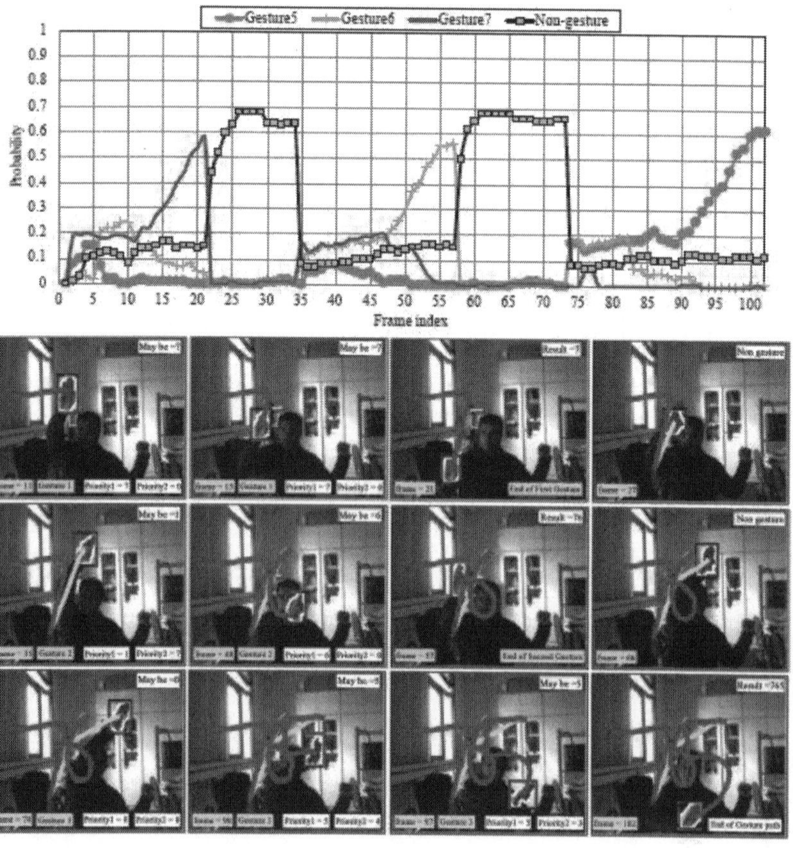

Figure 5. Temporal evolution of the probabilities of the gesture numbers "5", "6", "7" and non-gesture label "N".

The image sequences depicted in Figure 5 contain three key gestures "7", "6" and "5". The above graph of this figure considers only the temporal evolution of the probabilities of gestures "7", "6", "5" and non-gesture (for simplicity, the other curves are eliminated because their probabilities are low). The gesture "7" ends at frame index 21. Between frame index 22 and frame index 34, the highest priority is assigned to non-gesture label which means that the start point of second key gesture is not detected. At frame index 35, a new key gesture is started where the probability value of non-gesture label is not the highest value as compared to the other gesture labels. The gesture "6" ends at frame index 57. Between frame index 58 and frame index 73, the highest priority is assigned to non-gesture label. The gesture "5" starts at frame index 74 and ends at frame index 102.

4. CONCLUSION

This paper proposed a novel gesture spotting and recognition technique, which handled hand gesture from continuous hand motion based on Conditional Random Field in conjunction with Support Vector Machine. 3D depth map was captured by bumblebee stereo camera to neutralize complex background sense. Additionally, dynamic affine-invariants features like elliptic Fourier and Zernike moments, in addition to three orientations motion features were employed to CRF and SVMs. Finally, the discriminative model of CRF performed the spotting and recognition processes by using the combined of orientation features. Accordingly, Support Vector Machine verified the hand shape at the start and the end point of meaningful gesture by using elliptic Fourier and Zernike moments features. Experiments showed that our proposed method could successfully spot hand gesture from continuous hand motion data with 92.50% recognition rate.

REFERENCES

1. R.C. (1992) Discriminant Word Spotting Techniques for Rejection Non-Vocabulary Utterances in Unconstrained Speech. IEEE International Conference on Acoustics, Speech, and Signal Processing, 2, 105-108.

2. Chen, F.R., Wilcox, L.D. and Bloomberg, D.S. (1993) Word Spotting in Scanned Images Using Hidden Markov Models. IEEE International Conference on Acoustics, Speech, and Signal Processing, 5, 1-4.

3. Starner, T., Weaver, J. and Pentland, A. (1998) Real-Time American Sign Language Recognition Using Desk and Wearable Computer Based Video. IEEE Transaction on Pattern Analysis and Machine Intelligence, 20, 1371-1375.

4. Takahashi, K., Seki, S. and Oka, R. (1992) Spotting Recognition of Human Gestures from Motion Images. Technical Report IE92-134, 9-16.

5. Baudel, T. and Beaudouin, M. (1993) CHARADE: Remote Control of Objects Using Free-Hand Gestures. Communications of ACM, 36, 28-35.

6. Wexelblat, A. (1994) Natural Gesture in Virtual Environments. Proceedings of Virtual Reality Software and Technology Conference, Singapore, 23-26 August 1994, 5-16.

7. Lee, H.-K. and Kim, J.H. (1999) An Hmm-Based Threshold Model Approach for Gesture Recognition. IEEE Transactions on Pattern Analysis and Machine Intelligence, 21, 961-973.

8. Yang, H.-D., Sclaroff, S. and Lee, S.-W. (2009) Sign Language Spotting with a Threshold Model Based on Conditional Random Fields. IEEE Transactions on Pattern Analysis and Machine Intelligence, 31, 1264-1277.

9. Elmezain, M. (2013) Adaptive Foreground with Cast Shadow Segmentation Using Gaussian Mixture Models and Invariant Color Features. International Journal of Engineering Science and Innovative Technology (IJESIT), 2, 438-445.

10. Elmezain, M., Al-Hamadi, A., Niese, R. and Michaelis, B. (2009) A Robust Method for Hand Tracking Using Mean-Shift Algorithm and Kalman Filter in Stereo Color Image Sequences. International Conference on Computer Vision, Image and Signal Processing, PWASET, 59, 355-359.

11. Ding, C. and He, X.F. (2004) K-Means Clustering via Principal Component Analysis. Proceedings of the 21st International Conference on Machine Learning, New York, 225-232.

12. Nixon, M.S. and Aguado, A.S. (2002) Feature Extraction and Image Processing. Newnes, Central Tablelands.

13. Ahmad, M. and Lee, S.-W. (2008) Human Action Recognition Using Shape and Clg Motion Flow from Multi-View Image Sequences. Journal of Pattern Recognition, 41, 2237-2252.

14. 14. Dugad, R., Ratakonda, K. and Ahuja, N. (1998) Robust Video Shot Change Detection. Workshop on Multimedia Signal Processing, Redondo Beach, 7-9 December 1998, 376-381.

15. 15. Dalal, N. and Triggs, B. (2005) Histograms of Oriented Gradients for Human Detection. IEEE Computer Society Conference on Computer Vision and Pattern Recognition, San Diego, 25-25 June 2005, 886-893.

16. Elmezain, M., Al-Hamadi, A. and Michaelis, B. (2010) Robust Methods for Hand Gesture Spotting and Recognition Using Hidden Markov Models and Conditional Random Fields. IEEE Symposium on Signal Processing and Information Technology (ISSPIT), Luxor, 15-18 December 2010, 131-136

6

CHAPTER

A NOVEL MACHINE VISION SYSTEM FOR THE INSPECTION OF MICRO-SPRAY NOZZLE

Kuo-Yi Huang[1,*] and Yu-Ting Ye[2]

[1]*Department of Bio-Industrial Mechatronics Engineering, National Chung Hsing University, Tai-Chung 402, Taiwan*

[2]*Department of Mechatronic Engineering, Huafan University, New Taipei City 223, Taiwan*

ABSTRACT

In this study, we present an application of neural network and image processing techniques for detecting the defects of an internal micro-spray nozzle. The defect regions were segmented by Canny edge detection, a randomized algorithm for detecting circles and a circle inspection (CI) algorithm. The gray level co-occurrence matrix (GLCM) was further used to evaluate the texture features of the segmented region. These texture features (contrast, entropy, energy), color features (mean and variance of gray level) and geometric features (distance variance, mean diameter and diameter ratio) were used in the classification procedures. A back-propagation neural network classifier was employed to detect the defects of micro-spray nozzles. The methodology presented herein effectively works for detecting micro-spray nozzle defects to an accuracy of 90.71%.

Keywords: micro-spray nozzle; image processing; neural network

1. INTRODUCTION

Nozzles are a common mechanical component and are widely used in agriculture, manufacturing and the service industry. A micro-spray nozzle is an important component in an agricultural sprayer, which is used to spray water, pesticides and nutrients. Real-time flow uniformity depends on the internal quality of the micro-spray nozzle. Unstable flow will be created because of internal defects. The price and quality of micro-spray nozzles are down due to such defects. The internal defects of micro-spray nozzles usually result during cutting procedures with a CNC (computer numerical control) machine. Chang and Yu [1] proposed a triangular-pitch shell-and-tube spray evaporator featuring an interior spray technique. The dry-out phenomenon is prevented, and the heat transfer performance is improved in their study. In addition, micro-spray nozzles have to be sorted manually, because the surface of the micro-spray nozzle is heterogeneous, which makes auto-detection very difficult.

Image processing techniques are a powerful method and are widely used to inspect industrial products. Chen*et al.* [2] designed an automatic damage detection system of an engineering ceramic surface with image processing techniques, pattern recognition and machine vision. Paniagua *et al.* [3] proposed a neuro-fuzzy classification system to inspect the quality of industrial cork samples by incorporating techniques based on Gabor filtering techniques and neuro-fuzzy computing with three wavelet-based texture quality features. A microscopic vision system [4] has been employed to measure the surface roughness of the micro-heterogeneous texture in a deep hole, by virtue of the frequency domain features of microscopic images and a back-propagation artificial neural network optimized by the genetic algorithm. Indeed, neural networks, geometric, color and texture features were often employed in the classification of plants and crops [5,6,7]. Shen *et al.* [8] used the Otsu method, HSI color system and Sobel operator to extract disease spot regions and calculate leaf areas. Park *et al.* [9] employed an unsupervised segmentation algorithm by Gaussian mixture models to segment color image regions.

However, to the best of the authors' knowledge, there is no literature on the inspection of the internal quality of micro-spray nozzles using image processing techniques. Some research [10,11,12] talked about the determination of drop sizes and shapes for spray nozzles. The drop size distribution of an irrigation spray nozzle was determined using image processing techniques, and the relationship between drop size distribution, operating pressure and nozzle size were discussed [10]. The droplet shape and size of a diesel spray had been detected using wavelet transform, a Gaussian filter and sub-pixel contour extraction [11]. The gray level gradient, boundary curvature detection, the Hough transform and the convex-hull method were employed to count and size particles in the field of sprays [12].

Currently, the internal damages of micro-spray nozzles are manually inspected (sorted) using stereomicroscopes. The procedures are laborious and ineffective. The labor cost was about 80% of the total cost for micro-spray nozzle products. The detection process has to be automated to reduce the total cost. Thus, this paper aims to develop a machine vision system to correctly and automatically inspect the micro-spray nozzle. The specific goals are: (1) to develop an algorithm to segment the defect region; (2) to extract the gray level and texture features; and (3) to classify different grades using the aforementioned features by a classifier.

In summary, we develop a machine vision system to correctly and automatically inspect and classify micro-spray nozzles. The system includes an extraction algorithm of defect regions, a feature estimation algorithm for defect regions and a classifier for the quality of micro-spray nozzles.

2. MATERIALS AND METHODS

2.1. Micro-Spray Nozzle Structure and Defects

Micro-spray nozzles (shown in Figure 1) are provided by Natural Fog Multi-Tech Precision Industry Corporation Ltd. (Tai-Chung, Taiwan). The structure profile of the micro-spray nozzle is shown in Figure 2. The outlet diameter of the micro-spray nozzle is 0.1 mm. There are two inclined annular-planes, A and B (as shown inFigure 2), on the inside surface of the micro-spray nozzle. Figure 3 depicts the circle textures in the inner image of micro-spray nozzles after CNC machine manufacturing. The defects of micro-spray nozzles were made by the CNC machine during the manufacturing procedures. The defects appear on the outlet and inclined planes A and B. Four possible defects, which include the outlet shape and deckle edge, pellet and stripe metal filings on inclined planes, are shown in Figure 3. The purpose of this study is to inspect the defects of micro-spray nozzles automatically using a machine vision system.

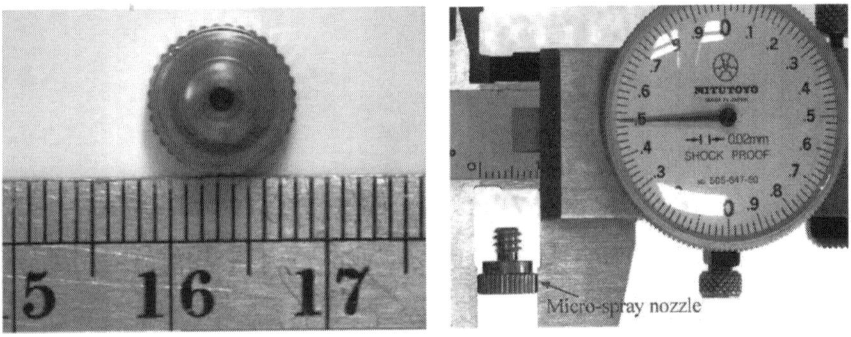

Figure 1. Micro-spray nozzle.

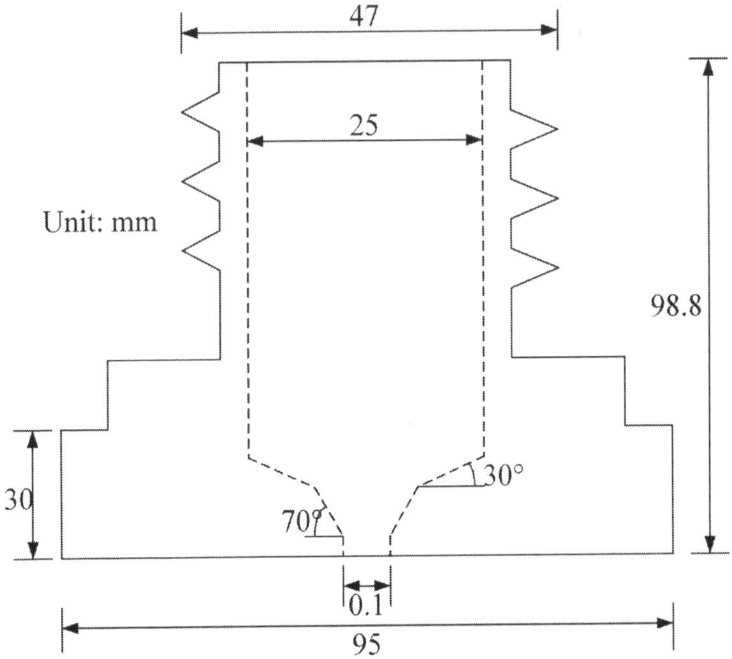

Figure 2. The profile of the micro-spray nozzle.

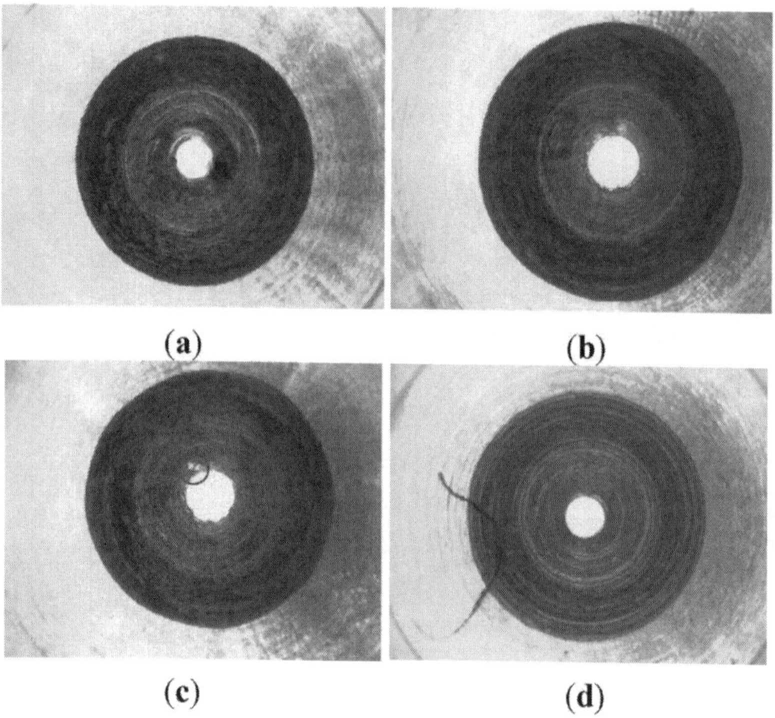

Figure 3. Four possible defects. (**a**) Small outlet; (**b**) Deckle edge of outlet; (**c**) Pellet metal fillings; (**d**) Strip metal fillings.

2.2. Hardware System

The machine vision system implemented to inspect the inner images of micro-spray nozzles is illustrated inFigure 4. This system includes an IEEE 1394 CCD color camera (DFK-31BF03, Imaging Source Inc., Bremen, Germany), a stereomicroscope (Stemi 2000-C, Zeiss Inc., Oberkochen, Germany), a front illuminating white light LED with a diffuse filter, a fixed table and a personal computer. Open Source Computer Vision Library (OpenCV1.0, Intel Corporation) and Visual C++ 6.0 programming are linked to the programs to grab images of 1024 × 768 pixels.

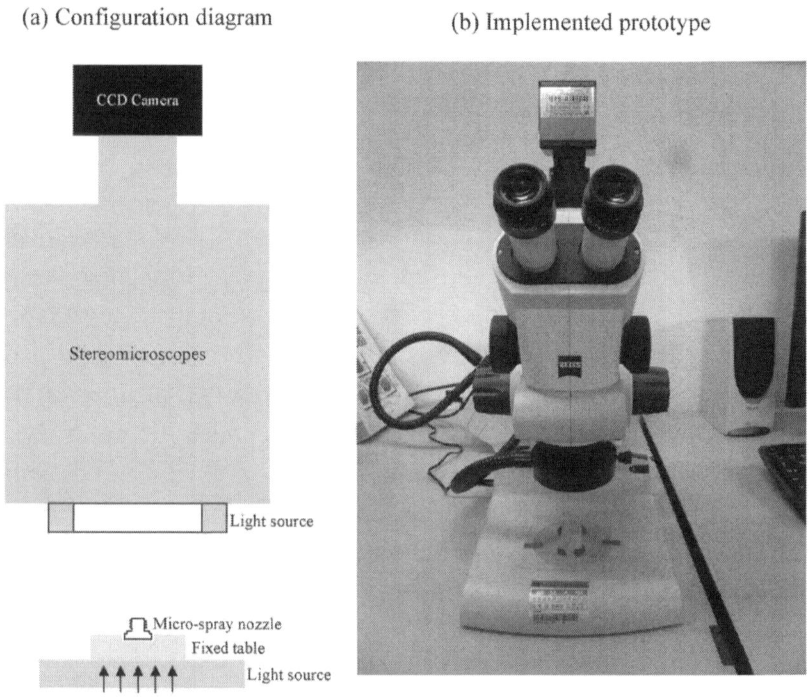

Figure 4. Illustration of the machine vision system for micro-spray nozzle defect inspection.

2.3. Region Segmentation and Features Extraction

Algorithms that include the estimation of the outlet's geometric feature and segmentation of the region of interest (ROI), a circle inspection (CI) algorithm and a classifier are proposed to detect micro-spray nozzle defects. Details of the proposed algorithms are described as follows.

2.3.1. Outlet Extraction

Segmentation of the ROI image is an essential procedure once the features of the micro-spray nozzle have been extracted. Firstly, the outlet image (as shown in Figure 5) is segmented using Otsu's auto-thresholding method and hole-filling operations [13]. By assuming that the binary image of the outlet is $f(x_i, y_i)$ (where $i = 1, 2, \ldots, m$and the total number of pixels is m), the centroid is obtained as $\overline{X} = \sum_{i=1}^{m} x_i / m$, $\overline{Y} = \sum_{i=1}^{m} y_i / m$. The covariance matrix is defined as $C = (\sum_{i=1}^{m} U_i U_i^T) / m - MM^T$, in which Ui is the *i*-th coordinate vector of the image andM=(∑i=1mUi)/m is the mean vector. *T* indicates vector transposition. A pair of orthogonal eigenvectors of the covariance matrix is then calculated. The geometric features—principle axis length (L_p), secondary axis (L_s), centroid, area (A), perimeter (P), compactness ($P^2/4\pi A$), diameter ratio (min./max. diameter, D_{mm}) and mean diameter (D_{mean}) of the outlet—are computed using eigenvectors. Secondly, two geometric features—diameter ratio and mean diameter—are employed in the micro-spray nozzle classification process.

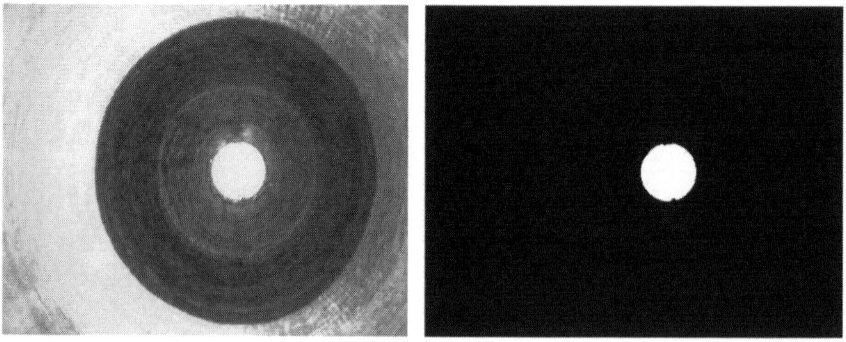

(a) (b)

Figure 5. Outlet image segmentation. (**a**) Orignal image; (**b**) Outlet image.

The ROI of inclined annular-planes is the internal image of the micro-spray nozzle, as shown in Figure 6. Segmenting the ROI effectively is an important procedure once the defects have been detected. Firstly, Canny edge detection [13], a randomized algorithm for detecting circles [14], hole-filling operation and the AND logic operator are used to segment the ROI of the inclined annular-planes.

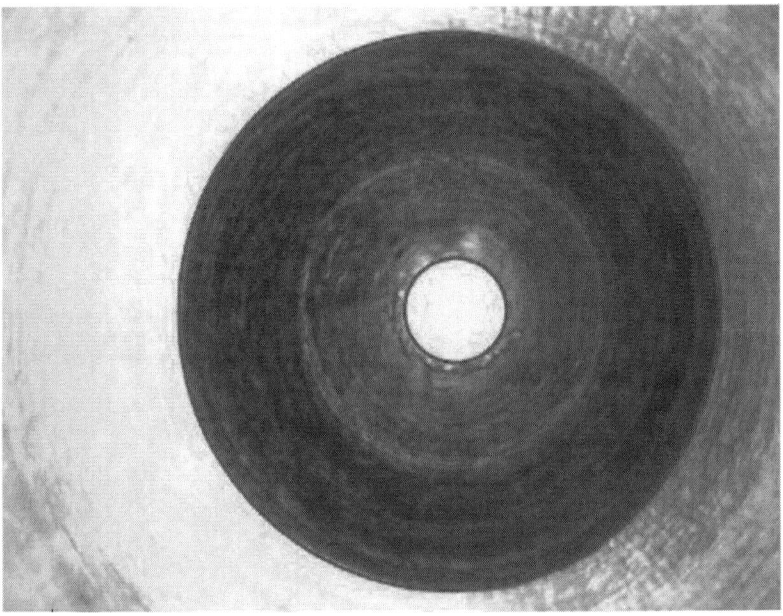

Figure 6. ROI diagram.

The procedures of extraction are as follows.

Step 1. Canny edge detection for the original image (Figure 7a), shown as Figure 7b.

Step 2. Randomized algorithm for detecting circles, shown as Figure 7c.

Step 3. The ring region is filled using a hole-filling operation, shown as Figure 7d.

Step 4. The ROI (shown as Figure 7e) is segmented using the AND logic operator for Figure 7a,d.

Step 5. Geometric features' computation.

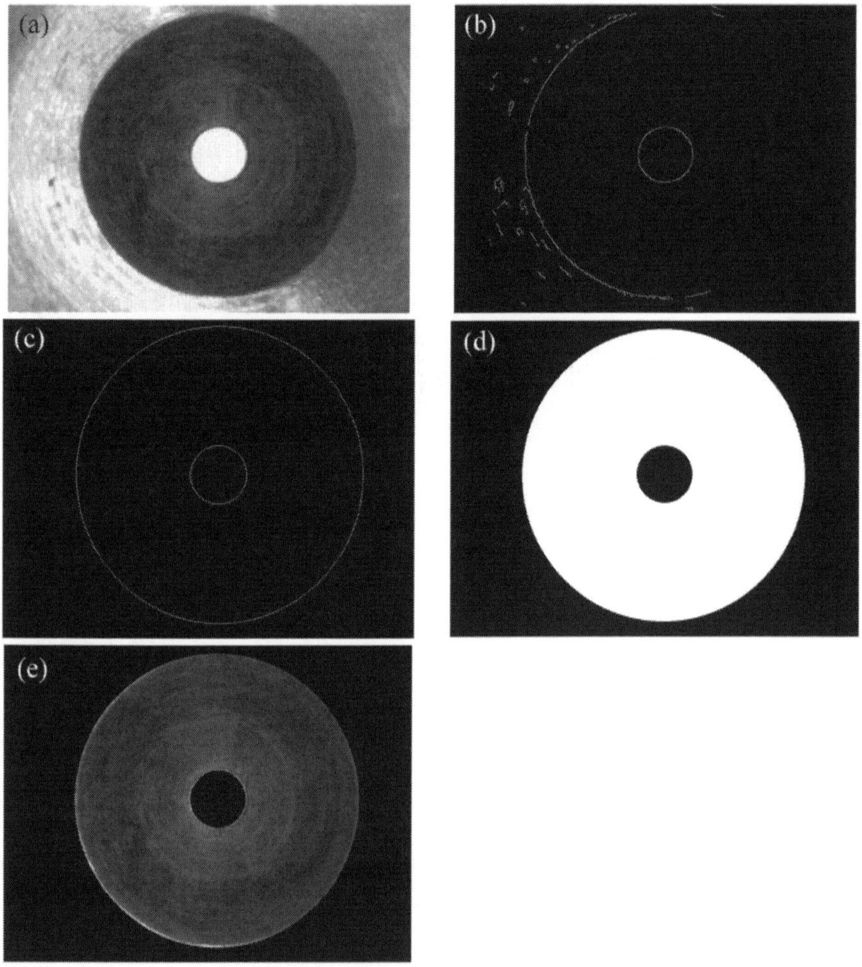

Figure 7. (**a**) Original image; (**b**) after Canny edge detection; (**c**) randomized algorithm for detecting circles; (**d**) the image after hole-filling operation; (**e**) ROI image with the AND logic operator for (a,d).

2.3.2. Possible Defect Segmentation

Segmenting defect regions is an important procedure before possible defects (including the deckle edge, pellet and stripe metal fillings) are detected and classified. A prior experiment proceeded as follows. Firstly, an inspection circle is used to find gray levels with scanning resolution in a pixel, as shown in Figure 8. There are different distribution forms of gray levels in different circles, as illustrated in Figure 9. However, the difference between defects and non-defects is difficult to distinguish using the thresholding method [13]. Therefore, a novel method, the circle inspection algorithm (CI algorithm), is proposed for defect region segmentation of micro-spray nozzles in this study.

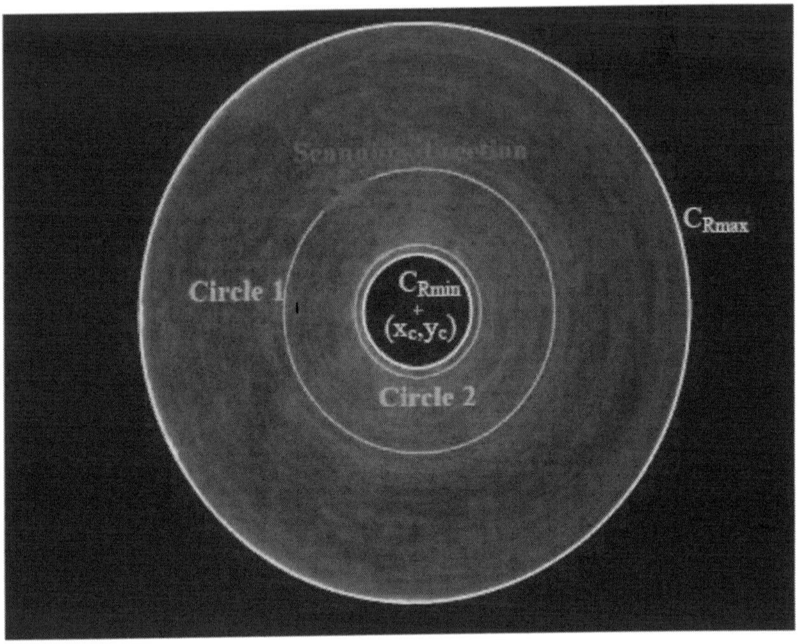

Figure 8. The scanning direction of the circle inspection for the ROI.

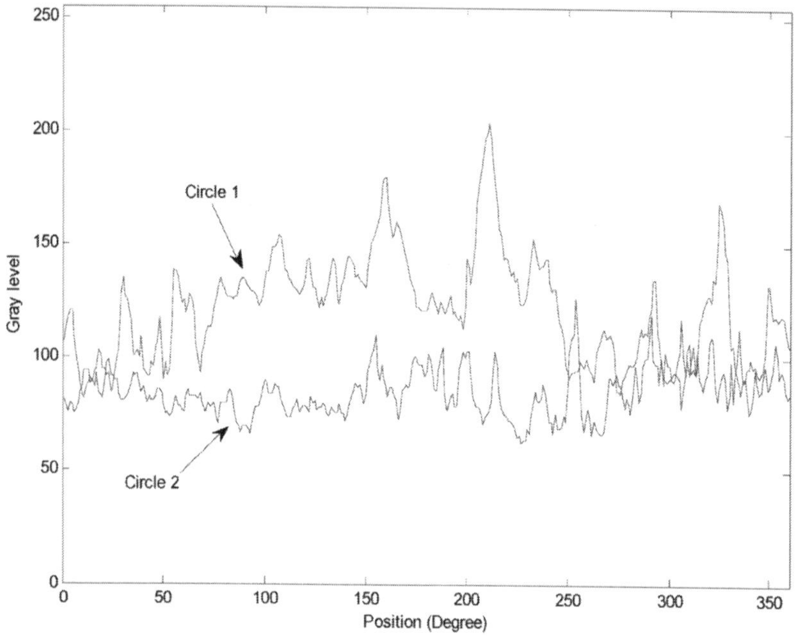

Figure 9. The distribution of gray levels of the circle inspection.

The CI algorithm is effectively executed to extract defect regions for internal images of micro-spray nozzles according to the differences of the gray level gradient. The CI algorithm is described as follows:

Step 1. The distribution of the gray level on the image is estimated along the circle C_{Rj} (with scanning resolution in a pixel); (x_c, y_c) is the center, and $R_{min} < R_j < R_{max}$.

Step 2. Compute the gray level gradient (Gi) of the circle, as demonstrated in Figure 10 on Circle 1.

$$G_i = \frac{1}{2}\left[\left(\frac{|g(i)-g(i-n)|}{n}\right)+\left(\frac{|g(i)-g(i+n)|}{n}\right)\right] \qquad (1)$$
$$= \frac{1}{2n}\left|2g(i)-g(i-n)-g(i+n)\right|$$

where $g(i)$ is the gray level of the circle, i is the position of the circle and n is the distance.

Step 3. Segment the possible defect regions (*PDR*).

$$\begin{cases} If \quad G_i \geq T, \quad then \quad g(i) \in PDR \\ If \quad G_i < T, \quad then \quad g(i) \in Normal \end{cases} \qquad (2)$$

where T is a threshold value.

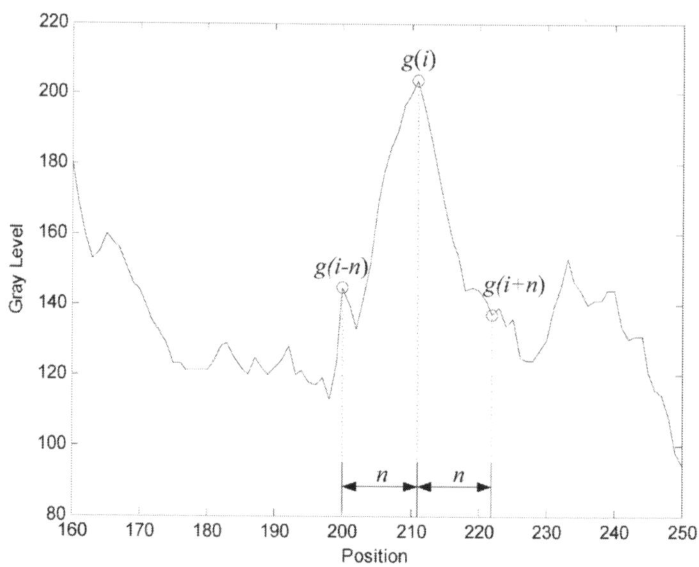

Figure 10. Parameters of gray level gradient computation.

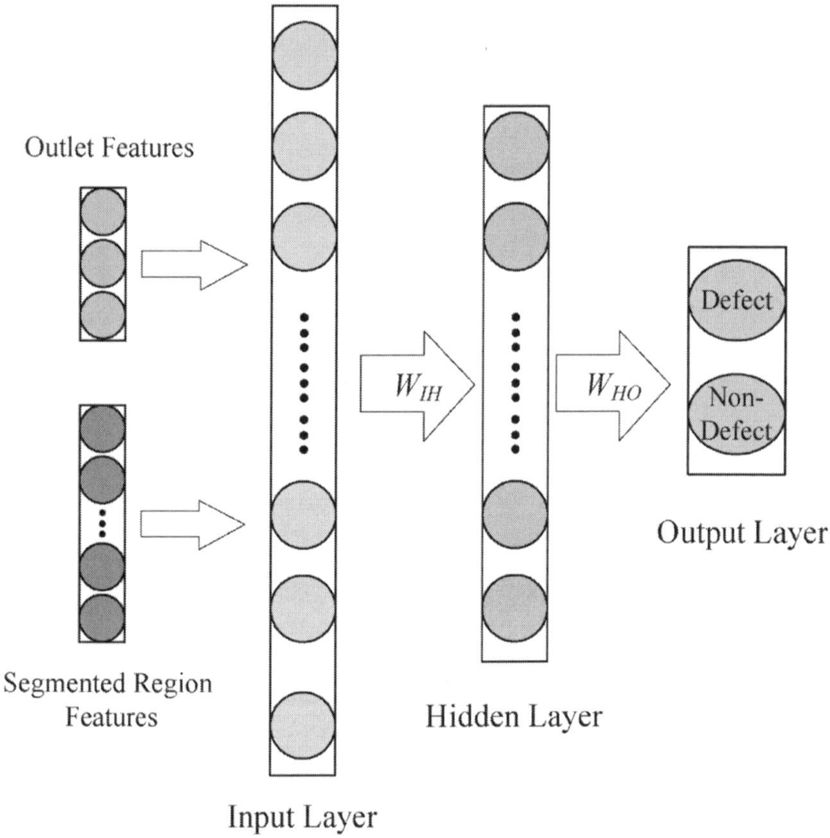

Figure 11. The structure of the back propagation neural network (BPNN) classifier.

2.4. Classification: Classifier

Geometric, texture and color features analysis have been widely employed in classification. With proper feature selections, the design of a classifier can be greatly simplified. This study adopts the geometric feature (mean diameter, diameter ratio, distance variance), the color features (mean gray level, variance of gray level) and texture features (contrast, energy and entropy from the gray level co-occurrence matrix (GLCMs) [15]) to classify defects and non-defects using a back propagation neural network [16] (BPNN, as shown in Figure 11). Mathematical formulations of these features are given in Table 1.

Table 1. Mathematical formulations of the features.

Distance Variance	Variance of $\frac{1}{N}\sum_{i}^{N}(D(x_i,y_i)-\overline{D})$
Mean gray level	$\overline{f}=\frac{1}{N}\sum_{i=1}^{N}f(x,y)$
Gray level variance	$\frac{1}{N}\sum_{i}^{N}(f(x_i,y_i)-\overline{f})$
Contrast (orientations 45°, 90°, 135° and 180°)	$\sum_{i}\sum_{j}(i-j)^2 p^2(i,j,d,\theta)$
Entropy (orientations 45°, 90°, 135° and 180°)	$-\sum_{i}\sum_{j}p(i,j,d,\theta)\log(p(i,j,d,\theta))$
Energy (orientations 45°, 90°, 135° and 180°)	$\sum_{i}\sum_{j}p^2(i,j,d,\theta)$

Note: $D(x_i, y_i)$ is the distance between location (x_i, y_i) and the outlet center, $p(i, j, d, \theta)$ represents the relative frequency of a gray level co-occurrence matrix (GLCM) of an image $g(x_i, y_i)$, where i is the gray level at location (x, y) and j represents the gray level of a neighboring pixel at a distance d and an orientation from location (x_i, y_i). The GLCM of distance 1 pixel and orientations 45°, 90°, 135° and 180° are used for the isolated image.

In this study, the BPNN classifier consists of three layers: an input layer, a hidden layer and an output layer (as shown in Figure 11). The input layer has 17 nodes, which are related to 3 geometric features, 2 color features and 12 texture features, normalized between 0 and 1. The output layer is made of nodes, related to two categories: defect and non-defect. Initially, the number of nodes n_H in the hidden layer is calculated using the following formula:

$$n_H = 0.5(n_I + n_o) + 2 \quad (3)$$

where n_I is the number of input nodes and n_o is the number of output nodes. The objective of the learning process is to find a relation in a pattern that was made by the features of each segmented region. The BPNN is trained, and the weights are changed until the error convergence criterion approaches 0.1. The error signal is given by:

$$E(t) = \sum_{k=1}^{2} (d_k(t) - y_k(t))^2 \quad (4)$$

where $d_k(t)$ is the desired response for neuron k ($k = 1\sim2$) and $y_k(t)$ is the output signal of neuron k at iteration t.

2.5. Overall Descriptions

The overall steps involved in the defect region segmentation and classification are shown in Figure 12. The algorithm for the classification of defects included image processing techniques, the CI algorithm and the BPNN classifier, are fully described in the previous two sections.

The program employed for detecting and classifying the defects is written in Microsoft Visual C++ 6.0 and OpenCV 1.0.

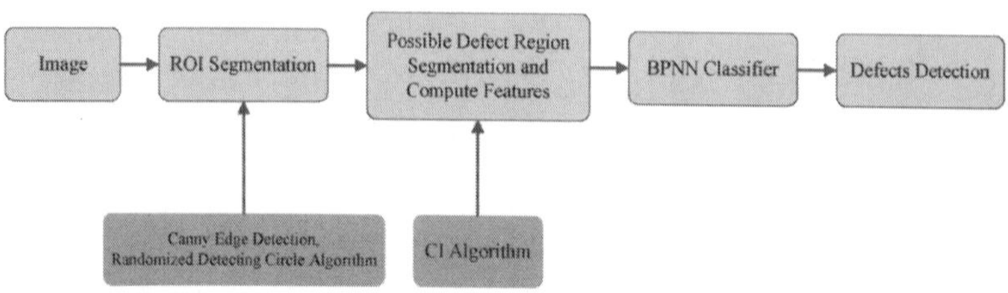

Figure 12. Segmentation and classification steps.

3. RESULTS AND DISCUSSION

In this paper, a defect detection (DD) software for a micro-spray nozzle is developed using image processing techniques and the CI algorithm (written in Visual C++ 6.0 with OpenCV 1.0), as outlined in the first few steps shown in Figure 12. The algorithm is summarized as follows:

Step 1. Two geometric features of the outlet are computed.

Step 2. The ROIs are segmented using Canny edge detection, a randomized algorithm for detecting circles, hole-filling and the AND logic operators.

Step 3. Possible defect regions are segmented by the CI algorithm.

Step 4. Estimate 15 features of the segmented regions.

Step 5. Establish and test the BPNN classifier to classify defects and non-defects.

The functions of DD include file operations (acquire, load and save images) and image analysis operations (binary operator, hole-filling, remove noises using closing, opening and Canny edge). The geometrics of the outlet, texture and color features of the segmented region are obtained, and defects can be detected by the DD computation accurately and rapidly.

The difference between defects and non-defect regions is not obvious in the original image of a micro-spray nozzle, as shown in Figure 13a. Possible defect regions, including defects and non-defects, are segmented using the CI algorithm (parameters $n = 6$, $T = 11$ are selected after some experimentations) and image processing techniques (such as hole-filling, erosion, dilation, opening, closing and Canny edge operators), as indicated inFigure 13b. Figure 13c results using the AND logic operator for Figure

13a,b. Hence, the defects of micro-spray nozzles (Figure 13d) are detected according to the BPNN classification.

In order to establish the BPNN classifier, 698 samples (with 565 non-defects and 133 defects) are randomly sampled. Eleven hidden nodes are obtained by Equation (3) according to 17 input features, and two output categories. The BPNN classifier is implemented using functions of MATLAB 8.0. For each configuration, the training sample set is randomly selected from all samples until the BPNN convergence is achieved. Over-fitting often occurs when the training set contains some incorrect samples in the BPNN. As the grades of micro-spray nozzles in training samples are already known before the training process, over-fitting is unlikely to occur. To ensure that the influence of over-fitting is trivial during the training process, the maximum number of iterations is set to 100,000. Further studies showed that the same inspection effect is obtained when the error rate convergence criterion is smaller than 0.1. Randomly-sampled images (1486 non-defects and 118 defects) are used to test the system. The accuracy of the classification is 90.71%. The accuracy of outlet shape and strip fillings is 100%. However, a few deckle edges and pellet fillings of the images can not be detected using the proposed algorithms, examples of classification failure and explanations are shown in Table 2.

In this study, the proposed system can detect and classify visible defects with a CCD camera accurately and efficiently. In the future, we hope that the detection and classification system can be applied to an auto-inspection system for micro-spray nozzles.

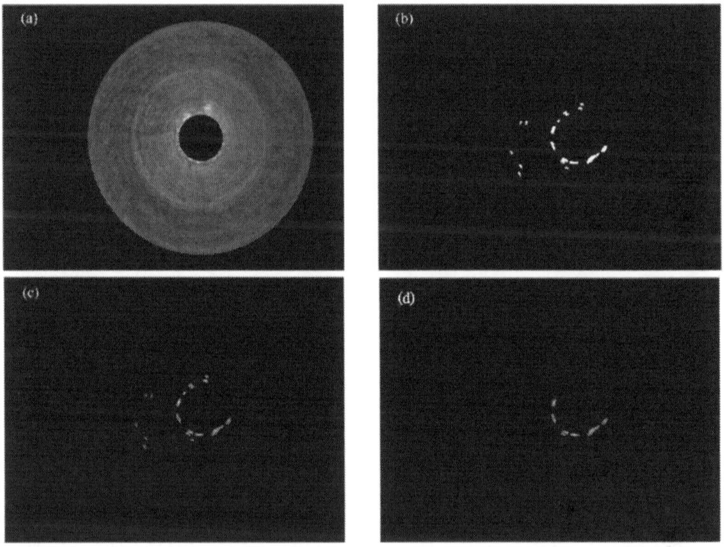

Figure 13. (**a**) Original image; (**b**) segmented binary image after the CI algorithm; (**c**) segmented image after the CI algorithm; (**d**) classification result.

Table 2. Examples of classification failure and explanations.

	Original Image	ROI	Explanation
Case 1: Deckle edge	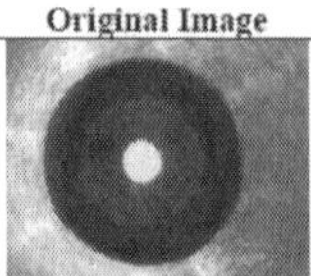	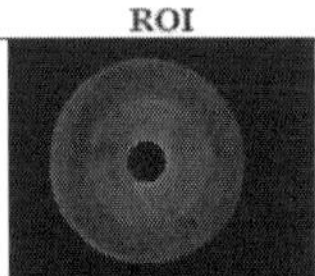	Deckle edges are removed after ROI segmentation operator.
Case 2: Deckle edge	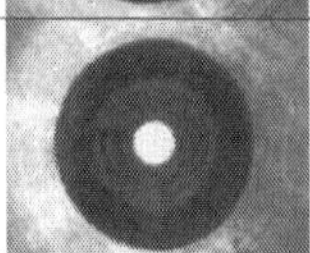	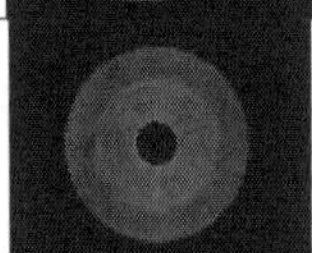	Deckle edges cannot be segmented by the CI algorithm because they are not obvious.
Case 3: Pellet filings	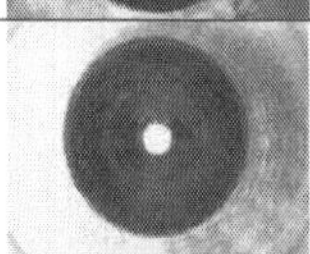	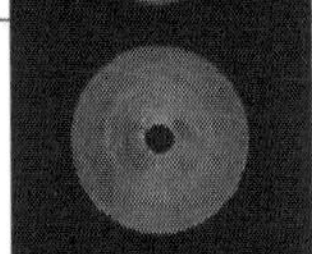	Pellet fillings cannot be segmented by the CI algorithm because they are not obvious.
Case 4: Dark image	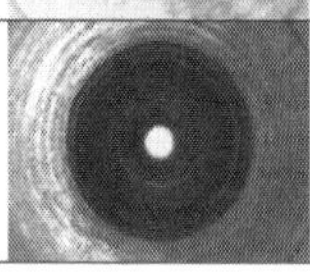	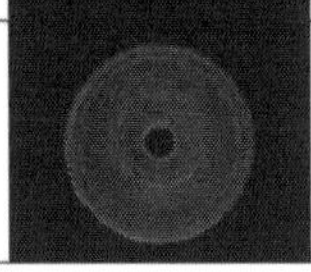	The image is blurred and dark.

4. CONCLUSIONS

Real-time flow uniformity depends on the internal quality of the micro-spray nozzle, and unstable flow will result because of internal defects. A novel inspection system for internal defects of micro-spray nozzles is developed in this study. The image processing techniques, Canny edge detection, a randomized algorithm for detecting circles, the circle inspection algorithm and the BPNN classifier are used to establish the micro-spray nozzle detection system. Possible defects can be segmented efficiently using the CI algorithm and image processing techniques. Geometric, color and texture features of the defects are obtained to establish a BPNN classifier. Testing results show that the defects of the micro-spray nozzles can be detected efficiently using the proposed system. In a future study, we aim to refine the inspection algorithm in order to increase the inspection accuracy for the production line of micro-spay nozzles.

AUTHOR CONTRIBUTIONS

All authors have made significant contributions to the paper. Huang K.Y. initiated the idea to develop the inspection system of micro-spray nozzles. Huang K.Y. and Ye Y.T. developed the inspection algorithms and the classifier together. Ye Y.T. wrote programs and performed the experiment. Huang, K.Y. contributed to the paper organization and technical writing to final version.

REFERENCES

1. Chang, T.B.; Yu, L.Y. Optimal nozzle spray cone angle for triangular-pitch shell-and-tube interior spray evaporator. *Int. J. Heat Mass Transf.* **2015**, *85*, 463–472.

Chen, S.; Lin, B.; Han, X.; Liang, X. Automated inspection of engineering ceramic grinding surface damage based on image recognition. *Int. J. Adv. Manuf. Technol.* **2013**, *66*, 431–443.

2. Paniagua, B.; Vega-Rodríguez, M.A.; Gómez-Pulido, J.A.; Sánchez-Pérez, J.M. Automatic texture characterization using Gabor filters and neurofuzzy computing. *Int. J. Adv. Manuf. Technol.* **2011**, *52*, 15–32.

3. Liu, W.; Tu, X.; Jia, Z.; Wang, W.; Ma, X.; Bi, X. An improved surface roughness measurement method for micro-heterogeneous texture in deep hole based on gray-level co-occurrence matrix and support vector machine. *Int. J. Adv. Manuf. Technol.* **2013**, *69*, 583–593.

4. López-García, F.; Andreu-García, G.; Blasco, J.; Aleixos, N.; Valiente, J. Automatic detection of skin defects in citrus fruits using a multivariate image analysis approach. *Comput. Electron. Agric.* **2010**, *71*, 189–197.

5. Kavdir, I. Discrimination of sunflower, weed and soil by artificial neural networks. *Comput. Electron. Agric.***2004**, *44*, 153–160.

6. Camargo, A.; Smith, J.S. An image-processing based algorithm to automatically identify plant disease visual symptoms. *Biosyst. Eng.* **2009**, *102*, 9–21.

7. Shen, W.; Wu, Y.; Chen, Z.; Wei, H. Grading method of leaf spot disease based on image processing. In Proceedings of the 2008 International Conference on Computer Science and Software Engineering, Wuhan, China, 12–14 December 2008; pp. 491–494.

8. Park, J.H.; Lee, G.S.; Park, S.Y. Color image segmentation using adaptive mean shift and statistical model-based methods. *Comput. Math. Appl.* **2009**, *57*, 970–980.

9. Sudheera, K.P.; Pandab, R.K. Digital image processing for determining drop sizes from irrigation spray nozzles. *Agric. Water Manag.* **2000**, *45*, 159–167.

10. Blaisot, J.B.; Yon, J. Droplet size and morphology characterization for dense sprays by image processing: Application to the diesel spray. *Exp. Fluids* **2005**, *39*, 997–994.

11. Lee, S.Y.; Kim, Y.D. Sizing of spray particles using image processing technique. *KSME Int. J.* **2004**, *18*, 879–894.

12. Gonzalez, R.C.; Woods, R.E. *Digital Image Processing*, 3rd ed.; Prentice Hall: Upper Saddle River, NJ, USA, 2002.

13. Chen, T.C.; Chung, K.L. An efficient randomized algorithm for detecting circles. *CVGIP Comput. Vis. Image Underst.* **2001**, *83*, 172–191.

14. Haralick, R.M.; Shanmugam, K.; Dinstein, I. Textual features for image classification. *IEEE Trans. Syst. Man Cybern.* **1973**, *3*, 610–621.

15. Fausett, L. *Fundamentals of Neural Networks: Architectures, Algorithms, and Applications*; Prentice-Hall: Upper Saddle River, NJ, USA, 1994.

7

CHAPTER

NUMBER DETERMINATION OF SUCCESSFULLY PACKAGED DIES PER WAFER BASED ON MACHINE VISION

Hsuan-Ting Chang *, Ren-Jie Pan and Hsiao-Wei Peng

Photonics and Information Laboratory, Department of Electrical Engineering, National Yunlin University of Science and Technology, 123 University Road, Section 3, Douliou, Yunlin 64002, Taiwan

ABSTRACT

Packaging the integrated circuit (IC) chip is a necessary step in the manufacturing process of IC products. In general, wafers with the same size and process should have a fixed number of packaged dies. However, many factors decrease the number of the actually packaged dies, such as die scratching, die contamination, and die breakage, which are not considered in the existing die-counting methods. Here we propose a robust method that can automatically determine the number of actual packaged dies by using machine vision techniques. During the inspection, the image is taken from the top of the wafer, in which most dies have been removed and packaged. There are five steps in the proposed method: wafer region detection, wafer position calibration, dies region detection, detection of die sawing lines, and die number counting. The abnormal cases of fractional dies in the wafer boundary and dropped dies during the packaging are considered in the proposed method as well. The experimental results show that the precision and recall rates reach 99.83% and 99.84%, respectively, when determining the numbers of actual packaged dies in the 41 test cases.

Keywords: automatic optical inspection; wafer; die; machine vision; IC packaging; sawing line

1. INTRODUCTION

Machine vision has been widely used in various fields because only simple devices are required, and various solutions have been proposed for different kinds of applications, such as industrial measurement [1], text recognition [2], finger recognition [3], medical image analysis [4], face recognition [5], and human computer interfaces [6]. As for the industrial measurement in a semiconductor factory, the automatic optical inspection for wafer-related processes has been widely studied in recent years, such as detecting a die in the open circuit [7], wafer defect detection [8], the LED grading system [9], and rotation calibration in wafer packaging [10].

The number of packaged dies is important information for the manufacturer. In general cases, the number of dies per wafer can be determined by existing counting algorithms [11,12,13,14], which can be found on websites [15] and [16] as well. In these methods, the number of gross dies per wafer can be estimated by entering the parameters such as wafer size, die width, die height, horizontal and vertical spacing. In Reference [11], the variables required in the proposed algorithm include the die dimensions (width and length), the size and orientation of the wafer flat, the size of the non-yielding periphery zone, and the die array relative the center of the wafer. The use and evaluation of the yield models in IC manufacturing are discussed in Reference [12]. Several die-per-wafer yield models, which are derived from Poisson, Binomial, and exponential probability density functions, are reviewed. Moreover, de Vries pointed out that there are different formulas used by different semiconductor manufacturing companies [13]. He found that the accuracy of an exact count algorithm depends on the die area and the aspect ratio. All the above methods require the input of the dimensions of the die and wafer.

Recently, computer vision based methods have received great attention in terms of detecting wafer die defects [17,18]. However, there are few studies that focus on the automatic counting of the die number in the wafer images without providing the size and dimension information for the dies and wafers. In addition to our preliminary work [19], Xu *et al.* proposed a wafer die-counting algorithm using the geometric characteristics [20] in the wafer images. In this work, RANSAC (Random Sample Consensus) algorithms [21,22] are used to detect the wafer location and the sawing lines. The incomplete dies at the wafer rim strip containing the circle pixels can be easily detected and are then eliminated. Both high counting accuracy and good computational efficiency can be achieved. However, this method does not deal with cases of fractured and randomly dropped dies on the wafer.

In practical situations, some situations that could lead to incorrect counting results should be considered. For example, with the IC testing programs, some dies in a wafer that do not pass the test will not be packaged. The dies not being packaged are left on the wafer and thus a number of dies that different from those successfully packaged are obtained. General commercial equipment [23] could automatically calculate the number of dies in the above case. However, in the cases of the remaining dies that are broken, displaced, or rotated, they cannot be determined straightforwardly. Thus a manual calculation is required if the actual number is desired. It is very time consuming to obtain the precise number of successfully packaged dies through manual wafer inspection. This number should be exactly the same as that determined from the pick and place robot. The clients of the die-packaging factory can only estimate the number, assuming that no abnormal cases occurred during the process. However, this number is usually less than that of actual packaged dies. If the difference between the two numbers is large, the clients will not accept the result and will ask for an explanation. Therefore, in this study we propose a computer-vision-based method that can automatically determine the exact number of actual packaged dies in the residual wafer image. As opposed to existing methods, the wafer and die parameters such as size, width, and length are not required. In addition, the determined die-per-wafer number can be more accurate when abnormal cases occur during the packaging process.

The remaining part of the paper is organized as follows. In Section 2, the proposed methods with the required image processing algorithms are described. The experimental results are provided in Section 3. Finally, the conclusions are drawn in Section 4.

2. METHOD

Figure 1 shows the systematic block diagram of the proposed system, which consists of five stages in order to determine the number of packaged dies per wafer: (1) wafer region detection: detect the actual wafer region from the input image; (2) wafer position calibration: calibrate the rotation angle of the input wafer image; (3) die region detection: detect the packaged die region from the wafer region; (4) detection of die sawing lines: determine vertical and horizontal segmentation lines in the wafer region, and then use them to partition off the rectangular die regions; (5) die number counting: determine the exact number of actual packaged dies. The detailed procedures are described in later subsections.

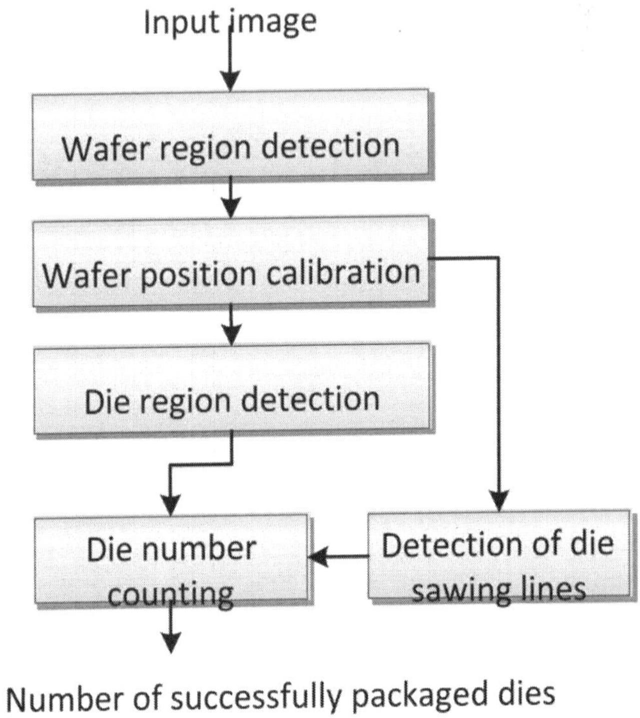

Figure 1. The system flowchart of the proposed method.

2.1. Wafer Region Detection

Figure 2a shows the input wafer image, which has redundant background information that should be removed for further processing. The detailed steps include: (1) color to grayscale transformation and binarization; (2) region labeling; (3) position calibration.

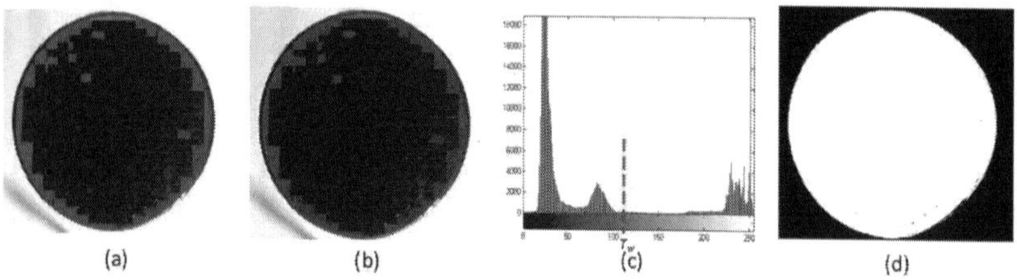

Figure 2. (**a**) Original image; (**b**) grayscale image; (**c**) histogram of the grayscale image; (**d**) binarized image.

2.1.1. Color-to-Grayscale Transformation and Binarization

A color image is composed of red, green, and blue components. Each component has a one-byte resolution, *i.e.*, 256 grayscale levels. A color image can be transformed to a grayscale image igray(x,y) by using the linear combination method shown in Equation (1).

$$i_{gray}(x,y) = 0.299 \times i_r(x,y) + 0.587 \times i_g(x,y) + 0.114 \times i_b(x,y) \quad (1)$$

where i_r, i_g, and i_b denote the grayscale values in red, green, and blue components, respectively, and (x,y) denotes the pixel coordinates.

The binarization process is often used in the object detection and segmentation framework in image processing. The main idea is to select a threshold T_w and to force all the pixel values into two fixed grayscale values, 0 and 255, as shown in Equation (2).

$$w_b(x,y) = \begin{cases} 0, \text{if } i_{\text{gray}}(x,y) > T_w \\ 255, \text{Otherwise} \end{cases} \tag{2}$$

where $w_b(x,y)$ is the pixel value after binarization. Figure 2b shows the grayscale image transformed from Figure 2a. Figure 2c shows the histogram of the image in Figure 2b. The threshold T_W can be automatically determined by applying Otsu's method [24] on the histogram of the grayscale image. Figure 2d shows the binarized result ofFigure 2b, based on Equation (2). The white wafer region is well extracted from the black background.

2.1.2. Region Labeling

In order to remove the background and keep the wafer information simultaneously, the mask must conform to the sharpness of the wafer. In Figure 2d, there are certain small regions (black points) in the white region boundary and they should be removed. The connected component labeling method [25] is used to determine the small black regions and the size of each region. Only the largest black area can be retained with the operation shown in Equation (3).

$$w'_b(x,y) = \begin{cases} 0, \text{if } w_{\text{label}}(x,y) = t \\ 255, \text{Otherwise} \end{cases} \tag{3}$$

where *t* is the label of the maximum black region and wlabel is a matrix that denotes the labeling result. Figure 3a,b show the mask w'b and the final wafer image w without the background information, respectively. As shown in Equation (4), the final wafer image is obtained as passing the input wafer image onto the mask w'b, *i.e.*,

$$w(x,y) = i(x,y) \cap w_b'(x,y) \tag{4}$$

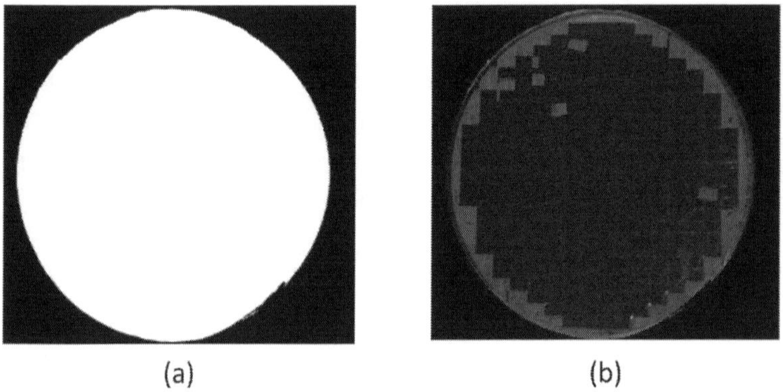

Figure 3. (**a**) The mask of capturing the wafer image; (**b**) Wafer image with black background.

2.2. Wafer Position Calibration

Due to the possible deviation on the wafer placement, the die sawing lines could not be exactly horizontal and vertical in the image, which is necessary in order to accurately determine the die number in the following processing steps. Here, the Canny edge detection [26] and Fourier transform methods are used to determine the wafer rotation angle. First, a Canny edge detector is utilized to obtain the edge information we(x,y) in the wafer image shown in Figure 3b. Figure 4a shows that many horizontal and vertical sawing lines appear in this image. This edge information can be transformed into the frequency domain $W_e(u,v)$ by using the two-dimensional Fourier transform shown in Equation (5).

$$W_e(u,v) = \iint_{-\infty}^{\infty} w_e(x,y) e^{-j2\pi(ux+vy)} dxdy \tag{5}$$

Figure 4b shows the corresponding spectrum image, We(u,v), in which the major components appear at the nearly horizontal and vertical directions. In order to determine the angle θ rotated from the exact horizontal and vertical axes, the threshold *Tc* shown in Equation (6) is used to binarize the spectrum image We(u,v). Figure 4c shows the binary image Ct(u,v) derived from the image shown in Figure 4b.

$$C_t(u,v) = \begin{cases} 0, \text{if } W_e(u,v) > T_c \\ 255, \text{Otherwise} \end{cases} \tag{6}$$

To determine the rotation angle of the wafer, two points $C_t(u_h,v_h)$ and $C_t(u_l,v_l)$ located on the points in the nearly vertical direction in the image $C_t(u,v)$ are selected. By using Equation (7), the deviation angle θ can be determined as

$$\theta = \frac{\pi}{2} - tan^{-1}\left(\frac{v_h - v_l}{u_h - u_l}\right) \tag{7}$$

The deviation angle θ can be used to calibrate the wafer image w(x,y) such that the sawing lines are as perfectly horizontal and vertical as possible. Equation (8) shows that the new coordinates (x', y') of the rotated image $W'(x', y')$ can be determined from the coordinates (x,y). However, if the coordinates (x', y') are non-integers, the bilinear interpolation is utilized to obtain the integer coordinates. Figure 5 shows the rotated image after using the position calibration.

$$\begin{bmatrix} x' \\ y' \end{bmatrix} = \begin{bmatrix} cos\,\theta & -cos\,\theta \\ sin\,\theta & sin\,\theta \end{bmatrix} \begin{bmatrix} x \\ y \end{bmatrix} \tag{8}$$

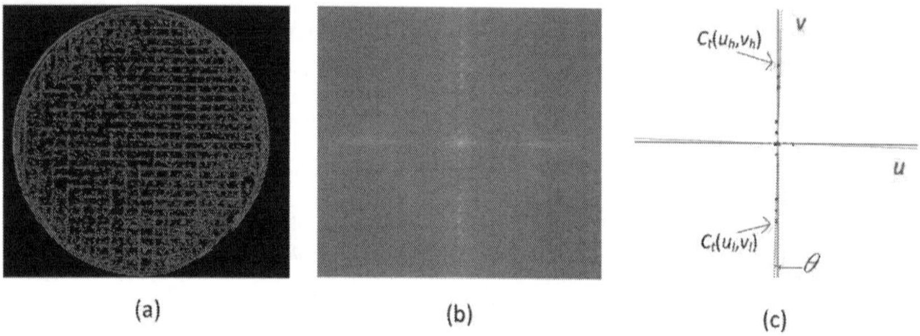

Figure 4. (**a**) Canny edge detection result of Figure 3b; (**b**) spectrum of the edge image shown in Figure 4a; (**c**) binary image in which the black points are corresponding to strong white points shown in Figure 4b.

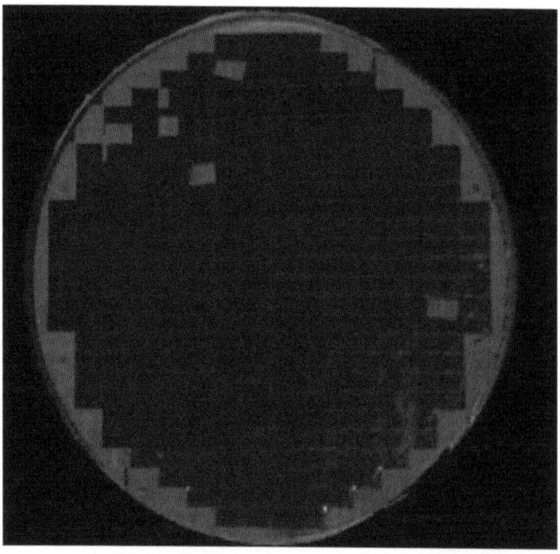

Figure 5. The wafer-region image after the position calibration.

2.3. Die region Detection

After the wafer region has been determined and its position has been calibrated in Subsection 2.2, the resident die regions, which are not taken away during packaging, are detected. In order to avoid the color saturation problem caused by the reflective points in the RGB color space, the YCbCr color space is utilized such that the brightness can be separated from its color components. Equation (9) shows the transformation function.

$$\begin{bmatrix} Y \\ Cb \\ Cr \end{bmatrix} = \begin{bmatrix} 16 \\ 128 \\ 128 \end{bmatrix} + \begin{bmatrix} 65.481 & 128.553 & 24.966 \\ -37.797 & -74.203 & 112 \\ 112 & -93.786 & -18.214 \end{bmatrix} \begin{bmatrix} R \\ G \\ B \end{bmatrix} \quad (9)$$

Figure 6a–c show the Y, Cb, and Cr components of the wafer image in Figure 5, respectively. As shown inFigure 6b, the Cb component has a more obvious contrast than the other components and is nearly unaffected by reflection. To extract the regions of the resident dies, a binarization process defined in Equation (10) is used.

$$W_{\text{dies}}(x, y) = \begin{cases} 255, \text{if } Cb(x, y) < T_{cb} \\ 0, \text{Otherwise} \end{cases} \quad (10)$$

where $Cb(x,y)$ denotes the pixel value in the Cb component, T_{cb} is the threshold value, which is determined by applying Otsu's method on the histogram of the Cb component image shown in Figure 7a; and Wdies(x,y)denotes the resident die image shown in Figure 7b.

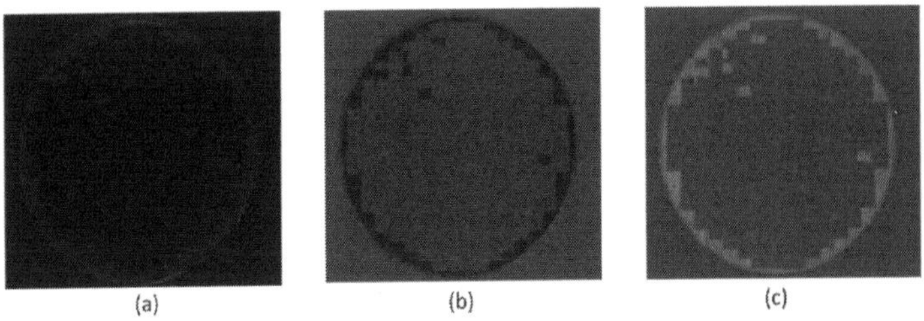

Figure 6. (**a**) The Y component image; (**b**) the Cb component image; (**c**) the Cr component image in the YCbCr color space.

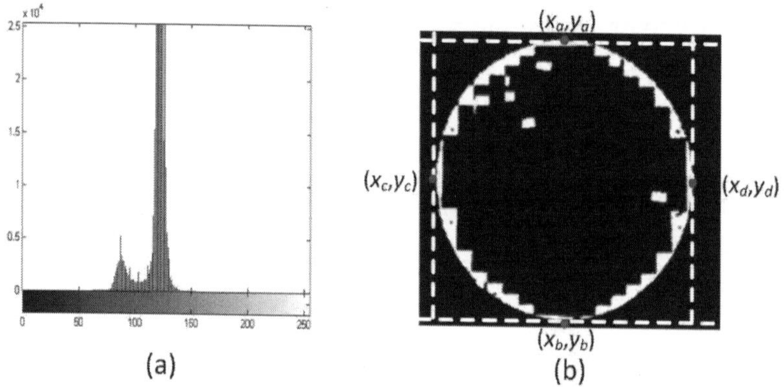

Figure 7. (**a**) Histogram of the Cb component; (**b**) the image of the resident die regions.

As shown in Figure 5, the rim strip of the wafer contains no dies and should be excluded to avoid possible confusion on die counting in further processing. In the third step, the area of the wafer region which does not include the rim strip is determined. The four non-zero value points (x_a,y_a), (x_b,y_b), (x_c,y_c), and (x_d,y_d) corresponding to the top, bottom, leftmost, and rightmost boundary points, respectively, are selected in the image Wdies shown in Figure 7b. The four points can be used to define an ellipse mask region WD using Equation (11).

$$W_D(x,y) = \begin{cases} 255, \text{if } \dfrac{(x-h)^2}{\alpha^2} + \dfrac{(y-k)^2}{\beta^2} \le 1 \\ 0, \text{Otherwise} \end{cases} \tag{11}$$

where

$$h = \frac{x_a + x_b}{2}, k = \frac{y_a + y_b}{2}, \alpha = \frac{x_d - x_c}{2}, \beta = \frac{y_a - y_b}{2}$$

Figure 8a shows a typical mask region, which is very close to a circle. By applying this mask onto the image inFigure 5, Figure 8b shows that the mentioned rim strip (shown in the white region) can be successfully removed.

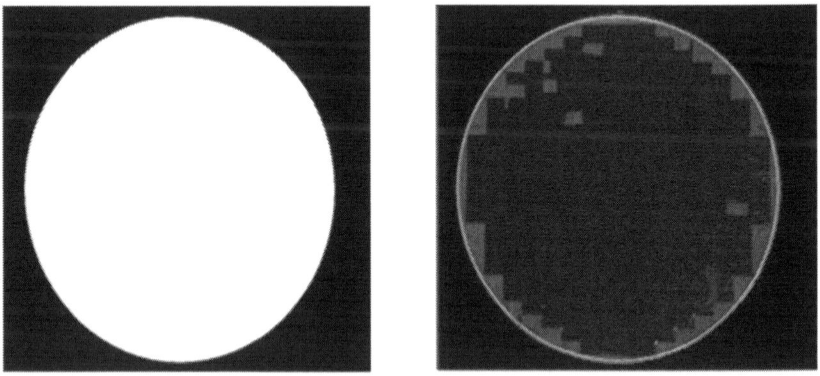

(a) (b)

Figure 8. (**a**) The mask of the wafer image; (**b**) the wafer image in which the region outside the white contour has been removed.

2.4. Detection of Die Sawing Lines

Prior to die counting, the geometrical information of a standard die, whose shape is rectangular and is defined by the sawing lines, should be derived. Therefore, detecting the die sawing lines in the wafer image is required. However, the sawing lines shown in Figure 9a are not obvious and thus are difficult to be easily detected. To overcome this problem, the histogram equalization method that can increase the global contrast in the image [27] is used. Figure 9b shows the enhanced result of Figure 9a. In this enhanced image e(x,y), the sawing lines have been intensified, thus they can be more easily detected. Equations (12) and (13) show that the pixel values of each column and row in the wafer image (Figure 9b) are accumulated to obtain the two vectors $v(j)$ and $h(i)$, respectively.

$$v(j) = \sum_{x} e(x,j) \tag{12}$$

$$h(i) = \sum_{y} e(i, y) \quad (13)$$

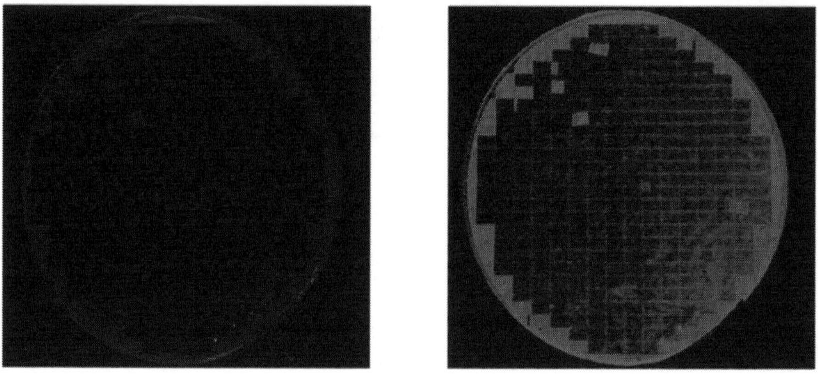

(a) (b)

Figure 9. (**a**) The grayscale image obtained from Figure 3b; (**b**) the enhanced image $e(x, y)$ obtained by applying the histogram equalization on Figure 9a.

Figure 10a,b show the projections of the accumulated pixel values in the columns and rows, respectively. In both projections, many obvious peaks appear in accordance with the sawing line positions in the wafer image shown in Figure 9b, because the pixel values in the sawing lines are much larger than that in the die regions. In addition, the intervals between two consecutive peaks should be very similar in these two projections. However, due to the incomplete dies and the non-uniform illumination condition, the peak and non-peak values vary a lot. Therefore, the peaks cannot be detected by directly applying a fixed thresholding scheme. Figure 11 shows the flowchart of the proposed method to detect the peak positions $v_p(j)$ in the vertical direction. Here j denotes the index of the detected peaks. The peak positions $h_p(i)$ in the horizontal direction can be detected with a similar strategy.

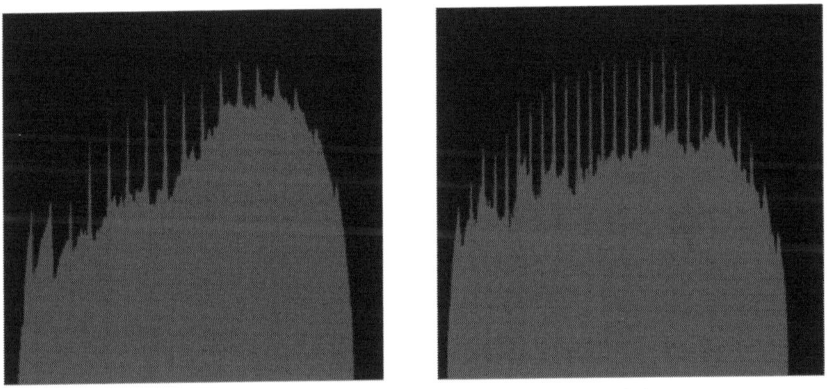

(a) (b)

Figure 10. The projections of the accumulated values in (**a**) the columns and (**b**) the rows.

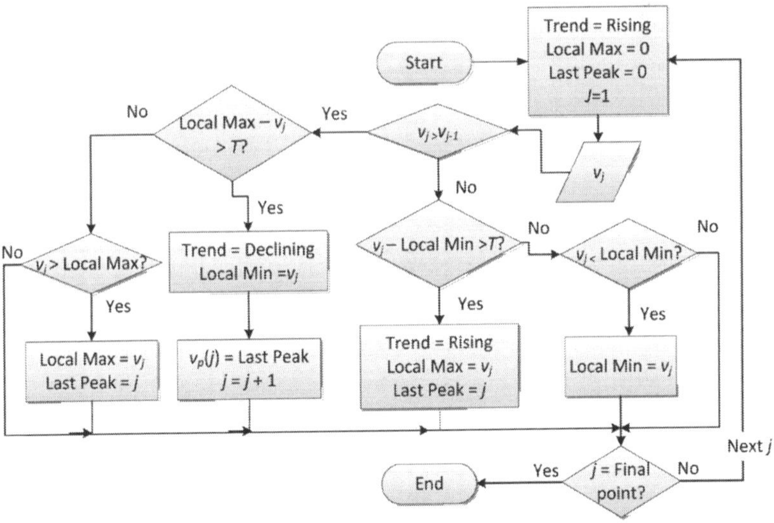

Figure 11. Peak detection flowchart in the vertical direction.

Figure 12 shows the detected die sawing lines in both the vertical and horizontal directions. The peak detection method described above shows that many incorrect sawing lines are detected. To solve this problem, the average line method is proposed to filter out the miss-detected sawing lines. Figure 13a,b show the depicted white lines representing the average values calculated by using Equations (14) and (15), respectively.

$$v'(j) = \frac{\sum_{j-l}^{j+l} v(j) + v(j)}{l+2} \tag{14}$$

$$h'(i) = \frac{\sum_{i-z}^{i+z} h(i) + h(i)}{z+2} \tag{15}$$

where v' and h' are the average values in the sliding windows of widths. Assume that l and w are the length and width of the die when the threshold *T* shown in Figure 11 is increased to a larger number in the peak detection method, respectively. As shown in Figure 11, a larger threshold *T* indicates a higher difference values between the two consecutive bins in the histogram. Figure 14a shows the detected peak positions with a large *T* value. The values l and z are calculated by using Equations (16)–(19), where we define the shortest distant between two peak positions to be length and width of the die in the histogram with a *T* value.

$$l = min\big(D_h(i)\big) \tag{16}$$

$$z = min\big(D_v(j)\big) \tag{17}$$

$$D_v(j) = \widehat{v_p}(j+1) - \widehat{v_p}(j) \tag{18}$$

$$D_h(i) = \widehat{h_p}(i+1) - \widehat{h_p}(i) \tag{19}$$

where vp^ and hp^ denote the detected peaks positions. Dv and Dh denote the distances between two consecutive peak positions in the vertical and horizontal directions, respectively. The die sawing lines v_p and h_p detected in the peak detection method are compared to the average values v' and h', respectively. If the condition $v_p(j)$ >v'(j) is satisfied, the new die sawing line is recorded as $v_r(k) = v_p(j)$. Figure 14b shows the detection result based on this average line method.

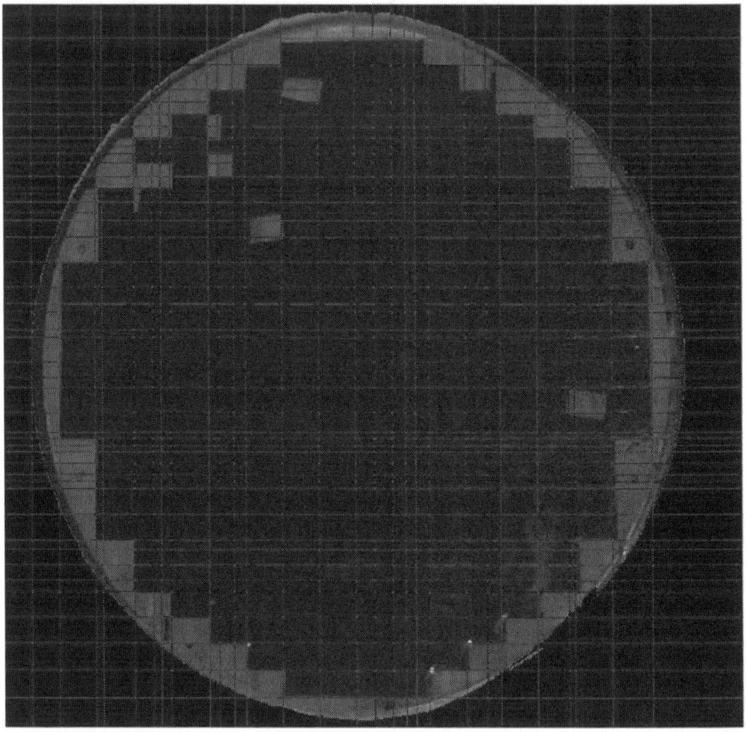

Figure 12. Result of the die sawing line detection.

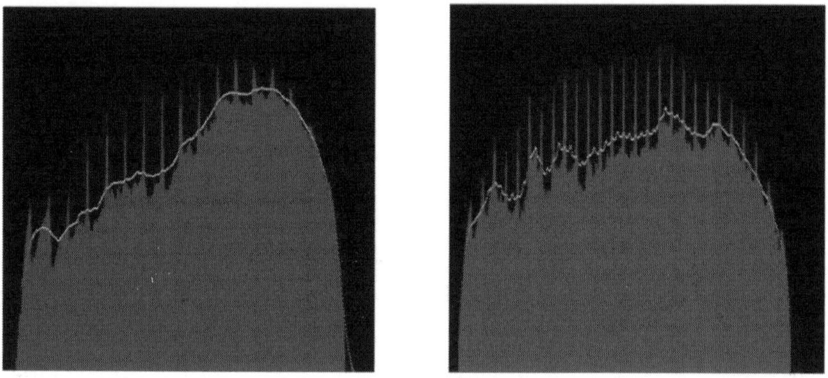

(a) (b)

Figure 13. The result of the average line method: (**a**) average values shown on a white line in the vertical direction; (**b**) average values shown on a white line in the horizontal direction.

The last step is to guarantee that the distance between the adjacent real wafer saw lines $v_r(k)$ and $v_r(k+1)$ is greater than a predefined value z. Figure 15 shows the flowchart of this process and Figure 16 shows the final result of the die sawing lines.

2.5. Counting the Packaged Dies Number

With the detected die sawing lines shown in Figure 16, the exact number of successfully packaged dies can be determined. In a normal case, the dies that have been taken away from the wafer can be determined. In special cases, some dies are broken, rotated, or displaced during the wafer sawing, wafer probing, or packaging processes. In counting the number of regular rectangular dies, both the normal and special cases must be considered.

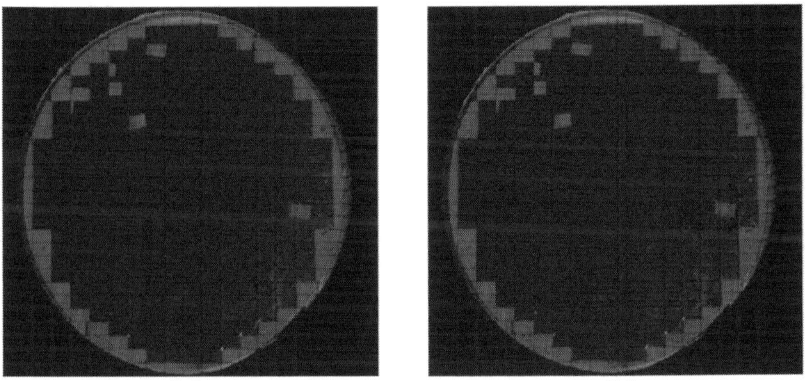

(a) (b)

Figure 14. (**a**) The result of the peak detection method with a *T* value; (**b**) the result of the average line method.

2.5.1. Normal Cases

Figure 17 shows that a matrix is constructed based on the die sawing lines. The binary entry value of the matrix is determined using Equation (20). The main idea is to evaluate the size of the wafer image WD in each corresponding local area, $N_c(m,n)$ and to use the threshold Tn1 for judging whether the die in this location has been packaged or not.

$$N_c(m,n) = \begin{cases} 1, \text{if} \displaystyle\sum_{x=v_f(m)}^{v_f(m+1)} \sum_{y=h_f(n)}^{h_f(n+1)} \frac{W_D(x,y)}{255} > T_{n1} \\ 0, \text{Otherwise} \end{cases} \quad (20)$$

where the coordinate (x,y) denotes the pixel position in the image, the coordinate (m,n) denotes the entry position in the matrix, and N_c denotes the area corresponding to the size of dies shown in Figure 18a. Some special dies, which should be taken away but in fact are not, or the opposite case, are also considered here. The information of the resident die image W_{dies} is utilized to identify the actual die number N in the normal case. Equations (21) and (22) show the steps to determine the number N. Figure 19b shows the resultant image in which the incomplete dies have been discarded.

$$\widehat{N_c}(m,n) = \begin{cases} 1, \text{if } N_c(m,n) = 1 \text{ and } \sum_{x=v_f(m)}^{v_f(m+1)} \sum_{y=h_f(n)}^{h_f(n+1)} \frac{d(x,y)}{255} < T_{n2} \\ 0, \text{Otherwise} \end{cases} \quad (21)$$

$$N = \sum_m \sum_n \widehat{N_c}(m,n) \quad (22)$$

where Tn2 is the threshold used to judge the location of the die which has been packaged or not, N denotes the number of the packaged dies in the normal case, and d(x,y) denotes the calibrated wafer image shown in Figure 5.

2.5.2. Abnormal Cases

If the resident dies are broken, rotated, or shifted from the normal position, they are abnormal cases, and should be treated in another way. Consider the calibrated wafer image shown in Figure 5. First, the intersection of the calibrated image and the actual packaged die image shown in Figure 18b is determined. The dies belonging to the abnormal case can be determined using Equation (23).

$$S_a(x,y) = d(x,y) \cap \widehat{N_c}(x,y) \quad (23)$$

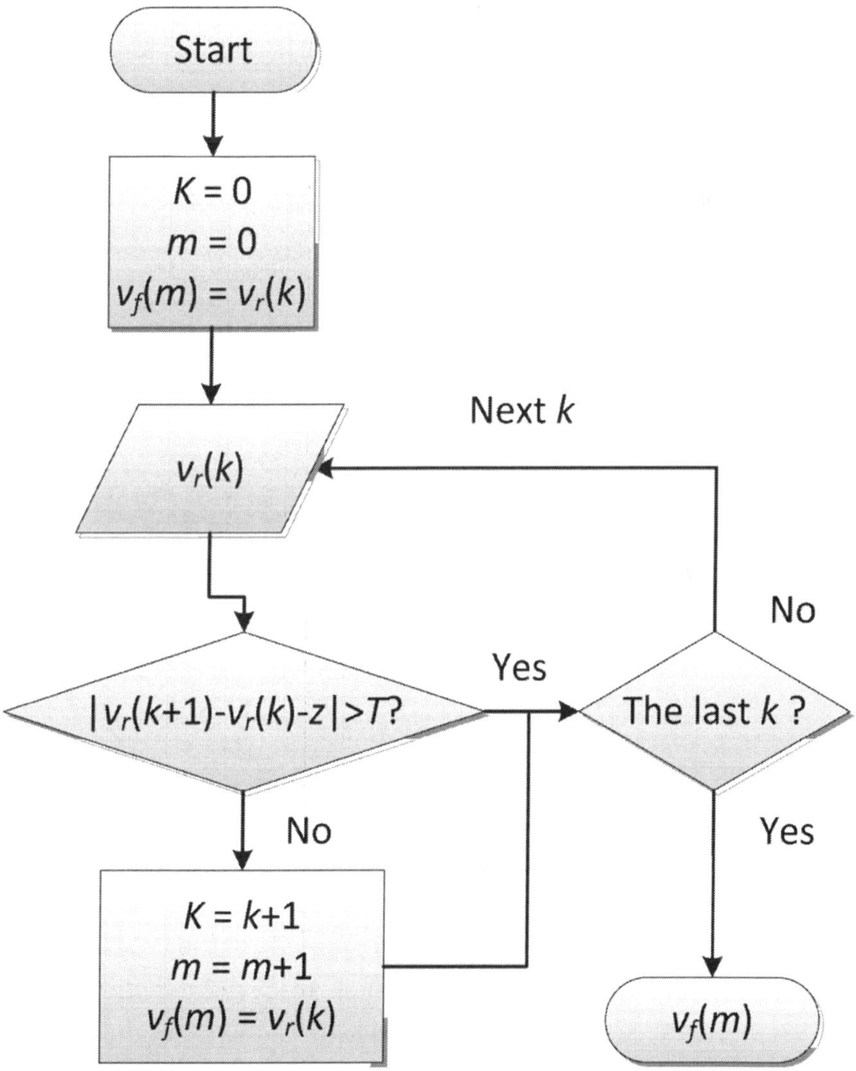

Figure 15. The flowchart of the last step.

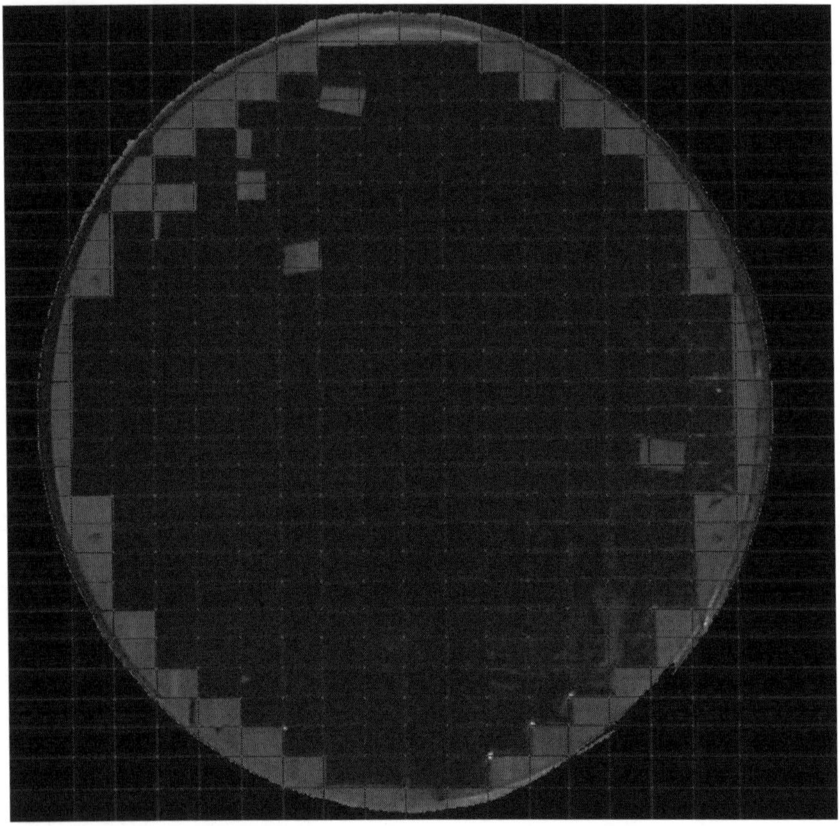

Figure 16. The final result of the detected die sawing lines.

where Sa denotes the image of the abnormal case shown in Figure 19a. It contains some deviation caused by the error introduced during the die sawing lines detection. Because the size of the deviation area is smaller than that of a normal die, the deviation could be removed by using the steps described in Equations (24) and (25).

$$S_c(m,n) = \begin{cases} 1, \text{if} \displaystyle\sum_{i=v_f(m)}^{v_f(m+1)-1} \sum_{j=h_f(n)}^{h_f(n+1)-1} S_a(i,j)/255 < T_{s1} \text{ and } S_n(m,n) = 1 \\ 0, \text{Otherwise} \end{cases} \quad (24)$$

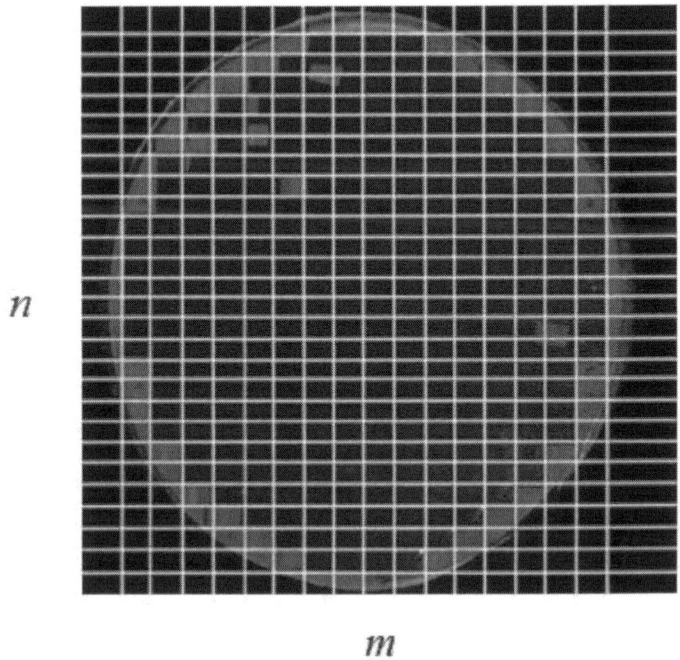

Figure 17. Wafer image mapped in the matrix defined by using the detected die sawing lines.

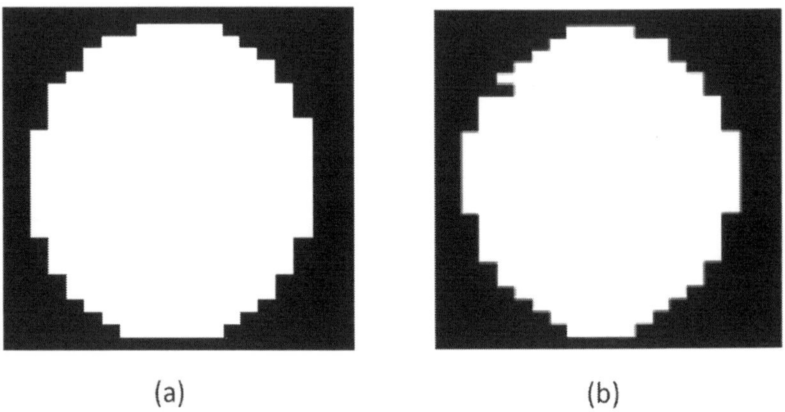

Figure 18. (**a**) The area that is judged to be packaged; (**b**) actual packaged area in the normal case.

$$S_n(m,n) = \begin{cases} 1, \text{if } \widehat{N_c}(m-1,n) < T_{n1} \text{ } or \text{ } \widehat{N_c}(m+1,n) < T_{n1} \\ or \text{ } \widehat{N_c}(m,n-1) < T_{n1} \text{ } or \text{ } \widehat{N_c}(m,n+1) < T_{n1} \\ 0, \text{Otherwise} \end{cases} \quad (25)$$

where Sc denotes the result after removing the small deviation regions. The condition Sn(m,n)=1 indicates the position that contained the deviation value. Figure 19b shows the resultant image Sn.

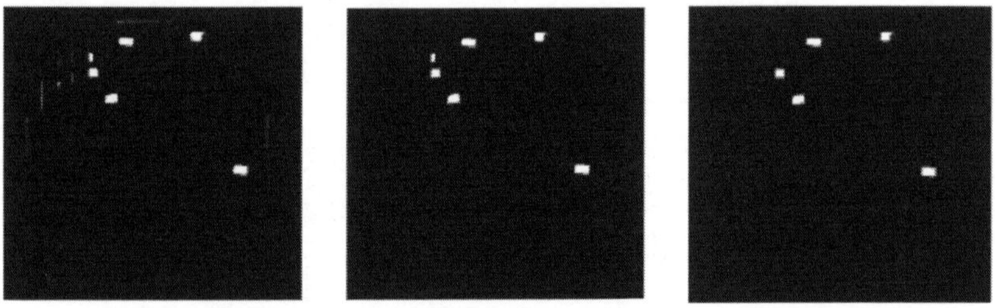

(a) (b) (c)

Figure 19. (**a**) The dies with small deviation regions in the abnormal case; (**b**) the result after removing the small deviation regions; (**c**) the final dies in the abnormal case.

In the second step, the small areas are filtered and the number S of dies is calculated by utilizing the labeling method. The result is shown in Figure 19c. Finally, the number of the successfully packaged dies is obtained by using Equation (26).

$$P = N - S \quad (26)$$

3. EXPERIMENTAL RESULTS

In our experiments, a Microsoft LifeCam Cinema image sensor was used, and the computer specifications were as follows: CPU: Intel Core i5-3570K, RAM: DDR3 1600MHz 4G. The programming was implemented using Visual Studio 2008. Figure 20 shows the photographic environment. Two illumination sources were used in the experimental set up to reduce reflection effects in the captured images. According to the empirical tests in our experiments, the various threshold values in the proposed method are given as follows: both T_w and T_{cb} are automatically determined by using the Otsu method, T_c = 185, T = 25, T_{n1} = 800, T_{n2} = 700, and T_{s1} = 450. The accuracy for evaluating the proposed method is defined in two aspects, the recall and precision rates, which are expressed as

$$\text{Precision rate} = \frac{\text{Number of correctly deteced dies}}{\text{Total number of detected dies}} \qquad (27)$$

$$\text{Recall rate} = \frac{\text{Number of correctly detected dies}}{\text{Total number of dies}} \qquad (28)$$

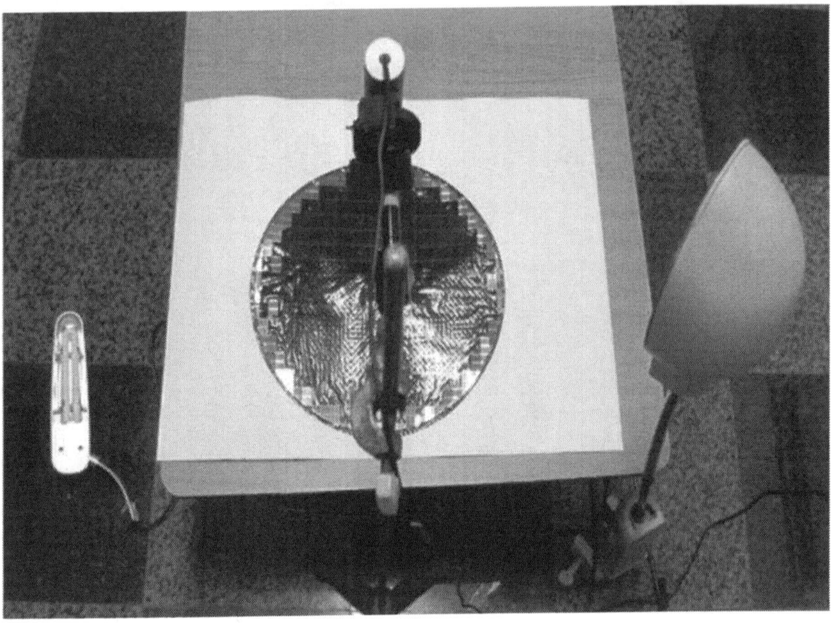

Figure 20. The experimental setup for taking the wafer images.

Figure 21a–j show ten samples of the all test wafer images in our experiments. Both normal and abnormal cases of the resident dies can be found in these images. Figure 22a–j show the corresponding detection results of the die regions. Figure 23a–j show the results of the detected die areas in the normal cases, while Figure 24a–j show the results of the detected dies area in the abnormal cases. Some tiny parts of the die, as shown in Figure 22b,c,f,g, can be discarded to prevent the inclusion of the number in the abnormal cases.

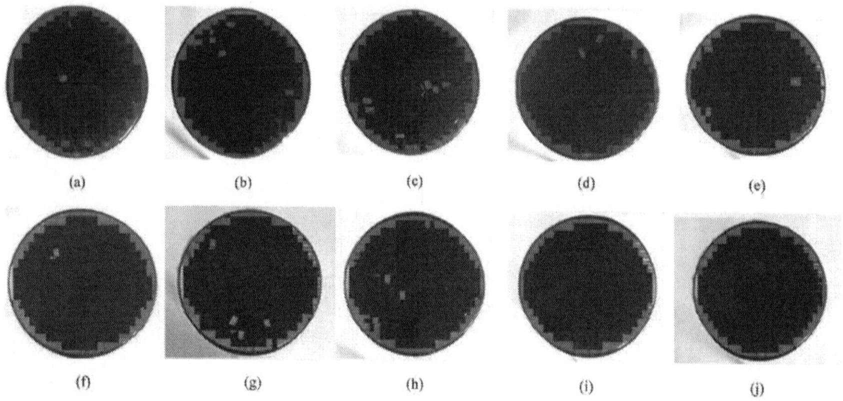

Figure 21. The ten test wafer images numbered from (a) to (j).

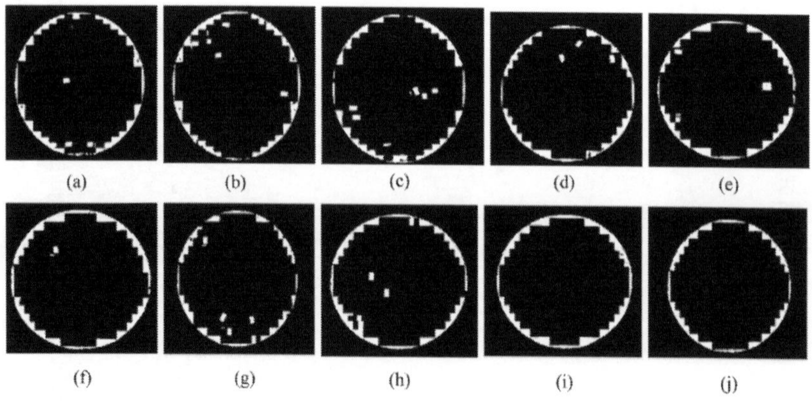

Figure 22. The results of the die region detection corresponding to the images shown in Figure 21a–j.

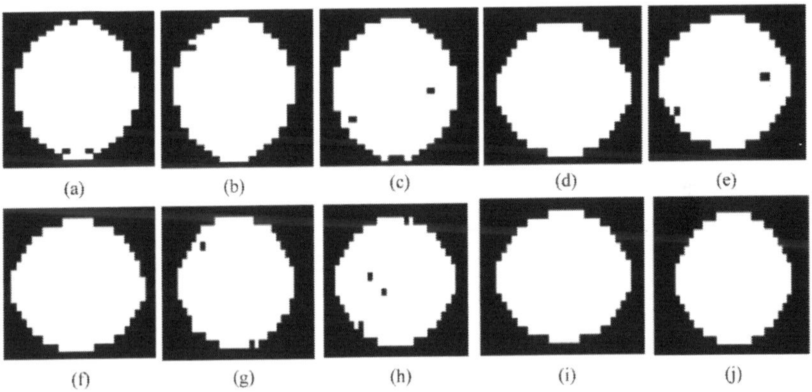

Figure 23. The packaged regions in the normal cases corresponding to the images shown in Figure 22a–j.

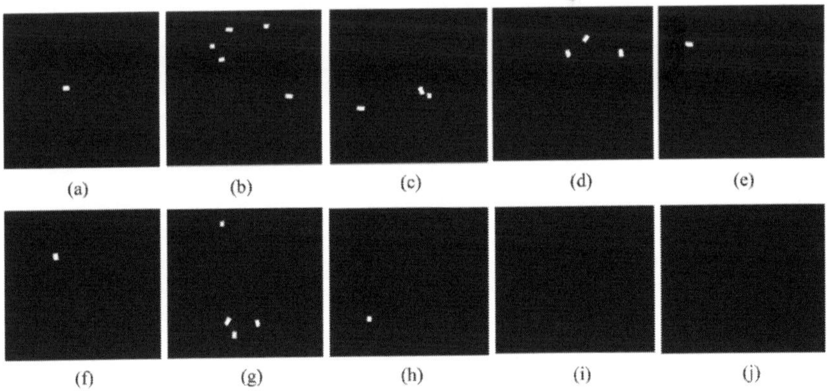

Figure 24. The results of the die regions in the abnormal cases corresponding to the images shown in Figure 22a–j.

There are 41 wafers images in total. The die numbers are divided into three situations: normal, abnormal, and packaged. As shown in this table, most of the dies in the abnormal cases can be correctly detected. Table 1summarizes the determined numbers in the normal, abnormal, and actual packaged cases. The recall and precision rates are provided as well. In this table, the precision and the recall rates are $(P/G) \times 100\%$ and 100%, respectively, when the detected number P is greater than the ground truth number G. On the contrary, the precision and the recall rates are 100% and $(P/G) \times 100\%$, respectively, when the detected number P is less than the ground truth number G. If the two numbers are equal ($P = G$), then both the precision and the recall rates are 100%. The recall and precision rates in the experimental results of the 41 test images achieve 99.82% and 99.84%, respectively. The computation time for each test image is around 0.7 s in average.

Table 1. The recall and precision results in the experiments.

Wafer Image	Normal (N)	Abnormal (S)	Packaged (P)	Ground Truth (G)	Precision Rate	Recall Rate
1	315	3	312	311	99.68%	100.00%
2	315	3	312	311	99.68%	100.00%
3	315	5	310	309	99.68%	100.00%
4	310	10	310	309	99.68%	100.00%
5	323	13	310	309	99.68%	100.00%
6	314	6	308	309	100.00%	99.68%
7	313	3	310	310	100.00%	100.00%
8	314	4	310	310	100.00%	100.00%
9	318	4	314	314	100.00%	100.00%
10	321	7	314	314	100.00%	100.00%
11	326	11	315	314	99.68%	100.00%
12	326	11	315	315	100.00%	100.00%
13	312	1	311	311	100.00%	100.00%
14	323	10	313	311	99.36%	100.00%
15	324	12	312	311	99.68%	100.00%
16	315	3	312	311	99.68%	100.00%
17	312	1	311	311	100.00%	100.00%
18	313	1	312	311	99.68%	100.00%
19	319	7	312	311	99.68%	100.00%
20	321	6	315	316	100.00%	99.68%
21	320	5	315	316	100.00%	99.68%
22	320	2	318	318	100.00%	100.00%
23	321	4	317	318	100.00%	99.69%
24	312	1	311	311	100.00%	100.00%
25	319	7	312	311	99.68%	100.00%
26	313	1	312	311	99.68%	100.00%
27	317	8	309	311	100.00%	99.36%
28	317	7	310	311	100.00%	99.68%
29	302	4	298	311	100.00%	95.82%
30	317	6	311	312	100.00%	99.68%
31	313	0	313	313	100.00%	100.00%

Table 1. *Cont.*

Wafer Image	Normal (*N*)	Abnormal (*S*)	Packaged (*P*)	Ground Truth (*G*)	Precision Rate	Recall Rate
32	315	2	313	313	100.00%	100.00%
33	315	2	313	313	100.00%	100.00%
34	316	3	314	313	99.68%	100.00%
35	322	7	315	313	99.37%	100.00%
36	318	2	316	316	100.00%	100.00%
37	325	9	316	316	100.00%	100.00%
38	330	11	319	316	99.06%	100.00%
39	320	3	317	316	99.68%	100.00%
40	319	2	317	315	99.37%	100.00%
41	316	1	315	315	100.00%	100.00%

4. CONCLUSIONS

This paper presents a machine-vision-based method to automatically determine the number of successfully packaged dies in a wafer image. The most significant contribution of the proposed method is that it can handle all the cases of the residual dies, including those in the wafer boundary, broken dies, fractured dies and dropped dies in the wafer. The precision and recall rates achieved were 99.82% and 99.84%, respectively, in the 41 test wafer images.

Figure 21a–j show that the brightness and position of each wafer image are slightly different. It is influenced by the ambient light and non-fixed photographic environment. In the future work, we will improve the image capture environment such that the number of system parameters can be reduced to make the system simpler. In addition, more test images will be collected to make the proposed method more robust in the various abnormal cases.

ACKNOWLEDGMENTS

This research is partially supported by the Ministry of Science and Technology (MOST), Taiwan under contract numbers MOST 103-2221-E-224-019 and MOST 103-2221-E-224-035 MY2. The authors thank for the reviewers' valuable comments and the English revision made by Resta S. Cheng.

AUTHOR CONTRIBUTIONS

Hsuan-Ting Chang has been responsible for the whole system modeling and the evaluation of the experimental results. Ren-Jie Pan and Hsaio-Wei Peng have been responsible for the experimental setup and the system implementation with Matlab coding.

REFERENCES

1. Driels, M.R.; Pathre, U.S. Vision-based automatic theodolite for robot calibration. *IEEE Trans. Robot. Autom.* **1991**, *7*, 351–360.

2. Madhvanath, S.; Govindaraju, V. The role of holistic paradigms in handwritten word recognition. *IEEE Trans. Pattern Anal. Mach. Intell.* **2001**, *23*, 149–164.

3. Kumar, A.; Yingbo, Z. Human Identification Using Finger Images. *IEEE Trans. Image Process.* **2012**, *21*, 2228–2244.

4. Lin, Y.S.; Lee, T.C.; Chang, H.T.; Peng, S.J.; Huang, J.W.; Wang, H.P.; Hung, C.W. A computer-aided method for automatic localization and thickness measurement of peritoneum in ultrasound images. In Proceedings of the Annual International Conference of the IEEE Engineering in

Medicine and Biology Society, MA, USA, 30 August–3 September 2011; pp. 8005–8008.

5. Gao, Y.S.; Leung, M.K.H. Face recognition using line edge map. *IEEE Trans. Pattern Anal. Mach. Intell.* **2002**,*24*, 764–779.

6. Hackenberg, G.; McCall, R.; Broll, W. Lightweight palm and finger tracking for real-time 3D gesture control. In Proceedings of the IEEE Virtual Reality Conference (VR), Singapore, Singapore, 19–23 March 2011; pp. 19–26.

7. Zeng, Z.; Dai, S.; Mu, P.A. Wafer defects detecting and classifying system based on machine vision. In Proceedings of the International Conference on Electronic Measurement and Instruments, Xi'an, China, 16–18 August 2007; pp. 4-520–4-523.

8. Wu, H.H.P.; Yang, J.G.; Hsu, M.M.; Wu, C.J. Automatic measurement and grading of LED dies on wafer by machine vision. In Proceedings of the IEEE International Conference on Mechatronics, Kumamoto, Japan, 8–10 May 2007; pp. 1–6.

9. Wang, G.; Li, D.; Wu, L.; Deng, Y.; Liu, R. Machine vision recognition of disconnection failure of IC wafer. In Proceedings of the International Conference on Electronic Packaging Technology, Shanghai, China, 26–29 August 2006; pp. 1–4.

10. Sharma, G.; Kumar, A.; Rao, V.S.; Soon, W.H.; Kripesh, V. Solutions strategies for die shift problem in wafer level compression molding. *IEEE Trans. Compon. Packag. Manuf. Technol.* **2011**, *1*, 502–509.

11. Croft, G.D.; Lomenick, R.L.; Youngblood, D.L.; Johnston, J.M. Die-counting algorithm for yield modeling and die-per-wafer optimization. *SPIE* **1997**, *3216*, 186–196.

12. Cunningham, J.A. The use of evaluation of yield models in integrated circuit manufacturing. *IEEE Trans. Semicond. Manuf.* **1990**, *3*, 60–71.

13. De Vries, D.K. Investigation of gross die per wafer formulas. *IEEE Trans. Semicond. Manuf.* **2005**, *18*, 136–139.

14. Magee, M.R.; Beer, M.D.; Erck, W.R. Computation of Die-Per-Wafer Considering Production Technology and Wafer Size. United States Patent US 6,529,790, 4 March 2003.

15. Die Per Wafer Calculator 1.00. Available online: http://mrhackerott.org/ semiconductor-informatics/ informatics/toolz/ DPWCalculator/ Input.html (accessed on 6 April 2015).

16. Die-per-Wafer Estimator. Available online: http:// www.silicon-edge.co. uk/j/ index.php/resources /die-per-wafer (accessed on 6 April 2015).

17. Mital, D.P.; Teoh, E.K. Computer based wafer inspection system. In Proceedings of the 1991 International Conference on Industrial Electronics, Control and Instrumentation, 28 October–1 November 1991; pp. 2497–2503.

18. Su, C.T.; Yang, T.; Ke, C.M. Neural-network approach for semiconductor wafer post-sawing inspection.*IEEE Trans. Semicond. Manuf.* **2002**, *15*, 260–266.

19. Chang, H.T.; Pan, R.J. Automatic counting of packaged wafer die based on machine vision. In Proceedings of the 2012

International Conference on Information Security and Intelligent Control (ISIC 2012), Douliu, Taiwan, 14–16 August 2012; pp. 274–277.

20. Xu, S.; Cheng, Z.; Gao, Y.; Pan, Q. Visual wafer dies counting using geometrical characteristics. *IET Image Process.* **2014**, *8*, 280–288.

21. Wafer Chip Counter—IVC12. Available online: http:// www.ivtech. com.tw / (accessed on 6 April 2015).

22. Fischler, M.A.; Bolles, R.C. Random sample consensus: A paradigm for model fitting with applications to image analysis and automated cartography. *Commun. ACM* **1981**, *24*, 381–395.

23. De la Fraga, L.G.; Dominguez, G.M.L. Robust detection of several circles or ellipses with heuristics. In Proceedings of the IEEE Congress Evolutionary Computation, New Orleans, LA, USA, 5–8 June 2011; pp. 484–490.

24. Otsu, N. A threshold selection method from gray-level histograms. *IEEE Trans. Syst. Man Cybern.* **1979**, *9*, 62–66.

25. Gonzalez, R.C.; Woods, R.E. *Digital Image Processing*, 2nd ed.; Prentice-Hall, Inc.: New Jersey, NJ, USA, 2002.

26. Canny, J. A computational approach to edge detection. *IEEE Trans. Pattern Anal. Mach. Intell.* **1986**, *PAMI-8*, 679–698.

27. Kim, Y.T. Contrast enhancement using brightness preserving bi-histogram equalization. *IEEE Trans. Consum. Electron.* **1997**, *43*, 1–8.

8

CHAPTER

ON-LINE ESTIMATION OF LASER-DRILLED HOLE DEPTH USING A MACHINE VISION METHOD

Chao-Ching Ho *, Jun-Jia He and Te-Ying Liao

Department of Mechanical Engineering, National Yunlin University of Science and Technology, Douliou, Yunlin 64002, Taiwan

ABSTRACT

The paper presents a novel method for monitoring and estimating the depth of a laser-drilled hole using machine vision. Through on-line image acquisition and analysis in laser machining processes, we could simultaneously obtain correlations between the machining processes and analyzed images. Based on the machine vision method, the depths of laser-machined holes could be estimated in real time. Therefore, a low cost on-line inspection system is developed to increase productivity. All of the processing work was performed in air under standard atmospheric conditions and gas assist was used. A correlation between the cumulative size of the laser-induced plasma region and the depth of the hole is presented. The result indicates that the estimated depths of the laser-drilled holes were a linear function of the cumulative plasma size, with a high degree of confidence. This research provides a novel machine vision-based method for estimating the depths of laser-drilled holes in real time.

Keywords: machine vision; on-line estimation; laser-drilled hole depth; laser drilling; laser machining

1. INTRODUCTION

The development of laser-based machining has been ongoing for a long time and is applied to all aspects of conventional industry, semiconductor manufacture, the biochemical and biomedical sectors, *etc.* Because lasers use very high energy, they have always previously been applied in conventional cutting and ablation processes. More recently, lasers have gradually also been applied to precision micromachining processes. The high energy produced by a laser makes precision control and monitoring difficult in micromachining. Therefore, a laser machining system that utilizes pulse laser machining rather than continuous laser machining has been developed. A pulse laser can be controlled more accurately than a conventional continuous laser system. However, the control is still not sufficient to apply to micromachining. In recent years, various measuring methods and technologies have been researched for laser machining monitoring and control systems, including electromagnetic fields, electric fields, acoustics, optodynamics, and optics.

1.1. Patent Research

In 1991, Koegl *et al.* disclosed a patent for a breakthrough detector that used magnetic field pickup coils placed upon the surface of a workpiece for the real-time detection of the magnetic field signal of laser-induced plasma during laser drilling. This method could detect whether the laser-drilled hole perforated the workpiece. The method claim to detect the depth of a laser-drilled hole in real time [1,2].

1.2. Acoustic Research

In 1996, Stauter *et al.* found that a short pulse laser generated shock waves during laser drilling. The shock wave energy reflected from the laser-machined region was detected using the laser beam deflection and a microphone. They demonstrated a system for the real-time control and measurement of the laser machining process [3]. In 2003, Palanco *et al.* presented a similar method of using a microphone to acquire the shock wave from the laser machining process and analyzed the spectra of the laser-machined shock waves of various metal materials in the time and frequency domains. Their experimental results showed a correlation between the spectra of the shock wave and the laser-induced plasma, but an accurate correlation was limited by the measurement configuration and equipment [4]. In 2010, Stournaras *et al.* established an experimental setup and performed a theoretical analysis to investigate the acoustic signal from laser drilling. The experiment results showed a good correlation between the signal's amplitude and the hole's depth based on the flow of gas-assisted machining, but it could not precisely estimate the depth of a laser-drilled hole [5].

1.3. Optodynamic Research

In 2002, Strgar *et al.* presented a real-time method for determining the depth of laser-drilled holes during laser drilling. The developed setup could detect the laser-induced ultrasonic waves in the workpiece and in the surrounding air. Because the depth of a hole increases with the machine time, the propagation times of the laser-induced ultrasonic wave traveling from the bottom of the hole to the bottom of the workpiece could be measured by a piezoelectric transducer at the bottom of the workpiece. Then, based on the propagation speed of an ultrasonic wave in various materials, the depth of the laser-drilled hole could be detected in real time [6,7]. In 2005, Stafe *et al.* used the same experimental method to research the depths of laser-drilled holes in various materials [8].

1.4. Electric Field Research

In 2002, Bredice *et al.* found that a pulse laser generated a discharge phenomenon in an electric field during laser machining. They placed the workpiece in the middle of two plates connected to an RC circuit, and the laser-induced plasma induced the discharge phenomenon. The quantum of the discharge signal of the RC circuit was then used to obtain a signal related to the plasma energy. This experiment measured the plasma energy successfully [9]. In 2007, Bredice developed a real-time measurement system that resembled the above measuring setup. By calibrating the curve of the experimental results, the system could predict the temporal evolution of the electron density of the generated plasma in real time [10]. In 2004 and 2008, Madjid *et al.* established another measurement mechanism which had two flat electrodes arranged in parallel, with a gap that allowed the plasma to be sandwiched between them. The machining region included the workpiece and flat electrodes placed in an acrylic chamber filled with air and He gas. By supplying a DC voltage to the flat electrodes, the induced current of the laser-processed plasma was detected using an oscilloscope. In addition to measuring the current of the laser-induced plasma, it also could detect whether the laser penetrated the target [11,12].

1.5. Optical Signal Research

In 2007, a method utilizing the detection of shock waves generated during the interaction between laser beam and irradiated material was presented by Walter *et al.* [13]. However, this method is not suited for detection of breakthrough unless the rear side of the workpiece is also monitored. It is not easy to deploy sensors for such a rear side configuration in many applications. Also, schlieren photography was employed to visualize the air flow, and resulted in the machining process was not assisted by an air jet to avoid image acquisition problems. The air jet function can aid in a cleaner-looking cut and enhance the material removal rates.

In 2010, a real-time measurement system based on the correlation between the optical signals of the laser-induced plasma from the processing region acquired by photodiodes and the geometrical characteristics of the laser-drilled hole was presented by Stournaras *et al.* [14]. In 2010, Lin *et al.* developed an optical measurement system based on the confocal principle. This system could precisely measure the depths of microholes during laser drilling in real time; the system achieved a sensitivity of 0.5 μm [15].

In this paper, we present a novel measuring method for the on-line monitoring of laser-drilled holes based on machine vision analysis. Therefore, on-line optical inspection system with low cost is developed to increase productivity. The monitoring of pulsed laser-induced plasma is used as the basis for on-line inspection control system for the hole drilling. Our measuring setup includes image acquisition units, laser machining equipment, and a computer analysis unit, as shown in Figure 1. First, we use the CMOS camera of the image acquisition unit for the on-line acquisition of an image of the laser machining zone of the workpiece's surface. The high laser energy will cause melting and vaporization of the metal material during laser machining, and cause the air and metallic vapor to ionize simultaneously. This ionization phenomenon will involve plasma and light, and it is captured by the CMOS camera. The images consist of both plasma and light information. Finally, the image data are sent to the computer analysis unit for an on-line analysis of the correlation between the geometrical forms of the machining zone, including the depth of a blind hole, and the image information. This experimental setup achieves the advantages of a lower cost, on-line monitoring, and good performance.

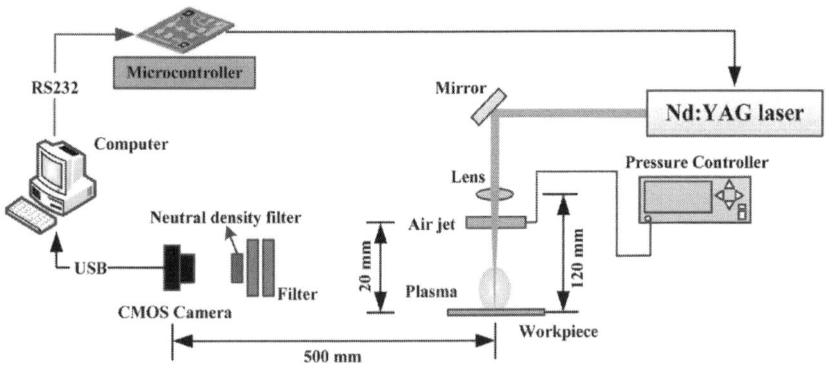

Figure 1. Experimental setup.

2. EXPERIMENTAL SETUP AND METHOD

2.1. Setup

The experiment setup, including the laser machining system, image acquisition unit, and computer control and analysis system, is shown in Figure 1. The computer is connected to a microcontroller, which controls the laser machining parameters, including the machining frequency and time, to trigger and control the laser machining system (LOTIS, LS-2134UTF, Nd:YAG laser system). The laser beam strikes the two kind of workpiece (aluminum, 5052, 0.6-mm thick, and stainless steel, 420, 0.8-mm thick) surface and induces the ionization phenomenon caused by plasma light. The plasma image of the ionization phenomenon passes through the wavelength filter (190–534 nm OD: 6.5, 850–1,070 nm OD: 5, 910–1,070 nm OD: 6) and neutral density filter (transmittance 13%) and is acquired by the CMOS camera mounted radially 500 mm from the work site. The microcontroller unit triggers the laser system to generate a single laser pulse and simultaneously delays a short time to control the image acquisition unit, which captures a single plasma image of the laser pulse. The plasma light is too bright for image analysis. To distinguish between the ionization phenomena for the air and material caused by the laser-induced plasma and to reduce the maximum brightness of the image acquired by the CMOS camera, a wavelength filter and neutral density filter are placed in front of the camera. The light from the laser-induced plasma that passes through the neutral density filter will remain at the wavelength of the ionizing material. The image analysis in this study focused on the ionization of the material from the laser-induced plasma. The ambient conditions and machining parameters of the experiment are listed in Table 1, where the air jet pressure is 300 Kpa.

2.2. Estimation Method

The laser-drilled machining, including breakthrough detection and blind hole depth analysis, were recorded and analyzed using 8-bit encoding and 120 × 120 pixel images. Through binarization during the image processing, we could determine the plasma emission region and calculate the total pixels of the plasma region. The

Table 1. Experiment parameters.

Laser				
Laser Pump Energy	**Radiation Energy**	**Pulse Duration**	**Pulse Repetition Rate**	**Wavelength**
18 J, 19 J, 20 J	145 mJ, 175 mJ, 200 mJ	6 ns	15 Hz	532 nm
Workpiece Material				
Material	**Focus Position**	**Thick**	**Ambient Temperature**	**Ambient Moisture**
Aluminum (Al, 5052)	Surface	0.6 mm	22 °C	60%
Stainless steel (SS, 420)		0.8 mm		
Camera and Lens				
Camera Aperture	**Camera Shutter Speed**	**Camera Object Distance**	**Camera Focus Length**	**Lens Focus Length**
16	117 μs	500 mm	75 mm	120 mm

images of aluminum and stainless steel after binarization are shown in Figure 2 and Figure 3, respectively. In breakthrough detection, the total pixels in the plasma region of a single image frame were recorded and analyzed. Breakthrough detection for laser drilling was successfully developed in a previous study [16]. Breakthrough detection can be briefly explained as follows. When a breakthrough occurs, the amount of plasma declines abruptly. The pixels in the plasma region of a single image frame would also decline abruptly and simultaneously at this time, as shown in Figure 4. Depth control and analysis for laser-drilled machining, the number of laser pulses is used to control the depth of a laser-drilled hole in the conventional control method. As the number of laser pulses increases, the depth of the hole would also increase. The conventional control method uses experience-based control rules to detect the completion of the ablation process off-line.

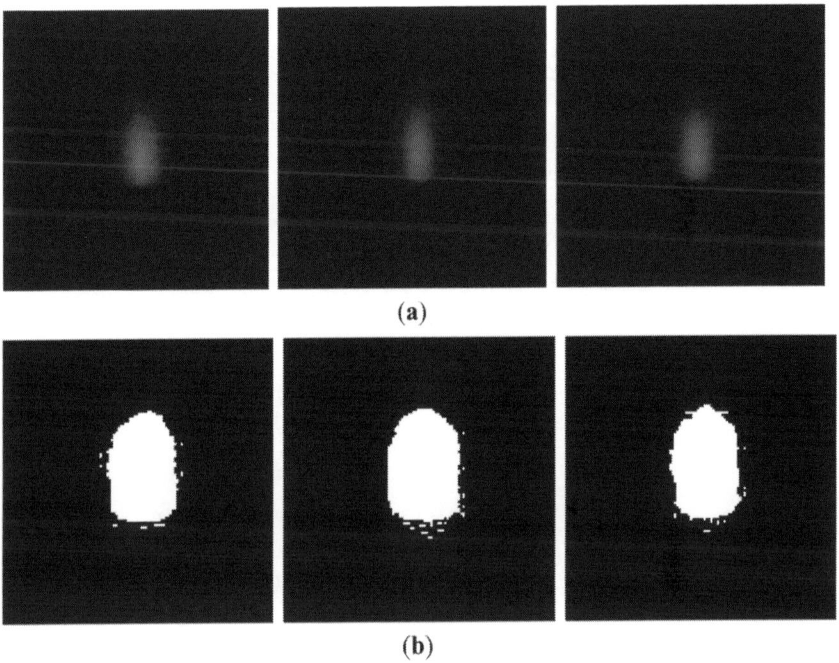

Figure 2. Plasma region of image of Al 5052 (**a**) acquired by CMOS camera and (**b**) after binarization.

This machine vision method of finding the relation between the laser-induced plasma region and laser-drilled hole depth is a novel estimation mechanism for determining the depth of a laser-drilled hole for laser machining. During laser-drilled machining, a plume is usually produced as the result of vaporization of material from the laser heated area. The evaporated material is ejected and collides with energetic electrons and result in a rapid increase in the level of ionization within the plume with the formation of the plasma. The force induced by evaporated material, together with assist air jet, expelled molten material at the cavity to its outer rim [17].

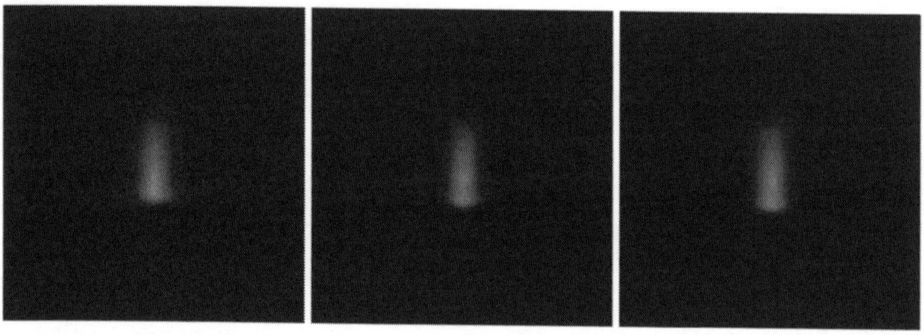

(a)

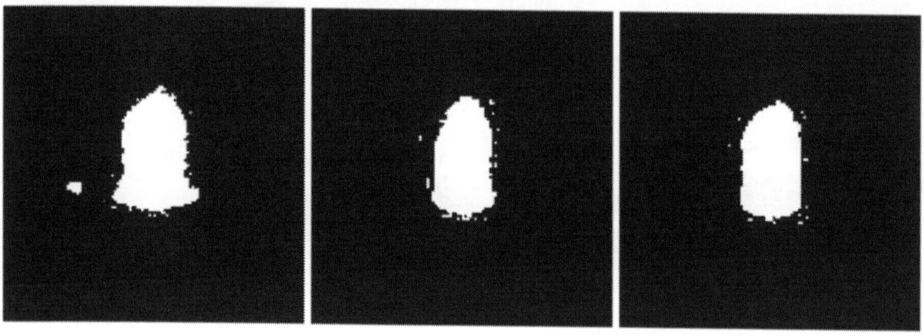

(b)

Figure 3. Plasma region of image of SS 420 (**a**) acquired by CMOS camera and (**b**) after binarization.

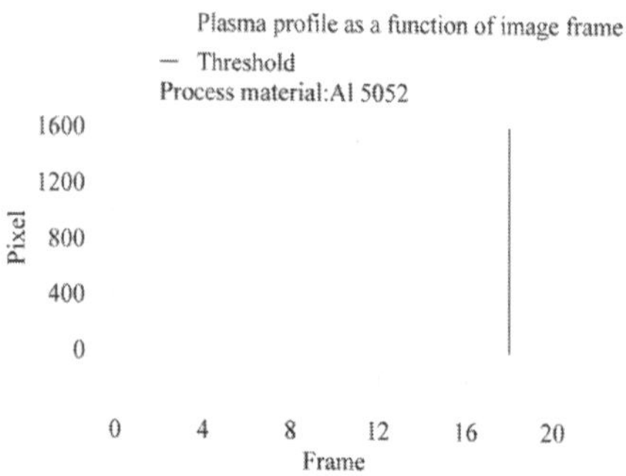

(**a**) Al 5052

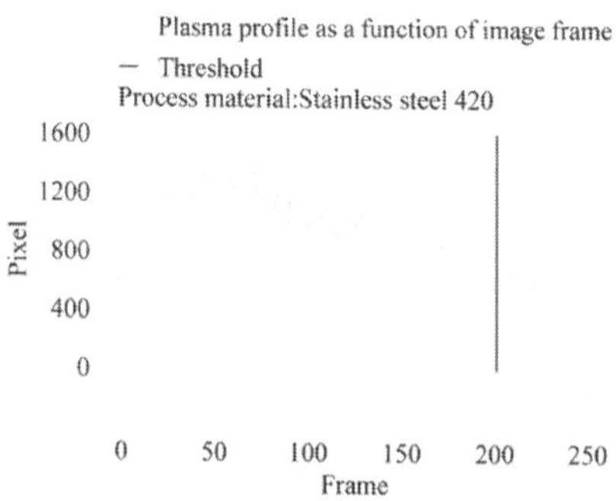

(**b**) SS 420

Figure 4. Breakthrough result based on abrupt decline in pixels of plasma region.

The vaporization of all material removed is observed by the camera setup radially. Because it is difficult to find the relation between the laser-induced plasma region size and hole depth, the laser-drilled hole depth detection adopts a pixel accumulation method to estimate the hole depth, as distinguished from the breakthrough detection, which uses a single image frame analysis. The pixels of the laser-induced plasma region for each single image frame from the beginning to end of the machining are determined by using image processing. We then accumulate the total pixels for the single image frames of the plasma region during laser machining and obtain the total pixels of the plasma region from beginning to end.

3. RESULTS AND DISCUSSION

In this study, an aluminum workpiece (aluminum, 5052, 0.6-mm thick) and a steel workpiece (stainless steel, 420, 0.8-mm thick) were used for the laser-drilled machining experiment, and the pulse laser machining system adopted a Nd:YAG laser (LOTIS, LS-2134UTF). The laser machining parameters are listed in Table 1. In these experiments, the drilling depth is determined after a couple of hours of careful grinding along vertical planes of the workpiece until the cavity is made visible. The depth and the diameter of holes and the thickness of recast are investigated by optical microscopy (OM).

The resulting profile images for laser-drilled machining using different process times, where the radiation energy of the pulse laser was 145 mJ, 175 mJ, and 200 mJ for aluminum and stainless steel are shown in Figures 5,6, 7, 8, 9 and 10, respectively. It is obvious that the depth of the laser-drilled holes increases with the process time. The relation between the machining hole depth and pixel value of the laser-induced plasma region is shown inFigure

11. In all cases, the depth of the laser-drilled holes could be described by a monotonically increasing function, and for both materials the ablation depth rate increases with large laser energy. Since the heat transfer mechanism near the ablation zone was heavily affected by the thermal response of the materials to the incident laser pulses. The vaporization thermal properties is known to be affected by the material boiling temperature, which is lower in aluminum (T_{vap} = 2,740 K) than stainless steel (T_{vap} = 3,134 K), thus leading to an earlier ablation under the same incident laser pulses. There, a faster depth removal rate on the aluminum material than in steel material was observed at the ablation process as expected.

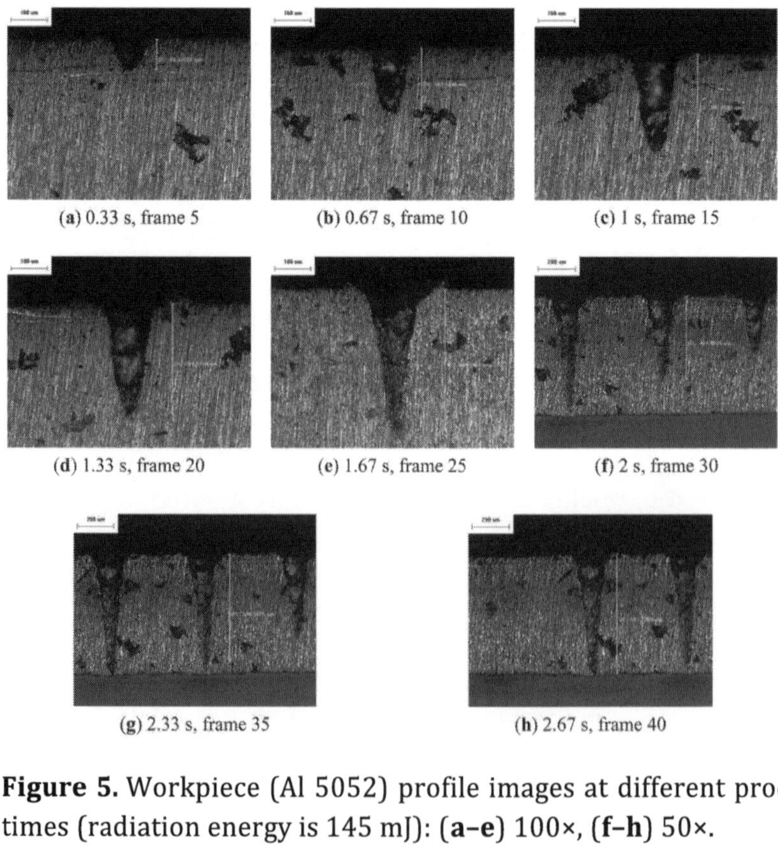

Figure 5. Workpiece (Al 5052) profile images at different process times (radiation energy is 145 mJ): **(a–e)** 100×, **(f–h)** 50×.

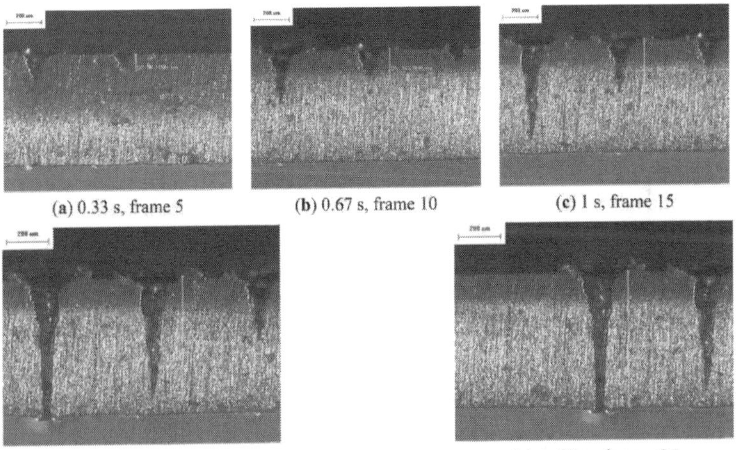

(a) 0.33 s, frame 5 (b) 0.67 s, frame 10 (c) 1 s, frame 15

(d) 1.33 s, frame 20 (e) 1.67 s, frame 25

Figure 6. Workpiece (Al 5052) profile images at different process times (radiation energy is 175 mJ): (**a–e**) 50×.

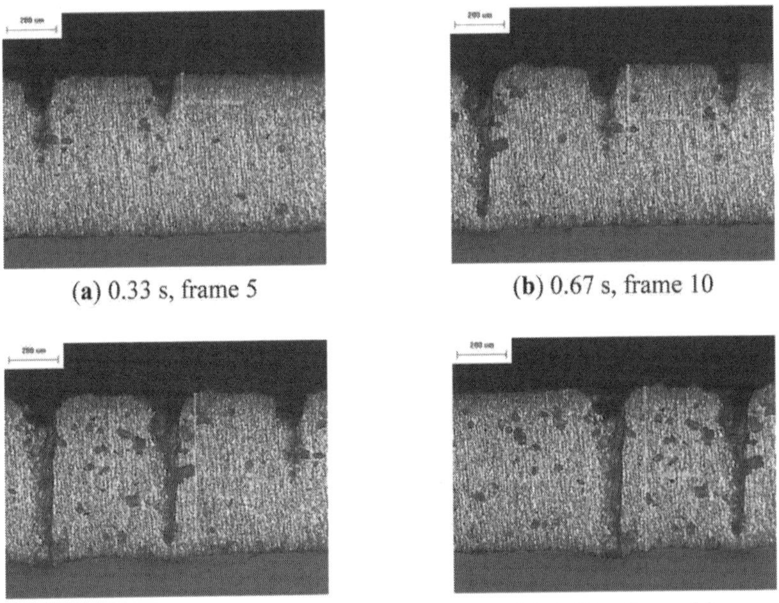

(a) 0.33 s, frame 5 (b) 0.67 s, frame 10

(c) 1 s, frame 15 (d) 1.33 s, frame 20

Figure 7. Workpiece (Al 5052) profile images at different process times (radiation energy is 200 mJ): (**a–d**) 50×.

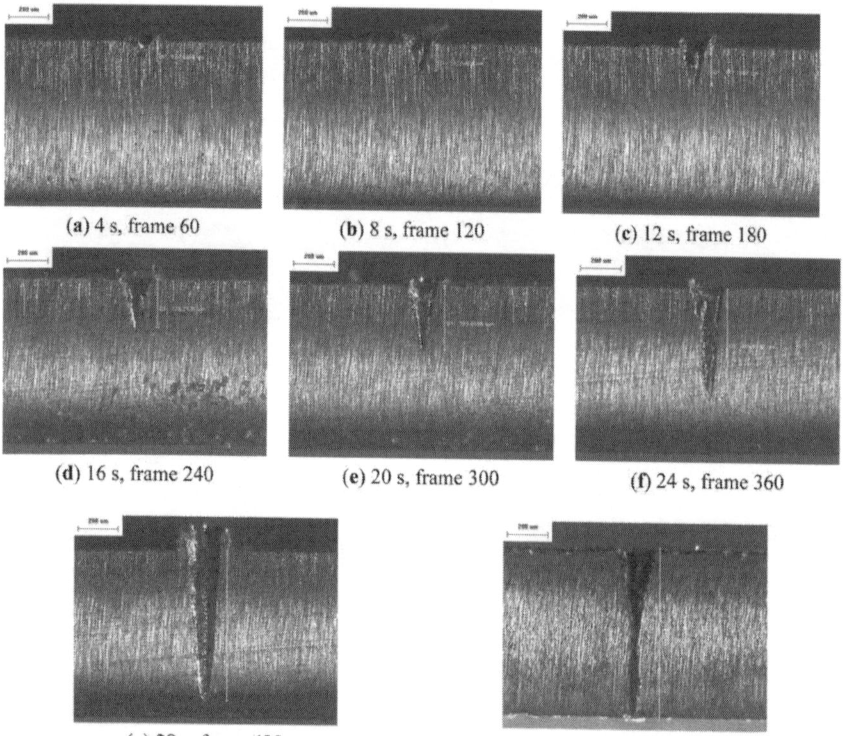

(a) 4 s, frame 60 (b) 8 s, frame 120 (c) 12 s, frame 180
(d) 16 s, frame 240 (e) 20 s, frame 300 (f) 24 s, frame 360
(g) 28 s, frame 420 (h) 32 s, frame 480

Figure 8. Workpiece (SS 420) profile images at different process times (radiation energy is 145 mJ): (**a–h**) 50×.

By investigating the depth of the laser-drilled hole as a function of the cumulative plasma size, we pave the way to fully control the process parameters. The depth estimated function D of the cumulative pixels of the total frame plasma region at the acquired ablation image frame n during laser machining is shown in Equation (1):

$$D[n] = \alpha \sum_{i=1}^{n} A_i + \beta \tag{1}$$

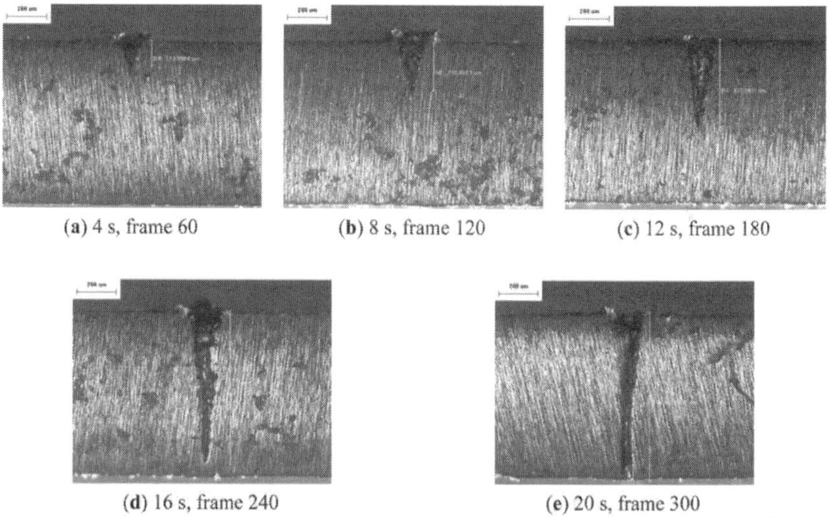

(a) 4 s, frame 60 (b) 8 s, frame 120 (c) 12 s, frame 180

(d) 16 s, frame 240 (e) 20 s, frame 300

Figure 9. Workpiece (SS 420) profile images at different process times (radiation energy is 175 mJ): (**a–e**) 50×.

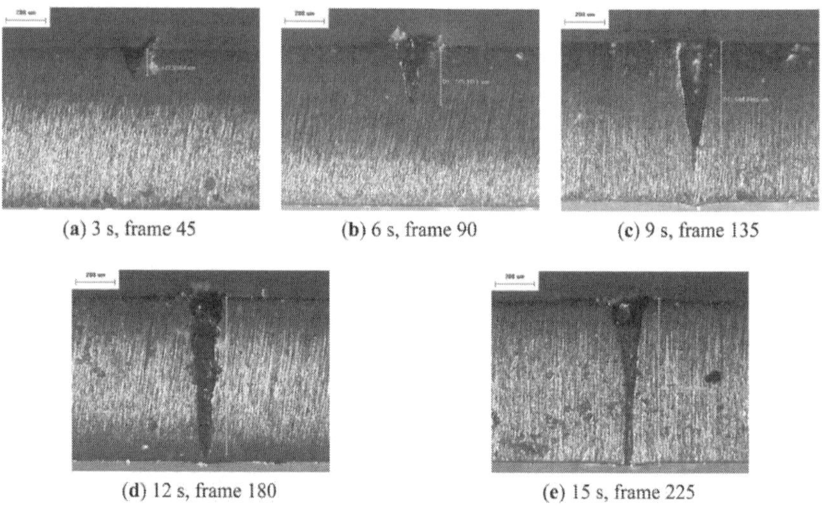

(a) 3 s, frame 45 (b) 6 s, frame 90 (c) 9 s, frame 135

(d) 12 s, frame 180 (e) 15 s, frame 225

Figure 10. Workpiece (SS 420) profile images at different process times (radiation energy is 200 mJ): (**a–e**) 50×.

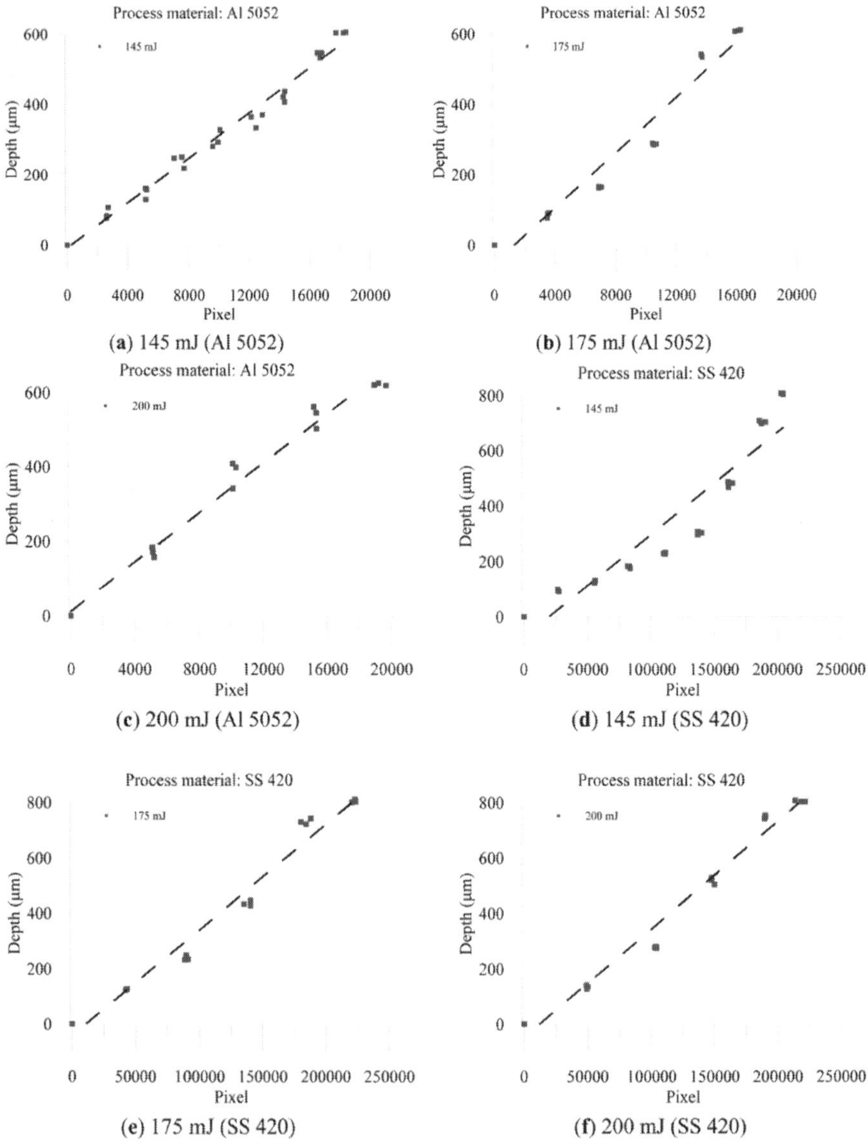

Figure 11. Relation between depth of laser-drilled hole and pixels of plasma region, at radiation energy of (**a**) 145 mJ (Al 5052); (**b**) 175 mJ (Al 5052); (**c**) 200 mJ (Al 5052); (**d**) 145 mJ (SS 420); (**e**) 175 mJ (SS 420); and (**d**) 200 mJ (SS 420).

where A_i represents the pixels of the plasma region of a single image frame, α depends on the thermal physical properties of the material (density, emissivity, thermal conductivity, specific heat, thermal diffusivity), and βdepends on the laser energy. The higher pulse energies lead to the more plasma region A_i, and hence a higher ablation rate can be expected. Same material under laser machined process reveals the same slope α. The higher laser pulse energy could ignite much more particle atmospheric plasma, and hence the parameter β depends on the radiation energy.

The results reveal that the cumulative plasma size has high coefficient of determination (R^2) of 0.984 (aluminum, 145 mJ), 0.95 (aluminum, 175 mJ), 0.983 (aluminum, 200 mJ), 0.892 (stainless steel, 145 mJ), 0.975 (stainless steel, 175 mJ), and 0.978 (stainless steel, 200 mJ) with the machining depth, respectively. The hole depth is directly proportional to the machining pulses and the sum of the pixels of all the frames of the plasma region. Based on the proportional relation, we could use the total cumulative pixel values to estimate and detect the laser-drilled hole depth. Also, higher laser energy could induce both a larger region and additional pixels of plasma. Considering the fact that the radiation energy of the laser machining also affects the machining depth, a higher energy could generate deeper holes for the same process time, as shown in Figure 12. We also found that when the laser beam struck the material surface, the higher energy induced a larger plasma region. In this study of image processing based on machine vision, we determined that the size of the laser-induced plasma region at the surface of the workpiece could be transformed into the value of the pixels. The laser energy conditions determined both the laser-drilled hole depth and size of the plasma region, along with the process time. Thus, we could analyze and obtain the total pixels of the plasma region in on-line during processing, and we achieved a on-line detection and estimation of the depth of a laser-drilled hole. However, as shown in the Figure 12, the variations in the cumulative plasma size and the drilling depth with the time were observed.

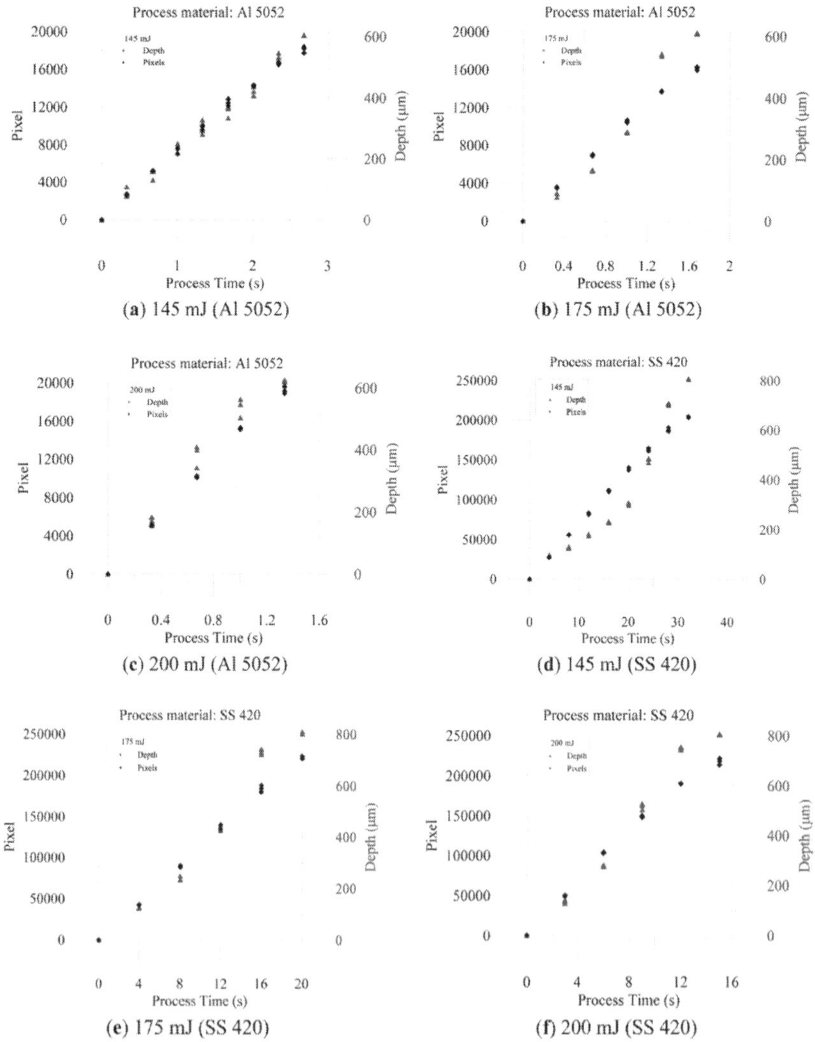

Figure 12. Relationship between pixels and depth, along with process time.

These variations include the thermal properties of materials with temperature during laser processing, unexpected variations of about 2% in the laser output power, the ablation process also sensitive to surface finishing conditions, a confined plasma within deeper depths leading to a more thermal mechanism of ablation and finally, a reduction in laser irradiance due to changes in the effective area exposed to the laser beam. Also, for holes with high aspect ratios, the multiple beam reflections along the wall of cavity will affect the amount of absorbed energy and the increase the variations on accuracy of the depth estimation. Comparisons between different measurements show an average error of 0.1% and an absolute average error of 4.1% for aluminum, and an average error of 5.1% and an absolute average error of 15.3% for stainless steel.

4. CONCLUSIONS

This paper presented a novel on-line estimation method for the depths of laser-drilled holes. Based on the laser-induced plasma region, transformed into a pixel value, we could obtain a correlation between the cumulative pixels and hole depth. Because the system could acquire and analyze images during laser machining in real time, the hole depth estimation was also in real time. The estimation mechanism based on a machine vision method could be combined with the depth control method for a conventional pulse laser to achieve more precise depth control for a laser-drilled hole.

ACKNOWLEDGMENTS

This research was partially supported by the National Science Council in Taiwan under Grant NSC 100-2221-E-224-016. Special thanks are given to anonymous reviewers for their helpful suggestions.

REFERENCES

1. Koegl, R.A.A.; Hogle, R.A. Real-Time Magnetic-Flux Breakthrough Detection Method and System for Laser Drilling. U.S. Patent 5,013,886, May 1991.

2. Koegl, R.A.A.; Hogle, R.A.; Bauer, S.D. Inductive Depth Sensing and Controlling Method and System for Laser Drilling. U.S. Patent 5,059,761, October 1991.

3. Stauter, C.; Gérard, P.; Fontaine, J.; Engel, T. Laser ablation acoustical monitoring. *Appl. Surface Sci.* **1996**,*109–110*, 174–178.

4. Palanco, S.; Laserma, J. Spectral analysis of the acoustic emission of laser-produced plasmas. *Appl. Opt.***2003**, *42*, 6078–6084.

5. Stournaras, A.; Chryssolouris, G. On acoustic emissions in percussion laser drilling. *Int. J. Adv. Manuf. Technol.* **2010**, *46*, 611–620.

6. Strgar, S.; Možina, J. An optodynamic determination of the depth of laser-drilled holes by the simultaneous detection of ultrasonic waves in the air and in the workpiece. *Ultrasonics* **2002**, *40*, 791–795.

7. Strgar, S.; Možina, J. An optodynamic method for the real-time determination of the depth of a laser-drilled hole. *Appl. Phys. A* **2002**, *74*, 321–323.

8. Stafe, M.; Negutu, C.; Popescu, I.M. Real-time determination and control of the laser-drilled holes depth.*Shock Waves* **2005**, *14*, 123–126.

9. Bredice, F.O.; Orzi, D.J.O.; Schinca, D.; Sobral, H.; Villagran-Muniz, M. Characterization of pulsed laser generated plasma through its perturbation in an electric field. *IEEE Trans. Plasma Sci.* **2002**, *30*, 2139–2143.

10. Bredice, F.O.; Sobral, H.; Villagran-Muniz, M.; Di Rocco, H.O.; Cristoforetti, G.; Legnaioli, S.; Palleschi, V.; Salvetti, A.; Tognoni, E. Real time measurement of the electron density of a laser generated plasma using a RC circuit. *Spectrochim. Acta Part B* **2007**, *62*, 836–840.

11. Madjid, S.N.; Kitazima, I.; Kobayashi, T.; Lee, Y.I.; Kagawa, K. Characteristics of induced current due to laser plasma and its application to laser processing monitoring. *Jpn. J. Appl. Phys.* **2004**, *43*, 1018–1027.

12. Idris, N.; Madjid, S.N.; Ramli, M.; Kurniawan, K.H.; Lee, Y.I.; Kagawa, K. Monitoring of laser processing using induced current under applied electric field on laser produced-plasma. *J. Mater. Process. Technol.* **2009**, *209*, 3009–3021.

13. Walter, D.; Michalowski, A.; Gauch, R.; Dausinger, F. Monitoring of the Micro-Drilling Process by Detection of Laser-Induced Shock Waves in Air. Proceeding of the 26th International Congress on Applications of Lasers & Electro-Optics, Orlando, FL, USA, 29 October–1 November 2007.

14. Stournaras, A.; Salonitis, K.; Chryssolouris, G. Optical emissions for monitoring of the percussion laser drilling process. *Int. J. Adv. Manuf. Technol.* **2010**, *46*, 589–603.

15. Lin, C.H.; Powell, R.A.; Jiang, L.; Xiao, H.; Chen, S.J.; Tsai, H.L. Real-time depth measurement for micro-holes drilled by lasers. *Meas. Sci. Technol.* **2010**, *21*, 25307:1–25307:6.

16. Ho, C.-C.; He, J.-J.; Hsu, J.-C.; Chang, Y.-J.; Kuo, C.-L. Machine-Vision-Based Real-Time Breakthrough Detection for Laser Drilling. Proceeding of the 11th International Conference on Automation Technology, Douliou, Yunlin, Taiwan, 18–20 November 2011.

17. Ion, J. *Laser Processing of Engineering Materials: Principles, Procedure and Industrial Application*, 1st ed.; Butterworth-Heinemann: Oxford, UK, 2005; p. 457.

9

CHAPTER

PARALLEL ALGORITHM FOR GPU PROCESSING; FOR USE IN HIGH SPEED MACHINE VISION SENSING OF COTTON LINT TRASH

Mathew G. Pelletier

United States Department of Agriculture, Agricultural Research Services, Lubbock Tx. USA

ABSTRACT

One of the main hurdles standing in the way of optimal cleaning of cotton lint is the lack of sensing systems that can react fast enough to provide the control system with real-time information as to the level of trash contamination of the cotton lint. This research examines the use of programmable graphic processing units (GPU) as an alternative to the PC's traditional use of the central processing unit (CPU). The use of the GPU, as an alternative computation platform, allowed for the machine vision system to gain a significant improvement in processing time. By improving the processing time, this research seeks to address the lack of availability of rapid trash sensing systems and thus alleviate a situation in which the current systems view the cotton lint either well before, or after, the cotton is cleaned. This extended lag/lead time that is currently imposed on the cotton trash cleaning control systems, is what is responsible for system operators utilizing a very large dead-band safety buffer in order to ensure that the cotton lint is not under-cleaned. Unfortunately, the utilization of a large dead-band buffer results in the majority of the cotton lint being over-cleaned which in turn causes lint fiber-damage as well as significant losses of the valuable lint due to the excessive use of cleaning machinery. This research estimates that upwards of a 30% reduction in lint loss could be gained through the use of a tightly coupled trash sensor to the cleaning machinery control systems. This research seeks to improve processing times through the development of a new algorithm for cotton trash sensing that allows for implementation on a highly parallel architecture. Additionally, by moving the new parallel algorithm onto an alternative computing platform, the graphic processing unit "GPU", for processing of the cotton trash images, a speed up of over 6.5 times, over optimized code running on the PC's central processing unit "CPU", was gained. The new parallel algorithm operating on the GPU was able to process a 1024×1024 image in less than 17ms. At this improved speed, the image processing system's performance should now be sufficient to provide a system that would be capable of real-time feed-back control that is in tight cooperation with the cleaning equipment.

Keywords: Machine vision; GPU; Image processing; Cotton; Sensing

1. INTRODUCTION

In the cotton ginning industry, knowledge of the cotton grade, during the processing stages, gives the cotton ginner a unique advantage and opportunity to reduce the amount of lint lost, during the lint-cleaning stage, while maintaining a quality product. This advantage is enhanced when the information, regarding the amount of trash in the cotton, is coupled with one of the new lint cleaning machines that have the ability to dynamically adjust how much cleaning they perform on the cotton, figure 1. By dynamically measuring the cotton trash content in real-time, the system could be automatically tuned to avoid wasting valuable lint as well as preventing fiber damage, from over-cleaning, which leads to a higher quality product and hence a more valuable commodity. This is beneficial to all aspects of the industry. New developments in the online classing of cotton, has recently seen the deployment of custom cotton classing systems that utilize computer vision systems to accomplish this task. There is however a lack of real-time sensors that are fast enough to allow for determination of the trash content immediately before the machine performs the cleaning. The lack of suitable rapid response sensing systems creates a disconnect between the cotton that's measured to the cotton that's being cleaned. Current state of the art sensors typically sense the product's trash levels after the cleaning has already taken place or so far before the cleaning takes place that it's impossible to synchronize the cleaning with the lint being cleaned. This disconnect, results in the users compensating through an increased dead-band range that in effect severely under-utilizes the dynamic cleaning technology. This research was undertaken with a view to developing new technology that is capable of analyzing the cotton fast enough to provide an immediate response to the cleaning equipment so the cotton that is being analyzed is the cotton that's being cleaned.

Figure 1. Lint cleaner developed by USDA-ARS that is dynamically adjustable. Photo's courtesy of Continental Eagle Corp.

2. BACKGROUND

To date, a limited amount of computer vision applications have been accomplished on general purpose microcontrollers due to the lack of computing power and the necessary high data transfer rates. Typical microcontrollers run at 20MHz or less with a few exceptions running at 40MHz-80MHz. In addition to these reduced central processing unit (CPU) speeds, the microcontrollers are further limited by being designed as 8 or 16 bit processors with only a general purpose instruction set and limited arithmetic logic unit (ALU). Under these constraints a computer vision application would take minutes if not hours to complete a single complex image analysis. These low powered embedded processors simply don't have the computational capability that an image processing system requires to be effective in a dynamically changing control system. This fact has kept the bulk of computer vision applications tethered to the PC or a high end digital-signal-processing (DSP) platform that consists of a DSP with either a video frame-grabbing chipset or a customized processor embedded directly into hardware via implementation onto an application specific

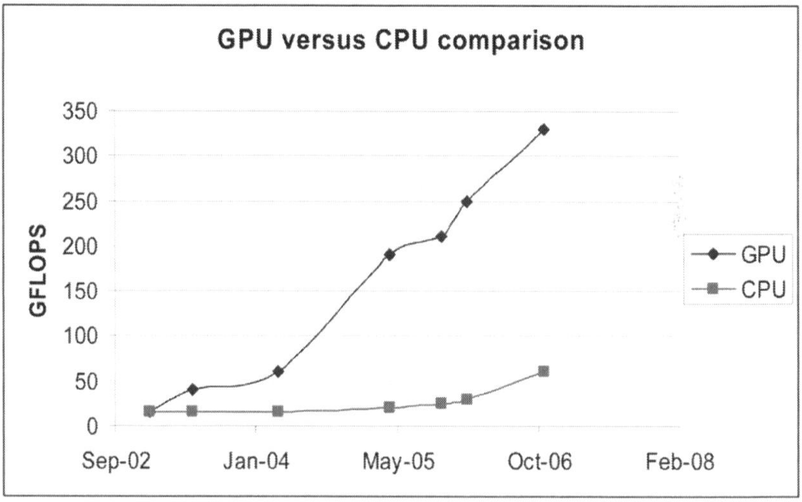

Figure 2. Graph detailing incredible performance increase over the last several years of the GPU over the traditional general purpose CPU on today's modern PC's. (Source: Nvidia 2006). Note: GFLOPS is defined as 1 trillion floating point operations per second.

processor (ASIC) or a field-programmable-gate-array chip (FPGA) (Buck et al., 2004; DeCoro and Tatarchuk, 2007; Galoppo et al., 2005; Kipfer et al, 2004; Kolb, 2005;Krueger and Westermann, 2003; Larsen and McAllister, 2001; Scheuermann and Hensley, 2007; Strzodka et al, 2005). In recent years however, a new alternative has emerged from the computer graphics arena targeted primarily at the PC based gaming industry. These new graphic processors "GPUs" have now evolved to the point where they have numerous CPUs on board the chip that are designed to run in a massively parallel architecture. Of particular interest are the recent advances of the GPUs towards fully programmable vector stream processing systems that are inherently parallel in nature. The results of these developments is to provide the scientific processing community with GPU architectures that have now advanced to the point where they provide a much faster alternative to computing of highly parallel algorithms, (figure 2) than the traditional single-pass Von Neumann architecture (Bell and Newell, 1971) of the traditional PC CPU design. This paper presents the development and testing of a highly parallizable algorithm for cotton trash image processing for use on one of the latest GPUs.

3. RESULTS AND DISCUSSION

In the interest of developing a rapid analysis system, a new machine vision processing algorithm has been developed that was designed to provide a highly parallel approach to the cotton trash identification problem. As the cotton trash system in practice is, in many instances, a retrofit system that is placed into existing systems, it's been found that controlled lighting is less controlled than would be considered optimal for alternative algorithms such as a pre-computed lookup table based on a Bayesian Classifier approach, (Pelletier 1999a,b, 2003). The main problem with the Baye's Classifier approach is the need for pre-computation of the Bayesian statistics, typically provided in the form of presorted classes obtained by an expert or human classer. Thus, it's not practical to dynamically adjust the Bayesian statistics as the expert is not available for periodic recalculation of the Bayesian statistics. This requirement forces the Bayesian approach to demand that the system provide a stable environment where the image statistics are unchanging. However, in trial deployments into several commercial installations, it was found that the static-image-statistic's criteria, was not valid. In practice, the changing lighting conditions and system placement as a retrofit onto various types of machines, typically creates a wide variation in the image statistics for each member of the feature set {trash, background, lint}; primarily due to the fact that each member of the feature set moves in and out of full or partially lit areas or becomes alternatively and repeatedly immersed in lighting and then later in shadows. To compensate for the widely changing lighting environments, encountered in typical commercial installations, required an alternative image processing algorithm to overcome the difficulties of the varying statistics. The new developments that have been brought about by this research were also coupled with the additional goal of increasing the processing speed of the algorithm to achieve a robust system that would also be capable of performing real-time trash feedback control. In an effort to obtain higher processing speeds, the research developed the algorithm with a goal to obtain a highly parallel algorithm suitable for use on highly parallel vector processors.

The basic overview of the image processing algorithm, figure 3, shows the steps required to process the image from raw color pixels into a set of statistics to inform the mechanical cleaning system of the quantity and type of trash; the basic information required by an optimal imaging/mechanical control system. The start of the image processing algorithm is to process each pixel, by analysis of the current target pixel against the target pixel's local neighboring pixels with the goal to determine or classify the target pixel into either lint or trash, figure 4. Noting that the bulk of the time required for the image processing algorithm is tied to this first step of pixel identification, the focus of the new development was to optimize the processing of this stage of the algorithm.

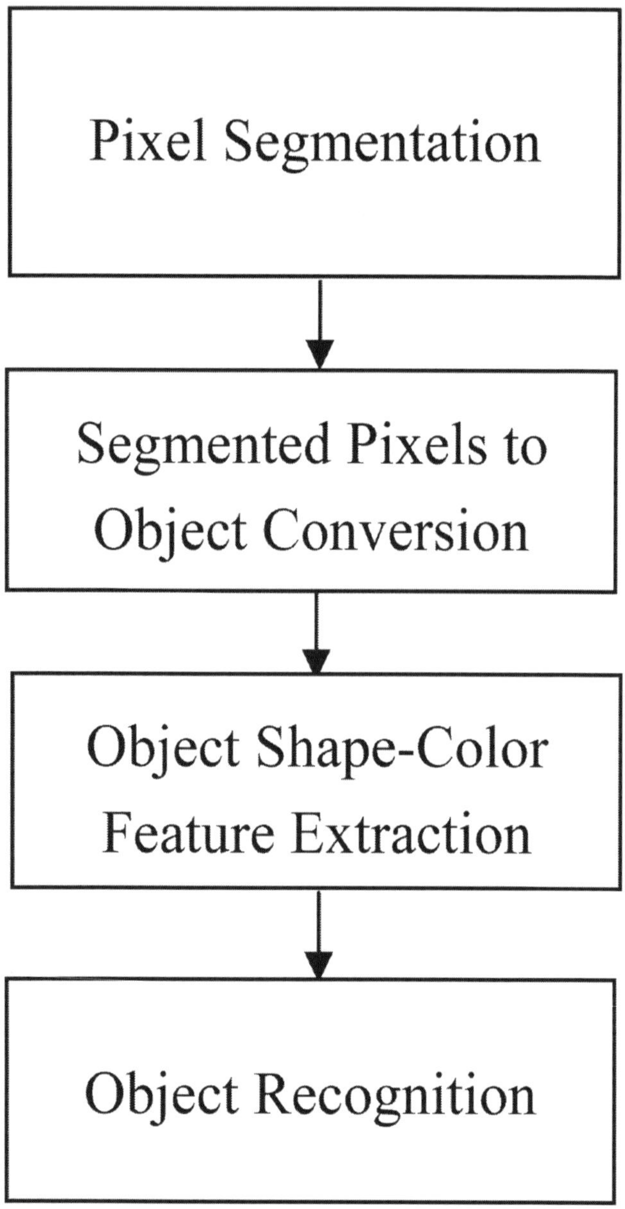

Figure 3. Image analysis to extract the quantities of the various trash constituents.

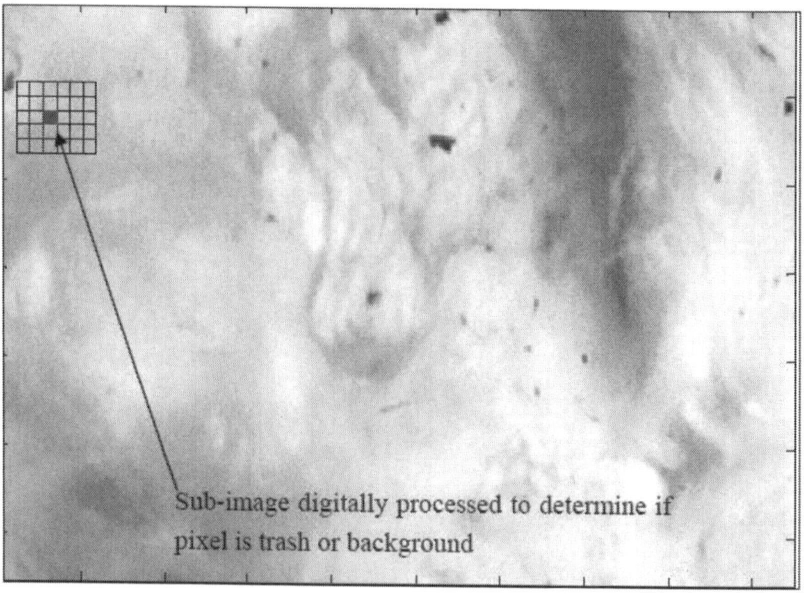

Figure 4. Sub-image is analyzed to determine if pixel is trash or lint.

The new algorithm, under investigation, was developed around a rapid single-pass Gaussian band-pass convolution kernel, "GBPCK", that effectively partitions the color space such that a simple threshold operation following the GBPCK will allow for the generation of a binary image where each pixel is classed to be either a trash or lint pixel. In practice, the GBPCK was shown to be remarkably robust across a wide variety of lighting situations. The single-pass Gaussian band-pass convolution kernel, "GBPCK", is implemented on a 7×7 finite impulse response, "FIR" two-dimensional convolution kernel or filter. As an FIR filter operates solely on the existing data and utilizes no feedback, the filtering operations operate solely on the incoming image without modifying it during the processing of the image. All results from the FIR filtering process are then stored in a second processed image. This non-feedback requirement of the FIR filter is a key enabling feature that allows for the implementation of the algorithm to be performed simultaneously on each pixel in parallel.

The basis for the Gaussian-normal band-pass filter is derived from the Gaussian low-pass filter, which is illustrated in equation 1:

$$G_{bpf}(r,\sigma) = 1/(\ \sigma\ \sqrt{(2\pi)}\ )\ \ e^{-r\wedge 2\ /\ (2\ \sigma)} \tag{1}$$

Where:

r := distance from center of non-causal filter

$r = \sqrt{(x^2 + y^2)}$

σ := Gaussian half-width

For illustration, we present a simplified form of the Gaussian band-pass filter that can be constructed from the difference of two Gaussian low-pass filters with differing extents, as shown in equation 2:

$$G_{bpf}(r) = 1/(\ \sigma\ \sqrt{(2\pi)}\ )\ \ e^{-r\wedge 2\ /\ (2\ \sigma)} - 1/(\ \rho\ \sqrt{(2\pi)}\ )\ \ e^{-r\wedge 2\ /\ (2\ \rho)} \tag{2}$$

Where:

r := distance from center of non-causal filter

$r = \sqrt{(x^2 + y^2)}$

ρ := spread of the Gaussian filter 1

σ := spread of the Gaussian filter 2

In practice the Gaussian band-pass filter was comprised of the sum of several Gaussian filters. By utilization of multiple-cascaded Gaussian filters, the shape of the Gaussian curve can be highly tuned for both extent and fall-off, allowing for optimum processing for the specific application. In order to optimize the calculation of the filter in real-time, the filter coefficients were pre-calculated. For the research subject under investigation, the discrete two-dimensional Gaussian band-pass filter was implemented from the consolidated cascade of multiple Gaussian-normal filters as detailed in equation 3:

$$G_{bpf}(m,n) = \beta * e^{-(1/4*r)^2} + 2\beta\, e^{-(1/2*r)^2} + (4\beta - \alpha) * e^{-r^2} + 8\beta\, e^{-(2*r)^2} + 16\beta\, e^{-(4*r)^2} \quad (3)$$

Where:

$r = \sqrt{(x^2 + y^2)}$:= distance from the center of the convolution kernel

$\beta = 0.0108$

$\alpha = 0.3182$

To gain insight into how the Gaussian band-pass filter, hereafter known as the GBPCK, is affecting the image, the frequency response of the discrete two-dimensional filter of equation 3 was calculated using the discrete-Fourier-Transform to transfer from the discrete spatial position domain to the discrete frequency domain (Strum and Kirk, 1988; Jain, 1989; Porat, 1998) where the two-dimensional discrete-Fourier-Transform is illustrated inequation 4:

$$H(k, g) = \sum \sum h(m,n)\, e^{-j(2\pi/N)\, k\, n}\, e^{-j(2\pi/M)\, g\, n} \quad (4)$$

Summed over the interval n = 0 to n = N-1 & m = 0 to m = M-1

Where:

N :- number image points in the sampled x-dimension

M :- number image points in the sampled y-dimension

$j := \sqrt{(-1)}$

The discrete frequency response of the filter, as calculated from equation 4, via the fast Fourier-Transform (FFT) algorithm, is shown in figure 5. For clarity, the one-dimensional cross-section of the filter is shown in figure 6.

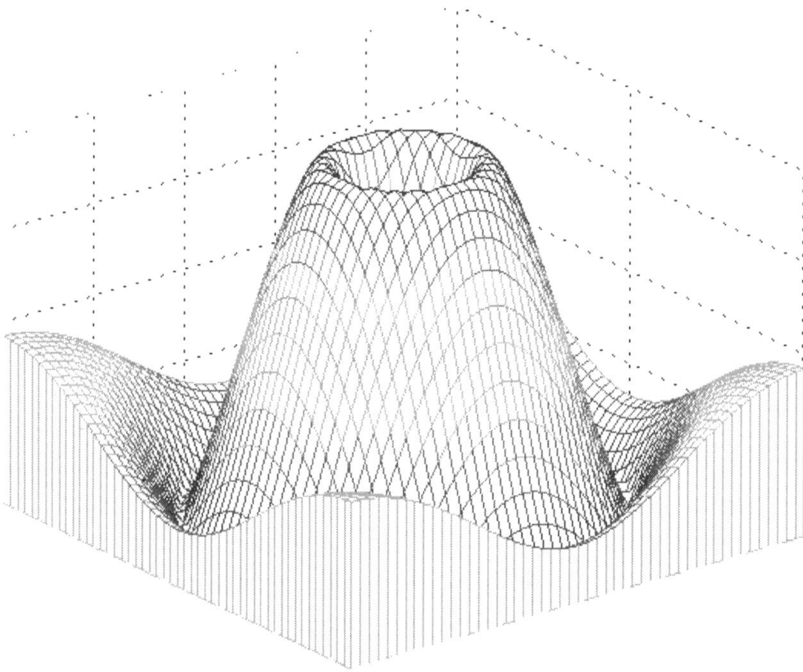

Figure 5. Frequency response of the two-dimensional Gaussian band pass filter for highly parallel, lighting independent, rapid trash analysis.

We note here that one of the key criteria's for online classing is the ability of the algorithm to separate cotton from trash in both lit and shadowed areas. One example of the performance of the GBPCK suitability for performing this task is detailed in figure 7.

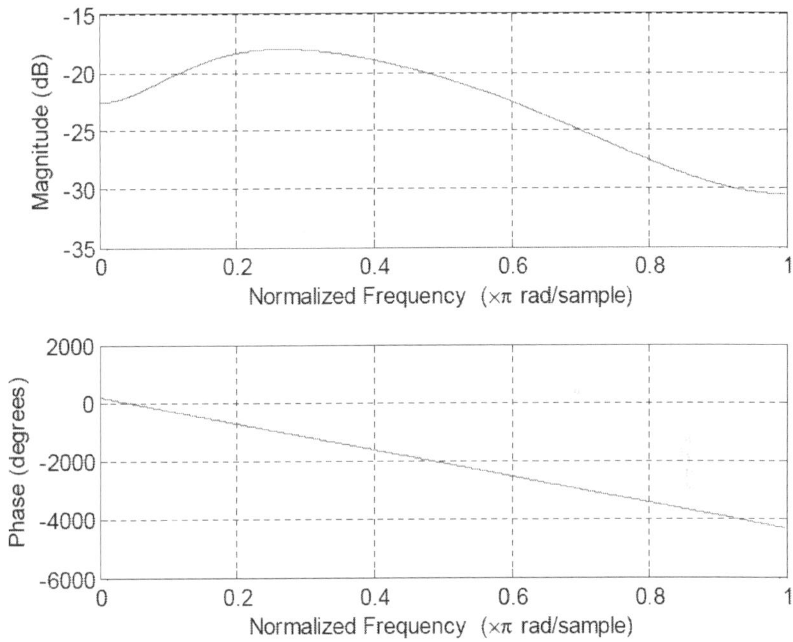

Figure 6. Frequency response of the one-dimensional cross-section of the 2D Gaussian band pass filter detailed in figure 5.

Once the development of a single pass filter was completed, the next task was to fine tune the implementation of the filter to effect the fastest processing on the given hardware. To gain insight into areas that would provide a meaningful speed-up, which was one of the primary goals of this research, it was also crucial to provide a baseline performance by which to judge the GPU approach. The algorithm was initially optimized for use on a Pentium 4 processor using the extended operation set for "Single Instruction for Multiple Data" or SIMD. The SIMD extension for the Pentium 4

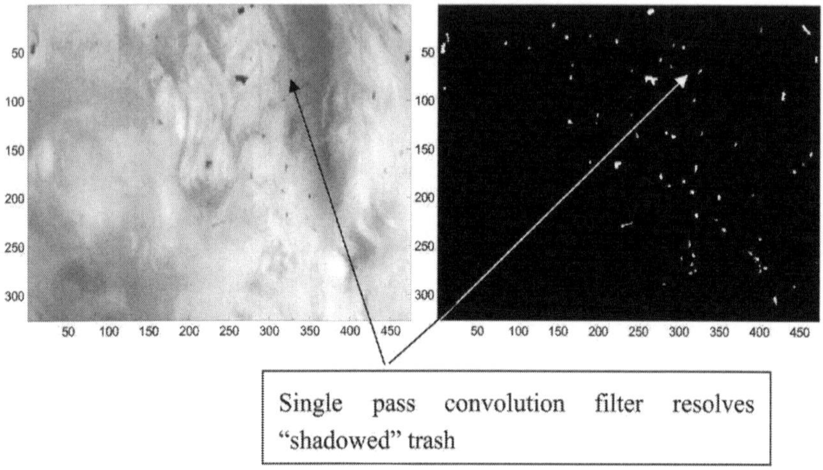

Figure 7. Performance of new single pass GCK algorithm.

provides a single vector processor that is capable of multiplying 4 single-precision floating point numbers in parallel. Performance of the algorithm after adjustment to take advantage of the Pentium's SIMD CPU chipset extensions as well as inline expanded and optimized C code, resulted in a processing time of 7.5 frames per second. This performance increase represents a significant speedup over the previous algorithm implementation of 2.5 frames per second. The next step in the development was to compare the optimized SIMD performance to the same algorithm running on an NVIDIA GeForce 8800 Ultra GPU graphics processing unit, housed on a pci-express bus card, where the code would then have the opportunity to take advantage of the GPU's 132 vector processors. We note here that while the GPU has 132 vector processors, each capable of multiplying 4 single precision floating point numbers in parallel, the core is only running at 500 MHz versus the Pentium's core at 3.0GHz. Given the speed disparity between the GPU processor to the Pentium core, one cannot expect a speedup of 132 times for the GPU over the CPU.

Other potential problem areas for implementation on the GPU platform lies in the bottle necks that are created by pushing large amounts of image data across the pci-express bus into the GPU's video ram, figure 8. In short, one may not even expect a 132-X times (500MHz/3000MHz) = 22-X gain from running on the GPU core versus normal operations that take place via computation on the CPU due to other hardware constraints.

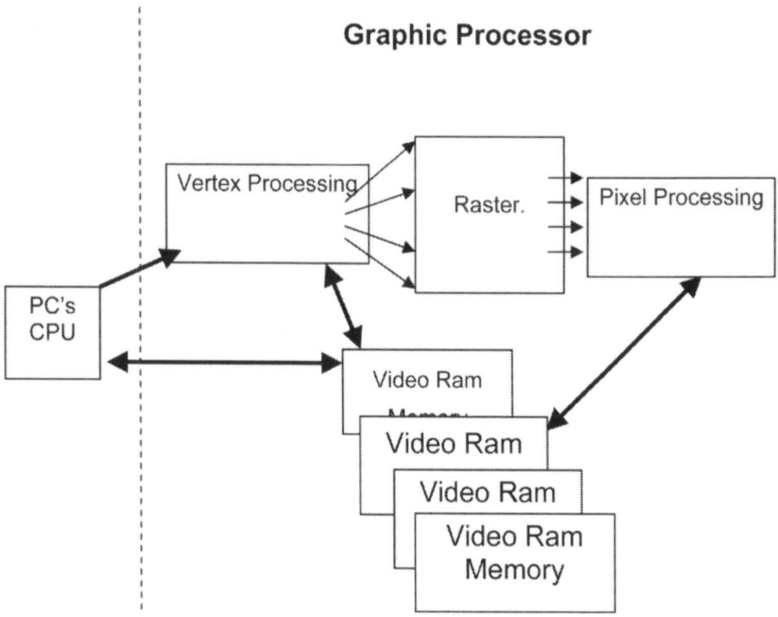

Figure 8. Processing flow using a GPU processor

In moving the algorithm off of the PC's traditional computing platform, the CPU, to the GPU; the developers of the modern GPUs have designed the system such that the CPU passes both an algorithm as well as the image and geometry data to the GPU. To effect efficient general computation on the GPU, the algorithm must be transformed to fit the highly specialized stream processing the GPU was designed to perform, figure 8. As such only certain algorithms that are inherently parallel in nature, can be converted, however for those suitable algorithms, once the transformation is made, the massively parallel architecture of the modern GPUs becomes available which enables dramatic increases in performance over the traditional CPU style computations. To ease the transformation process, the graphic card developers have developed an augmented C programming language that allows one to specify how the image is to be broken into numerous sub-images that will all be computed concurrently as well as the algorithm each vector processor should execute. By combining both the GBPCK algorithm with the threshold and non-linear median-filter shot-noise reduction operation, to form a combined GBPCK-TM analyzer, it allowed the algorithm to be moved completely off of the CPU and onto the GPU. The new cotton trash analyzer processing program now has the ability to break the large image into numerous sub-images that can all be analyzed concurrently as detailed in figure 9. Once the GPU analyzes the data per specification of the GBPCK-TM, it then transfers the fully analyzed binary image solution back to the CPU along with trash statistics such as trash content. In testing of the GBPCK-TM algorithm for cotton trash identification, we found the following:

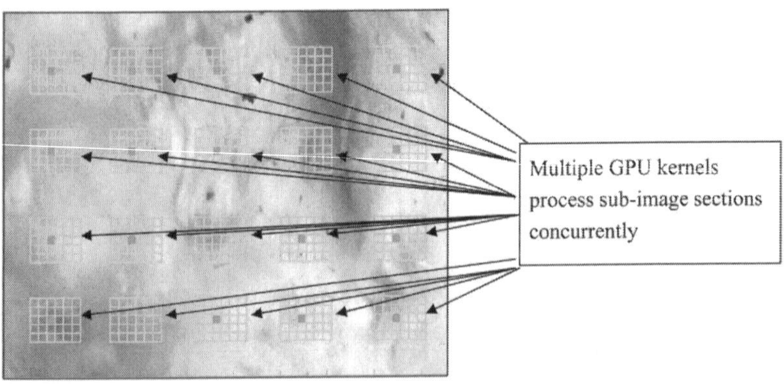

Figure 9. Massively parallel approach to image processing showing how numerous sub-images are all analyzed concurrently using 132 vector processors on a GPU.

- Transitioning from the Bayesian Classifier to a single pass GBPCK, was enabling technology as commercial use dictated retro-fitting the system into on-line environments which resulted in wide fluctuations in the positioning of the lint bat, which in turn created large fluctuations in both the light intensity as well as large variations depth and quality of the shadowed lint. These lighting inconsistencies resulted in large degradations in the quality of the performance of the Bayesian classifier. When tested against these same lighting fluctuations, the GBPCK performance was significantly improved over the Bayesian Classifier.

- In practice the Bayesian Classifier in practice required extensive on-site training. In contrast, the GBPCK provided a robust rapid startup as no on-site training was required and eliminated the need for ambient light shielding, thereby improving system's ability to be retrofit into a wider variety of machine designs as well as reducing manufacturing and installation system costs.

- We note herein for those not familiar with cotton classification, that the standard by which all cotton lint is graded, is the human visual system. An elaborate process has been developed over the last century that enables for a stable transition from year to year of the cotton classing grade. Each year in Memphis Tennessee, a standard set of boxes, holding lint samples that are representative of the color and trash grade. Each classing office throughout the US utilizes a set of these boxes as the defacto standard for any lint sample that is in question as to the correct grade. As such, the human visual system is the standard which is judged against a contiuously changing historical standard. Given this standard, the best test for performance of the system is a visual analysis of the quality of the recognition, which can be best judged by examination of the included figure 7. We also note that when the system was run against the official photograph prints of the cotton classing standards, used daily by USDA-AMS cotton classers, the system was able to predict the grade with a coefficient of determination of r^2=0.99. While it is also recognized that with the shadowing, the performance will be degraded, field tests indicated a level of performance comparable to the correlations achieved between human classers during periodic re-grading of the lint that occurs across the course of the season at the request of customers, typical r^2=0.80-0.85. In house testing suggests the performance with shadows is within ½ leaf grade, which is typically within 1 standard deviation of the natural variability of the lint in the ginning process.

- By transitioning from the Bayesian Classifier to a single pass GBPCK, along with optimizations of the algorithm, improvements over processing speed was gained.
    - Optimization of algorithm effected a speed up of 2.5 times (7.5 frames/sec).
- By moving the code from the CPU to the GPU and utilizing the combined GBPCK-TM algorithm, further improvements were gained:
    - When utilizing a single Nvidia GeForce 8800 GPU with 132 vector processors; a speed up of 20 times was gained (60 frames/sec) over the Bayesian Classifier and a speed up of eight was gained over running highly optimized code on the CPU.
- At 60 Frames/second:
    - 71 sq-m.of cotton can be imaged/bale with the new GBPCK-TM algorithm running on the GPU.

- versus 2.5 Frames/second, utilizing the previous Bayesian Classifier approach:
    - 3.5 sq-m.of cotton can be imaged/bale.

4. CONCLUSIONS

As the cotton ginning industry moves toward machines that have the ability to dynamically adjust the amount of cleaning the machine performs, a great deal of valuable lint is saved and there is a significant reduction in fiber damage as well. The missing element at this time is the ability of the sensors to determine the required amount of cleaning for the cotton as it is feed into the machine. This research has demonstrated that through the use of massively parallel processing, that is now possible on today's programmable GPUs, a machine vision algorithm suitable for real-time classing of cotton, can be processed in a significantly reduced time that is sufficient to open the door for the possibility of processing the trash content of the incoming lint in time to set the machine so that it cleans the cotton that was just analyzed. This just-in-time analysis provides the enabling technology with the capacity to allow for a system that is optimized to clean the cotton that is being fed into the machine at the precise optimal cleaning level. Once this transition from the current system, that looks at a sample of cotton taken either way before processing or after the cleaning has already taken place, moves toward one where the machine is cleaning the cotton that was analyzed as it is being fed into the machine; performance gains are expected to be upwards of 30% in reduction of valuable lint loss. This level of improvement can be expected due to the fact that today's systems use a very large dead-band to protect the users against both the inherent wide variability in the cotton lint's trash distribution, as well as the potential for changes to take place before the machine can react to the changing cotton trash levels. It is also expected that this technology will likely drive new machine designs that can not only optimize the cleaning across the entire width of the machine, which effectively cleans 100% of the cotton to remove the trash from the 4% of the cotton that actually have trash particles, towards a machine that only cleans the 4% of the cotton that actually contains the trash. Once this level of automation is reached, significant reductions in lint loss as well as subsequent reductions in fiber damage will also become possible as there should be an additional 96% reduction in lint loss and fiber damage. As the typical first stage lint cleaners generate upwards of 4.5-7 kg of lint loss, if 4.5 kg of lint per bale can be saved, this would represent a $100 million U.S. of added annual revenue to US cotton growers as well as a similar amount for the international growers.

REFERENCES

1. Buck, I.; Foley, T.; Horn, D.; Sugerman, J.; Fatahalian, K.; Houston, M.; Hanrahan, P. Stream computing on graphics hardware. *ACM Proc. SIGGRAPH* **2004**, *23*, 777–786.

2. Jain, A.K. *Fundamentals of Digital Image Processing*; Prentice-Hall: New Jersey, 1989; pp. 15–18.

3. Kipfer, P.; Segal, M.; Westermann, R. Uberflow. A GPU-based particle engine. Proceedings of the ACM SIGGRAPH/EUROGRAPHICS conference on Graphics hardware, Grenoble, France; ACM: New York, NY, USA; pp. 115–122.

4. Kolb, A.; Latta, L.; Rezk-Salama, C. Hardware-based simulation and collision detection for large particle systems. Proceedings of the ACM

SIGGRAPH/EUROGRAPHICS conference on Graphics hardware, Grenoble, France; ACM: New York, NY, USA; pp. 123–131.

5. Krueger, J.; Westermann, R. Linear algebra operators for GPU implementation of numerical algorithms.*ACM Transactions on Graphics* **2003**, *22*(3), 908–916.

6. Pelletier, M.G.; Barker, G.L.; Baker, R.V. Non-contact image processing for gin trash sensors in stripper harvested cotton. *ASAE* **1999**, Paper #991126. 9.

7. Pelletier, M.G.; Barker, G.L.; Baker, R.V. Image processing for stripper harvested cotton trash content measurement: a progress report. *Proc. Beltwide Cotton Prod. Res. Conf.* **1999**, 1412–1415.

8. Pelletier, M.G. Real time measurement system for seed cotton or lint. U.S. Patent, No. 6,567,538, 2003.

9. Porat, B. *A course in digital signal processing*; John Wiley and Sons, Inc.: New York, 1997; pp. 93–159.

10. Strum, R.D.; Kirk, D.E. *First Principles of Discrete Systems and Digital Signal Processing.*; Addison-Wesley Publishing Co.: Reading, MA, 1988; pp. 363–527.

11. Strzodka, R.; Doggett, M.; Kolb, A. Scientific computation for simulations on programmable graphics hardware. *Simulation Modelling Practice and Theory* **2005**, *13*(8), 667–680, (Special Issue: Programmable Graphics Hardware)

10

CHAPTER

TRACKING BY IDENTIFICATION USING COMPUTER VISION AND RADIO

Rok Mandeljc *, Stanislav Kovačič, Matej Kristan and Janez Perš

Machine Vision Laboratory, Faculty of Electrical Engineering, University of Ljubljana, Tržaška 25, SI-1000 Ljubljana, Slovenia

ABSTRACT

We present a novel system for detection, localization and tracking of multiple people, which fuses a multi-view computer vision approach with a radio-based localization system. The proposed fusion combines the best of both worlds, excellent computer-vision-based localization, and strong identity information provided by the radio system, and is therefore able to perform tracking by identification, which makes it impervious to propagated identity switches. We present comprehensive methodology for evaluation of systems that perform person localization in world coordinate system and use it to evaluate the proposed system as well as its components. Experimental results on a challenging indoor dataset, which involves multiple people walking around a realistically cluttered room, confirm that proposed fusion of both systems significantly outperforms its individual components. Compared to the radio-based system, it achieves better localization results, while at the same time it successfully prevents propagation of identity switches that occur in pure computer-vision-based tracking.

Keywords: person localization; identification; tracking; radio; computer vision; multi-camera; sensor fusion; tracking-by-identification

1. INTRODUCTION

In the past two decades, the problem of object detection, localization and tracking received significant attention. This coincides with the rising demand for information about objects' location and identity, which stems from applications in various fields, such as manufacturing, military, surveillance and security, transport and logistics, medical care, childcare, performance analysis in sports and sports medicine. Various localization solutions based on different sensor modalities have been proposed [1], with two most prominent research areas being detection and tracking using video cameras [2] and localization using radio technology [3]. Sensor fusion has also gained prominence as a paradigm for overcoming limitations of individual sensor modalities [1].

The need for recovery of individuals' positions and trajectories, measured in the world coordinate system (*i.e.*, room coordinate system as opposed to an image plane), can be found in different scenarios, most notably in closed-world surveillance, intelligent environments and performance analysis in sports. In surveillance, knowing individuals' position and identity enables us not only to determine their presence or absence, but also analyze their behavior, detect abnormalities in it and reconstruct events. Similarly, in sports, obtaining athletes' trajectories allows a consistent analysis of game measures, such as movement of the individual players or the whole team, physiological demands and intensity of the game, and strategy assessment, which has proven to be very valuable for coaches and sports physiologists. Therefore, a person localization system can be regarded as a measuring device that measures individuals' positions and determines their identities. As can be seen from the short survey on currently-used player tracking techniques in sports [4], attempts have been made to use both radio-based and camera-based approaches.

Both radio and video sensor modality have their advantages and disadvantages, which are often of complementary nature. The main disadvantage of radio-based localization and tracking systems is that they are intrusive; they comprise a network of radio receivers (sensors) and radio-emitting tags that people need to wear. While inconvenient, this is still acceptable in environments where people are already expected to wear identification tags, for example in some surveillance applications and intelligent environments. In sports, however, intrusive systems are discouraged because the tags might hamper the athletes' movement or, in event of body contact, even cause injuries. In some sports, intrusive techniques may violate sport regulations. Additionally, the update frequency of individuals' positions is limited due to the nature of radio signal and, due to time-slotting, decreases as the number of tracked individuals increases.

Video cameras used in computer-vision-based approaches, on the other hand, enable unobtrusive recovery of individuals' positions and trajectories. This can be done at comparatively high frequency, which is, especially if off-line processing is permissible, limited only by cameras' frame rate. However, computer-vision-based approaches have difficulties with maintaining individuals' identities over longer periods of time; many modern multi-view approaches rely on identification by tracking, meaning that they propagate the identities along the track, with little or no appearance-based validation. This can lead to propagation of identity switches when individuals come close and then disperse again. This problem is even more evident in uniformed environments, such as sports or high-security facilities, where individuals become visually indistinguishable due to similar clothing.

In this paper, we present a person detection and localization system that performs tracking by identification. The proposed system is composed of two subsystems. The first component is a commercially-available localization solution that is based on Ultra-Wideband radio technology. The second component is a state-of-the-art computer-vision based system that performs identification by tracking; anonymous detections are obtained from multiple views on frame-by-frame basis and then linked into trajectories by a global optimization method. The proposed combination performs all three steps—detection, localization and identification of individuals—on a frame-by-frame basis, and only then links these independent, identified, detections into tracks. Due to use of radio tags, the proposed system is currently suitable for closed-world surveillance applications and intelligent environments; however, we expect that eventual progress in miniaturization of radio tags will enable wider adoption in sports applications as well.

The subsystems are combined in two stages. In the first stage, we fuse information from the radio-based system directly into the camera-based detection algorithm to improve anonymous person detection and localization. In the second stage, we augment the anonymous detections with identity information from the radio system, before linking them into trajectories and thereby performing tracking by identification. We present evaluation methodology and metric, which is based on 2-D localization error, and use it to evaluate the performance of the system and its individual components. The experimental results on a challenging indoor dataset show that the proposed combination of computer vision and radio performs better, both in terms of localization error and maintaining the identities of individuals. To enable further research in the field of multi-modal sensor fusion, we offer our dataset to the research community as a free download [5]. To the best of our knowledge, this is the first publicly-available multi-modal dataset combining multiple calibrated cameras and a radio-based localization system.

The remainder of the paper is organized as follows. In Section 2, we provide an overview of related work in the field of person detection and tracking using multiple cameras, multi-modal sensor fusion and existing metrics for their performance evaluation. In Section 3 we introduce both components of our system, the radio-based and the computer-vision-based localization system. This is followed by both stages of fusion, presented in Section 4; the first stage improves the anonymous detection and localization, and the second stage results in tracking by identification. Section 5 describes the evaluation methodology and metric that we use to evaluate the proposed system and its components. Finally, in Section 6, we present experimental validation of the proposed approach, along with the dataset that we use, and conclude the paper in Section 7.

2. RELATED WORK

The task of tracking multiple people using video cameras has a long tradition in the field of computer vision; an overview of existing multi-target tracking literature can be found in [2]. Here, we focus on approaches that use multiple cameras with overlapping fields of view, as such are usually required for recovery of individuals' positions and trajectories in the world coordinate system. The existing approaches can be roughly divided into two groups. The first are so-called detection-by-tracking approaches, which rely on sequential detection, usually using Kalman filter (e.g., [6,7]) or particle filters ([8,9]). Such trackers are causal; they consider only previously-processed frames, which is why they still represent state-of-the-art in the real-time tracking. However, relying on recursive detection may result in irrecoverable errors when a person fails to be detected or when detections are incorrectly linked. Such errors tend to propagate and multiply in the subsequent frames, eventually causing a tracker to fail. Tracking-by-detection approaches mitigate this issue by first employing robust frame-by-frame detection [10,11], on top of which global optimization methods are applied for tracking (e.g., [12]), usually off-line and in batch manner. However, when it comes to maintaining the identities of tracks, these approaches perform identification by tracking; they rely on identity propagation along the track, with none or limited appearance-based validation, and as such, they are prone to propagation of identity switches after people come close and disperse again. Recently, Shitrit *et al.* [13], extended state-of-the-art tracking approach [12] to preserve identities of players in sports, based on the color of their jerseys and their numbers. However, to reliably distinguish between individuals, a much larger assortment of visual cues is usually needed.

In their detection stage, many tracking-by-detection approaches aggregate information from multiple cameras using an occupancy map. Occupancy map, also referred to as occupancy grid or plan view, is a well-established concept in mobile robotics [14]. It involves discretizing the ground plane of area of interest into a grid, followed by estimation of occupancy probability for each of its cells. It was introduced in the field of computer vision with works of Beymer [15] and Yang *et al.* [16], both in the context of estimating the number of people in a room. In the work of Franco and Boyer [17], an occupancy map is used as a framework for fusion of multi-view silhouette cues. These approaches are bottom-up; they project points of the foreground likelihood, either stereo disparities of foreground regions obtained by background subtraction, of each view into the ground plane and then infer the occupancy likelihood from the amount of points projected in each cell. Works of Delannay *et al.* [18] and Muoz [19] also fall into this category. Similarly, Khan and Shah [11] warp the foreground regions from all views into a reference plane, producing a 2-D grid of occupancy likelihoods, which they call a synergy map. They use multiple planes, parallel to the reference plane, and stack the resulting synergy maps into a 3-D volume representing sampled scene space. Losada *et al.* [20] use multiple calibrated cameras and 3-D occupancy grid for localization of multiple mobile robots in an intelligent environment.

The state-of-the-art Probabilistic Occupancy Map (POM) by Fleuret *et al.* [10] uses a top-down approach. A generative model that approximates silhouettes with rectangles is used to back-project currently estimated occupancy probabilities into all views; the occupancy map is obtained by iterative optimization of the probability field, so that the difference between the back-projected and the input binary images, obtained by background subtraction, is minimized. Due to iterative nature and use of back-projection, the algorithm implicitly handles occlusions between people. Berclaz *et al.* [21] use the same framework, but instead of foreground images, output of a people detector is used. Alahi *et al.* [22] also obtain occupancy map from foreground images in a top-down manner, using sparsity-constrained inverse problem formulation.

The anonymous detections obtained by aforementioned approaches can be incorporated into a tracking framework, resulting in tracking by detection. In [11], graph cuts are used to link the frame-by-frame-detections, while in [10], tracking is done using dynamic programming and a local color appearance model. In recent work by Berclaz *et al.* [12], multi-object tracking on top of an occupancy map is formulated as a global optimization problem and solved using K-Shortest Paths algorithm. Their approach completely ignores the appearance and yet it has been shown to outperform other methods, therefore it represents state of the art in identification by tracking. Recently, Shitrit *et al.* [13] extended this approach to preserve identities based on sparsely-available visual cues. In our system, we achieve tracking by identification by augmenting anonymous detections with identity information from a radio-based localization system.

Fusion of visual information with other sensor modalities is also an active research topic. A popular choice appears to be a combination of one or more video cameras and a laser range finder, especially in mobile robot navigation (e.g., [23]), but also for pedestrian detection on autonomous vehicles and in driver assistance systems. For example, in [24], multiple baselines and a laser ranger finder are fused, whereas [25] proposes a combination of a stereo camera and a laser scanner. In [26], multiple sensor modalities—GPS, inertial sensors, stereo camera and a-priori 3-D model of environment—are used to improve pedestrian positioning accuracy in an urban environment. The work of Meingast *et al.* [27] proposes a method for automatic calibration of a heterogeneous sensor network, in which nodes consist of a video camera and a wireless sensor mote. This is achieved via fusion of data coming from both types of sensors; cameras are auto-calibrated up to scale factors from correspondences, obtained from detected moving objects, whereas scale factors are estimated with help of wireless motes and radio interferometry. A prominent area of multi-modal sensor fusion is also fusion of audio-visual information [28], which also deals with problem of localization and identification of speakers in a room.

For this task, Bayesian networks with particle-filter-based inference are commonly used.

An overview of commonly used technologies and techniques for radio-based object detection and localization can be found in the survey paper by Liu *et al.* [3]. In addition to ubiquitous IEEE 802.11 (WiFi) wireless network infrastructure, Radio-Frequency Identification (RFID) and Ultra-Wideband (UWB) radio technology are commonly used. In case of passive RFID, the radio tag must pass close by the RFID reader to be detected. Such technology can be used for tracking assets and individuals in large-scale environments (*i.e.*, whole building, campus), by equipping them with RFID tags and placing RFID readers at checkpoints. In [29], a combination of passive RFID and cameras is proposed to avoid exposing privacy of authorized people in video streams; if a person authenticates themselves with an RFID card when entering a room, their faces in video stream are blurred. Active RFID enables detection of more distant tags. Therefore, it can be also used for navigation in large-scale environments, by equipping a person or robot with RFID reader and using tags as landmarks [30]. RFID has also been fused with single camera with aim of improving object and human recognition [31,32].

WiFi and active RFID are commonly used for localization using Received Signal Strength Indication (RSSI), where distance between emitter and receivers is estimated from signal strength. This allows person and asset localization and tracking in large-scale environments, and also navigation using RSSI fingerprints of WiFi access points. There have been several attempts at fusing computer vision and WiFi signal strength for person localization, e.g., [33,34]. Anne *et al.* [35] propose indoor person localization by combining computer vision, WiFi signal strength and RFID, where RFID tags are installed in the floor and RFID reader is placed in individual's shoes. Cucchiara *et al.* [36] propose a combination of a network of video cameras and an active RFID system for detection of intruders in wide open areas. However, contrary to the system we propose, their system is not concerned with localization of individuals; their division of area of interest in relatively crude locations is done solely to allow association of detections from video cameras with those from the RFID system. Yu and Ganz [37] aim to prevent identity switches in longer video sequences by associating identities from a signal-strength-based active RFID system with tracklets that are obtained from a calibrated video camera. Later, they extended their approach to use raw (uncalibrated) radio measurements, and perform tracking and identity association in image plane instead on the ground plane [38].

Ultra-Wideband (UWB) radio [39], due to high bandwidth of signals, offers much higher temporal (and thus spatial) resolution than RFID-based solutions. Due to increased resolution, in addition to RSSI, Angle of Arrival (AoA), Time of Arrival (ToA) and Time Difference of Arrival (TDoA) can be used to precisely localize objects in smaller areas, such as a single room. Several commercially-available systems based on UWB are available on the market; in this paper, we use the solution offered by Ubisense [40], which localizes radio tags using AoA and TDoA measurements. Similarly to this paper and our previous work [41], Dibitonto *et al.* [42] also propose fusion of Ultra-Wideband radio localization system and computer vision. However, they use a single camera, and are concerned only with correlation of trajectories and not with localization performance.

When it comes to evaluation of localization results, different metrics are used by different authors. For example, in their survey paper on localization systems, Hightower *et al.* [1] suggest that researchers report 2-D localization error distribution. However, this information does not include information about missing and phantom detections. Several authors of computer-vision-based approaches ([10,18,21,22]) report number of false positive and negative detections or related metrics from information retrieval theory, such as precision and recall or false positive and false negative rate. Authors of [10,11] additionally report average localization error. Yet, although all perform localization on ground plane, some perform evaluation in image plane and some on ground plane, and they use different criteria to determine whether a detection is a true positive, a false positive or a false negative. Recent approaches [12,13] have adopted CLEAR Multi-Object Tracking (MOT) metrics [43]. However, it appears that the preferred formulation is the one from [44], which is based on evaluation in the image plane using bounding box overlap. While suitable for monocular approaches that perform detection and tracking in the image plane, such evaluation is less suitable for approaches that perform detection and tracking in world coordinate system, where, as argued in Section 5, localization error on ground plane should be considered instead.

3. RADIO-BASED SYSTEM AND COMPUTER-VISION-BASED SYSTEM

In this section, we present the radio-based system and the computer-vision-based system, which are the main components of our tracking-by-identification system. Table 1 summarizes the comparison of radio-based and camera-based detection and localization, which is based on our previous work [41] and re-confirmed by experimental results in Section 6.2. As can be seen, the radio-based system provides very reliable detection, with practically no false positive and negative detections, but with considerable localization error in a cluttered environment. On the other hand, computer-vision-based approach offers better localization, but the detection sometimes suffers from false positives and false negatives. These findings form the baseline for fusion in Section 4.

Table 1. Summarized comparison of radio- and camera-based detection and localization, based on our previous work [41] and experimental results from Section 6.2.

	Radio-based detection (Section 3.1)	Camera-based detection (Section 3.2)
False positive detections	none	some
False negative detections	practically none	some
Localization of detections	poor	very good
Identity information	strong (tag ID)	none
Data capture frequency [Hz]	4.6 (five people)	20 (cameras' framerate)

3.1. Radio-Based System

The radio-based localization system that we use is a commercially-available solution from Ubisense [40]. It is based on Ultra-Wideband (UWB) radio technology [39] and comprises a network of radio receivers (sensors) that are installed in a room and small radio-emitting tags that are worn by people. There are two types of tags available—omnidirectional compact tags (http://www.ubisense.net/en /resources/factsheets/series-7000-compact-tag.html) and directional slim tags (http://www.ubisense.net/en/ resources/factsheets/ series-7000-slim-tag.html), both of which are shown in Figure 1. Tags are localized with combination of Angle-of-Arrival (AoA) and Time-Difference-of-Arrival (TDoA) measurements [3], which makes 3-D localization possible even when only two sensors detect a tag.

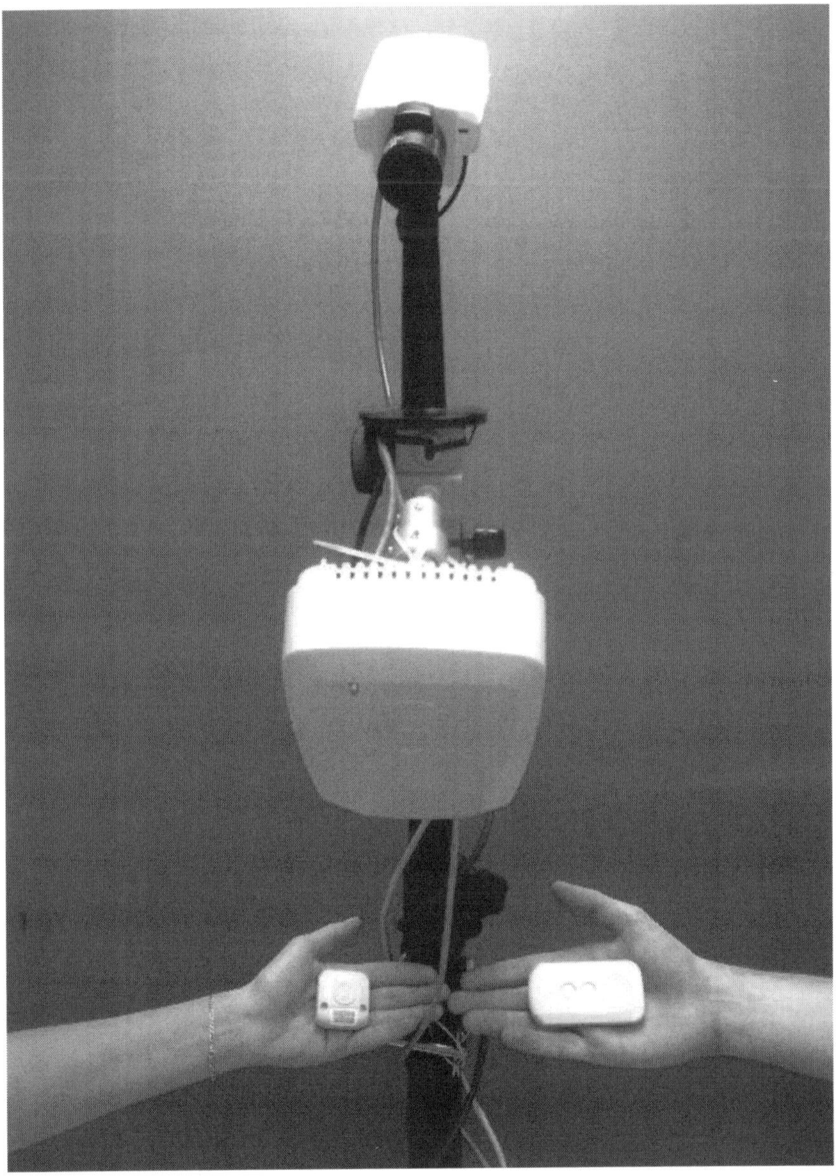

Figure 1. An AXIS P1346 IP camera and a Ubisense sensor mounted on a stand. The hand on the left side is holding a Ubisense compact tag, while the hand on the right side is holding a slim tag.

To prevent interference between tags, each tag is allocated time slots during which it emits signal. Combined with limitations stemming from the nature of the radio signal, this caps the position refresh frequency for a tag at 33.75 Hz, which is achievable when only a single tag is used and decreases with increasing number of tags. Using five tags, we measured the median update frequency of an individual tag to be 4.6 Hz.

For each tag, its position and unique identifier can be obtained from system's software platform. Since identity is encoded in the radio signal, the system inherently does not suffer from identity switches, and can be considered as a tracking-by-identification system. The advertised localization accuracy of the system is 15 cm, with 99% of errors being within 30 cm, however our experiments indicate that performance in a realistic, cluttered indoor environment is much lower due to occlusions (both from other people and from inanimate objects) and presence of metallic surfaces, which reflect radio signals. These cause non-line-of-sight (NLOS) signal propagation, which is the main cause of errors in radio-based localization.

3.2. Computer-Vision-Based System

The computer-vision-based system uses multiple calibrated and time-synchronized video cameras with overlapping fields of view. It is based on the state-of-the-art Probabilistic Occupancy Map (POM) algorithm [10] for frame-by-frame person detection and localization, and K-Shortest Paths (KSP) [12] algorithm for linking independent detections into trajectories.

The POM algorithm operates by discretizing the ground plane of area of interest into a rectangular grid, typically of resolution 20 cm. It then, on frame by frame basis, iteratively estimates the probabilities of occupancy for all cells in the grid, based on input binary images, which are usually obtained by means of background subtraction. It uses a simple and robust appearance model that approximates the silhouette of a person at each possible location with a rectangle of fixed height. Typically, rectangles correspond to width of 50 cm and height of 175 cm. Using this model, currently estimated occupancy probabilities are back-projected into input views. Estimation begins by assigning all cells uniform initial probabilities of occupancy, and then the probability field (occupancy map) is iteratively optimized so that the difference between input binary images and synthetic back-projected images is minimized.

Here, we briefly summarize the mathematical model used by POM, as we refer to it in Section 4.1; for complete formulation, see [10]. Given a discretization of ground plane in N cells, we denote by $\mathbf{X}$ a vector of binary random variables $(X_1,..., X_N)$, standing for the occupancy of each cell ($X_k = 1$ if k-th cell is occupied and $X_k = 0$ if it is vacant). The goal is to estimate the posterior probability over occupancy maps, $P(\mathbf{X}|\mathbf{B})$, given the information from C video cameras $\mathbf{B} = (B_1,...,B_C)$. This problem is, under independence assumption, broken down into estimating probability of occupancy for each cell, $P(X_k = 1|\mathbf{B})$. The authors derive expression for estimated probability that k-th cell is occupied, $q_k = Q(X_k = 1)$, via minimization of Kullback-Liebler divergence between the estimated posterior $Q(\mathbf{X}|\mathbf{B})$ and the "true" posterior $P(\mathbf{X}|\mathbf{B})$. Here, we write the expression from [10] in a bit more general form:

$$q_k = \frac{1}{1 + \exp\{\lambda_k + \sum_c \mathcal{O}_c(k, \mathbf{X})\}} \quad (1)$$

where λ_k is log-ratio of the prior probabilities,

$$\lambda_k = log \frac{P(X_k = 0)}{P(X_k = 1)} \quad (2)$$

and $\mathcal{O}_c(k, \mathbf{X})$ is a term that encapsulates all information from the c-th camera about the occupancy of k-th cell:

$$\mathcal{O}_c(k, \mathbf{X}) = E_Q\{\log P(B_c \mid \mathbf{X}) \mid X_k = 0\} - E_Q\{\log P(B_c \mid \mathbf{X}) \mid X_k = 1\} \quad (3)$$

In the above equation, $E_Q\{\cdot\}$ denotes the expectation under the approximation $\mathbf{X} \sim Q$. In the original formulation, B_c denotes binary image obtained from view c using background subtraction, however Equation (3)is general enough to allow inclusion of any sensor modality

For visual sensors (cameras), a generative model that relates the values of $\mathbf{X}$ to the input binary images is used; at each iteration step, for each view, it generates a synthetic image from the currently estimated values of $\mathbf{X}$. The authors define a normalized pseudo-distance between the input binary image B_c and a synthetic image A_c, which roughly corresponds to pixel overlap between the two. The conditional distribution is then modeled as $P(B_c \mid \mathbf{X}) = \frac{1}{Z} e^{-\Psi(B_c, A_c)}$ where $\Psi(B_c, A_c)$ denotes the pseudo-distance between the images. In order to make the problem solvable, the following approximation is made under assumptions that are detailed in [10]:

$$E_Q\{\Psi(B_c, A_c) \mid X_k = \xi\} \approx \Psi(B_c, E_Q(A_c \mid X_k = \xi)) \quad (4)$$

The term in Equation (3) therefore becomes:

$$\mathcal{O}_c(k, \mathbf{X}) = \log \frac{e^{-\Psi(B_c, E_Q\{A_c \mid X_k = 0\})}}{e^{-\Psi(B_c, E_Q\{A_c \mid X_k = 1\})}} = \Psi(B_c, E_Q\{A_c \mid X_k = 1\}) - \Psi(|B_c, E_Q\{A_c \mid X_k = 0\}) \quad (5)$$

The conditional synthetic images $E_Q(A_c|X_k = \xi)$, $\xi = \{0, 1\}$ correspond to the average synthetic images $E_Q\{A_c\}$ with q_k forced to 0 and 1, respectively. The first case represents the hypothesis that the k-th cell is vacant, and the second that it occupied.

For each frame, a set of anonymous detections is obtained in the form of cells with high resulting probability of occupancy. These are linked into trajectories using K-Shortest Paths (KSP) tracker [12], which formulates the tracking task as a global optimization problem on a Directed Acyclic Graph, resulting in a convex optimization function. The obtained trajectories inherently have no identities; these must be assigned manually, for example using the identity of a person that the trajectory was initialized on. This is state-of-the-art identification-by-tracking, since linking is based solely on spatio-temporal proximity. Linking is performed off-line and in batch manner.

To capture video, we use Axis P1346 IP cameras (http: //www.axis.com /products/cam_pl346) with wide-angle lenses. Therefore, lens distortion is first calibrated and corrected using OCamCalib toolbox [45] and then intrinsic and extrinsic parameters are calibrated on rectified images using Camera calibration toolbox for Matlab [46]. The binary foreground images are obtained using implementation of background subtraction algorithm [47,48] provided by OpenCV library. We use publicly-available implementations of POM (http://cvlab.epfl.ch/software/pom) and KSP algorithm (http: //cvlab.epfl.ch /software/ksp).

For computer-vision-based system, the data capture frequency is limited only by cameras' frame-rates, in our case 20 frames per second. This is also the highest possible temporal resolution of the position data, which is achievable by offline processing. Since the detection algorithm relies on back-projection, its speed depends both on the number of locations (occupancy map resolution) and the size of input images. For illustration, times required to process a single four-view frame with grid resolutions 25 cm (899 locations) and 10 cm (5,396 locations) are listed in Table 2. Since the algorithm uses very simple appearance model, there is no significant change in result as images are scaled down in order to gain processing speed. The tracking step is applied in batch mode, therefore all data processing is assumed to be performed off-line, with position update frequency of 20 Hz.

Table 2. Time required for constructing an occupancy map with resolution 25 cm (899 locations) and 10 cm (5,396 locations, respectively) from four views as the images are scaled down. Measurements were performed on computer with Intel® Core™ i7 950 CPU, clocked at 3.07 GHz, and 18 GB RAM, using single-threaded POM implementation.

Image size	Processing time [s]	
	25 cm grid	10 cm grid
2,048 × 1,536	6.37	16.77
1,024 × 768	1.54	4.10
512 × 384	0.34	1.07
256 × 192	0.08	0.31
128 × 96	0.03	0.15

4. FUSION OF SYSTEMS

In this section, we present the fusion of both systems that were introduced in Section 3. The most obvious advantage of the radio-based system is that it provides detections with reliable identity information, even though their localization might be relatively poor. On the other hand, anonymous camera-based detections are generally better localized, although they occasionally suffer from gross errors. Therefore, the logical way to fuse both systems is to combine the best of both worlds: good camera-based localization and reliable radio-based identities. This is achieved in two stages. In the first stage, described in Section 4.1, we improve anonymous detection and localization of camera-based algorithm by adding location information from the radio system. The resulting anonymous detections are then augmented with identity information from radio tags in the second stage, which is described in Section

4.1. Improvement of Anonymous Detection and Localization

The first fusion stage aims to improve anonymous detection and localization. We use the approach from our prior work [41] and expand it by offering a different, more formal view on how it operates. The idea of the approach is to anonymize detections from radio-based system and fuse them directly into the POM algorithm in order to reduce the number of gross errors (false positive and false negative detections) it produces. This is done by introducing additional data term, $\mathcal{O}_{radio}(k,\mathbf{X})$, in Equation (1):

$$q_k = \frac{1}{1 + \exp\{\lambda_k + \mathcal{O}_{radio}(k, \mathbf{X}) + \sum_c \mathcal{O}_c(k, \mathbf{X})\}} \quad (6)$$

The term $\mathcal{O}_{radio}(k,\mathbf{X})$ encapsulates all radio system's information about k-th cell's occupancy. Generally, it is of form for sensor data terms from Equation (3), however, since we model it as being independent of currently estimated probabilities **X**, it is simplified to:

$$\mathcal{O}_{radio}(k, \mathbf{X}) = \mathcal{O}_{radio}(k) = \log \frac{P(R \mid X_k = 0)}{P(R \mid X_k = 1)} = -\log \omega_k \quad (7)$$

where *R* denotes information from the radio system. As per [41], we model the inverse of the likelihood ratio in the above equation as:

$$\omega_k = \frac{P(R \mid X_k = 1)}{P(R \mid X_k = 0)} = \alpha \cdot \max_t \{G_t(x_k, y_y)\} + \beta \quad (8)$$

where G_t is a Gaussian centered on the coordinates of tag *t* detection, (x_t, y_t), and evaluated at the center of the cell*k*, (x_k, y_k):

$$G_t(x_k, y_k) = e^{-\frac{(x_k - x_t)^2 + (y_k - y_t)^2}{2\sigma_t^2}} \quad (9)$$

We can see from Equation (6) that, since they are both independent from currently estimated probablities **X**, we can combine terms λ_k and $\mathcal{O}_{radio}(k)$ into a new log prior ratio term:

$$\lambda_k' = \lambda_k \cdot \mathcal{O}_{radio}(k) = log \frac{P(X_k = 0)}{P(X_k = 1)} \cdot (-\log \omega_k) = \log \frac{P(X_k = 0)}{\omega_k \cdot P(X_k = 1)} \quad (10)$$

Let ρ_k denote the old prior, $\rho_k = P(X_k = 1)$, and ρ'k the new prior, ρ'k=P'(Xk=1):

$$\lambda_k' = \log \frac{1 - \rho_k'}{\rho_k'} = \log \frac{1 - \rho_k}{\omega_k \cdot \rho_k} \quad (11)$$

From Equation (11), we can derive the expression for the new occupancy prior for *k*-th cell:

$$\rho_k^{'} = \frac{\omega_k \cdot \rho_k}{1 - \rho_k(1 - \omega_k)} \tag{12}$$

Therefore, we can see the proposed fusion of information from radio-based system as introduction of non-uniform priors, with high values in cells close to locations where radio tags are detected and low values in cells far away from such locations. Figure 2(a) shows the value of likelihood ratio ω_k from Equation (8) as the distance from a radio tag increases. We use the parameters from [41]: $\alpha = 12, \beta = 0.5$ and default uniform prior for POM, $\rho_k = 0.01$. From the results presented in Section 6.2, we have estimated $\sigma_t = 1/3$ m. Figure 2(b) shows the resulting prior value ρ'k from Equation (12). As can be seen, the chosen parameters result in prior that is, compared with the static uniform prior, roughly eleven times higher in cells that contain radio system tags, and roughly halved for cells that are far away from cells containing radio tags.

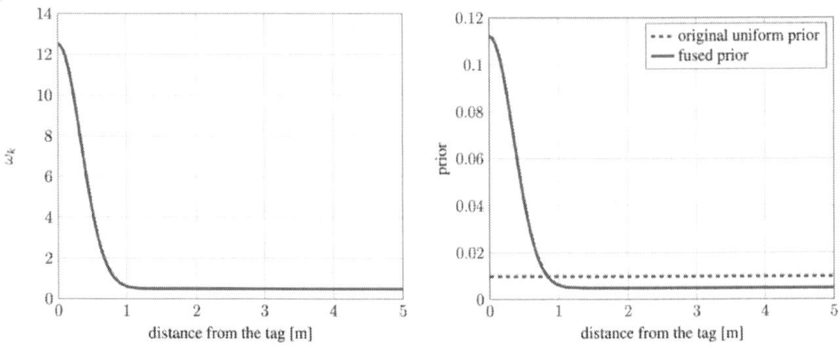

(a) value of likelihood ratio ω_k

(b) value of prior $\rho_k^{'}$

Figure 2. The value of likelihood ratio ω_k and resulting fused prior.

Consequently, given the same visual evidence, a cell will more likely be recognized as occupied when a radio tag is present in its vicinity In such fusion scheme, the majority of information required for detection is provided by the cameras, whereas information from radio system increases robustness. In cases when the ambiguity of visual information causes the algorithm to favor convergence to an incorrect solution, yet there is also sufficient visual evidence for the correct solution, the modified prior helps the algorithm to converge to the correct solution. On the other hand, even if information from radio system is incorrect, it does not disrupt the algorithm's convergence to the correct solution, as long as visual information is good.

4.2. Tracking by Identification

In the second stage, we augment the obtained anonymous detections with identity information from radio tags. As shown in Section 3, radio tags offer reliable identity information, while their localization might be relatively poor. Conversely, computer-vision-based system produces well-localized anonymous detections, with some gross errors corrected by the first stage of fusion, described in Section 4.1.

The augmentation of anonymous detections with identity information is done on frame-by-frame basis. At each time instant, the first stage of fusion results in P anonymous detections, comprising their coordinates on ground plane: danoni=(xanoni,yanoni); $i = 1...P$. Similarly, radio system produces R identified detections, consisting of coordinates on ground plane and identity information, denoted by γ: dradioj=(xradioj,yradioj,γradioj); $j = 1...R$. We find optimal assignment between both sets of detections based on their spatial configuration. We construct a cost matrix M with costs of assigning each detection danoni to each detection dradioj, based on Euclidean distance between them, and find optimal assignment using Hungarian method [49]:

$$\begin{array}{c|ccc} M & \mathbf{d}_1^{anon} & \dots & \mathbf{d}_P^{anon} \\ \hline \mathbf{d}_1^{radio} & m_{11} & \dots & m_{1P} \\ \vdots & \vdots & \ddots & \vdots \\ \mathbf{d}_R^{radio} & m_{R1} & \dots & m_{RP} \end{array} \tag{13}$$

$$m_{ij} = \|\mathrm{d}_i^{anon} - \mathrm{d}_j^{radio}\| = \sqrt{(x_i^{anon} - x_j^{radio})^2 + (y_i^{anon} - y_j^{radio})^2} \tag{14}$$

This assumes that although individual radio tags might be poorly localized, their overall spatial configuration remains similar to that of the anonymous detections, which turns out to be a reasonable assumption most of the time. We obtain new identified detections in following way:

- For each assigned pair $(\mathbf{d}_j^{radio}, \mathbf{d}_i^{anon})$, we augment coordinates of $\mathbf{d}_i^{anon}$ with identity from $\mathbf{d}_j^{radio}$.
- For all unassigned $\mathbf{d}_i^{anon}$ (happens when $R > P$), their original coordinates are used.
- All unassigned $\mathbf{d}_i^{anon}$ (happens when $R < P$) are discarded as false positives, as our system assumes that all individuals wear radio tags. In a different application, for example an intruder detection system, this information could be used differently.

The above procedure results in *R* new identified detections:

$$\mathbf{d}_j^{result} = \begin{cases} (x_i^{anon}, y_i^{anon}, \gamma_j^{radio}) & \text{if } \mathbf{d}_j^{radio} \text{ is assigned; } (\mathbf{d}_j^{radio}, \mathbf{d}_i^{anon}) \\ (x_j^{radio}, y_j^{radio}, \gamma_j^{radio}) & \text{otherwise} \end{cases} \tag{15}$$

$$j = 1 \ldots R \tag{16}$$

These frame-by-frame identified detections can either be used on their own, or additionally post-processed by applying a tracking step to smooth the resulting trajectories and correct possible gross errors, as we illustrate in Section 6.4. In this case, each sequence of identified detections is separately linked into an identified trajectory, thereby performing tracking by identification.

5. EVALUATION METHODOLOGY

In this section, we present our evaluation methodology, which is based on 2-D localization error on ground plane. We believe this is appropriate for evaluating person detection and tracking systems that perform localization in the world coordinate system, even for approaches that are based solely on computer vision. Evaluation with bounding box overlap, as suggested by [44], is suitable only for monocular approaches that perform detection and tracking in the image plane. It is less suitable for multi-view approaches that perform detection and tracking in world coordinate system, where such an evaluation would favor approaches whose appearance model (*i.e.*, the size of bounding boxes) matches that of the ground-truth annotations. This might not be fair, as due to multi-view geometry, better-fitting bounding boxes in individual image planes might not necessarily mean better localization on the ground plane. Furthermore, it is specific to computer-vision-based approaches and does not allow evaluation of approaches based on other sensor modalities. It is worth noting that MOT metrics, based on 2-D localization error on ground plane, have been used in certain tasks of CLEAR evaluation, such as 3-D visual person tracking [43].

Our evaluation methodology is based on the same idea as the general formulation of the MOT metrics. At each time instant, we wish to find mapping between given detections and ground-truth annotations, and then estimate both the localization error and the amount of missing and false positive detections. However, in contrast to Multiple-Object Tracking Accuracy (MOTA) metric, which merges statistics for all error types into a single number, we report statistics for each error type separately. We believe this both offers better insight into system's performance and also allows easier comparison; it should be up to the person performing the comparison to compute the single-number metric from all the components and weight them according to the requirements of specific application. Furthermore, we find the mapping between detections and ground-truth annotations using different cost functions, each resulting in a mapping that reveals a different aspect of a system:

- *detection*: does the system correctly determine the number of individuals in a room (*i.e.*, are there any false positive and missing detections)
- *localization*: how well does the system determine positions of detected individuals
- *identification*: how well does the system determine/maintain identities of detected individuals (if it performs identification at all)

As shown in the following subsections, the three aspects are not always completely de-coupled. For example, a co-occurring false positive and false negative detection cannot be distinguished from a detection with a gross localization error. Similarly, identity switches also manifest themselves as gross localization errors.

5.1. Evaluation for Systems that Perform Anonymous Detection and Localization

A system that performs anonymous detection and localization is concerned only with recovering correct number of individuals in the room, along with their positions. Such system can be used in applications where positions of individuals are important, but their identities are not, for example in person counting or determining which locations are most frequented.

At each time instant (e.g., a video frame), the system produces *D* anonymous detection hypotheses, comprising their 2-D coordinates on the ground plane: $\mathrm{d}_i = (x_i^d, y_i^d);\ i = 1 \ldots D$. Similarly, we have a group of *G* anonymous ground-truth annotations on the ground plane: $\mathrm{g}_j = (x_j^g, y_j^g); j = 1 \ldots G$. Since we do not have any identity information that could be used for assigning detections to ground-truth points, we find an optimal assignment based on their spatial configuration. We construct a cost matrix *C*, whose elements describe the cost of assigning each detection d_i to each ground-truth point g_j:

$$\begin{array}{c|ccc} C & \mathbf{d}_1 & \dots & \mathbf{d}_D \\ \hline \mathbf{g}_1 & c_{11} & \dots & c_{1D} \\ \vdots & \vdots & \ddots & \vdots \\ \mathbf{g}_G & c_{G1} & \dots & c_{GD} \end{array} \tag{17}$$

Different cost functions can be used to obtain assignments that reveal different aspects of the system. In this paper, we define three different cost functions, and refer to their use for evaluation as using *Metric A*, *Metric B*and *Metric C*. The first two are presented in this subsection, whereas the third one is presented in the next one. Primarily, all three cost functions are based on the Euclidean distance between a detection and a ground-truth point:

$$c^A_{ij} = c^A(\mathbf{d}_i, \mathbf{g}_j) = \|\mathbf{d}_i - \mathbf{g}_j\| = \sqrt{(x^d_i - x^g_j)^2 + (y^d_i - y^g_j)^2} \tag{18}$$

The optimal assignment, which minimizes the overall assignment cost, can be found using Kuhn-Munkres algorithm (Hungarian method) [49]. If matrix C is non-square (*i.e., $D \neq G$*), it should be augmented to square matrix by introducing dummy elements, which is often already handled by the algorithm implementations. After running the algorithm and obtaining the optimal assignment, the unassigned detections are considered to be false positive (phantom) detections and the unassigned ground-truth points are considered to be missing (false negative) detections. For assigned detection/ground-truth pairs, their distances c_{ij} correspond to the resulting localization error. From now on, we refer to use of cost function c^A from Equation (18) for constructing assignments as *Metric A*. Examples of assignments with a false positive and a false negative detection are shown in Figure 3.

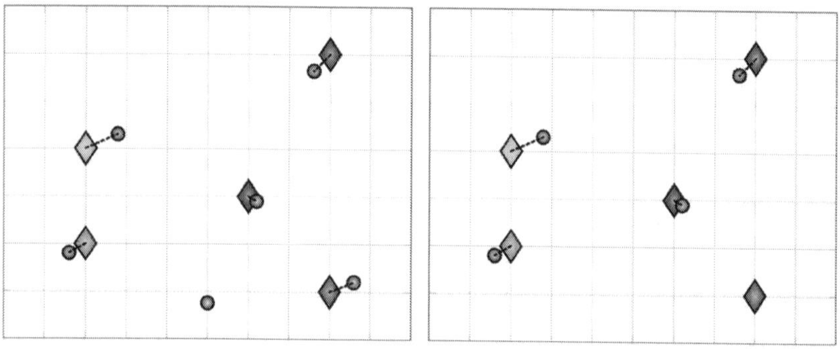

(a) A *phantom* (false positive) detection. (b) A *missing* (false negative) detection.

Figure 3. Examples of assignments obtained with proposed evaluation methodology, illustrating a false positive (**a**), and a false negative detection (**b**). Diamonds represent ground-truth points and gray circles represent anonymous detections. The dotted black lines denote assigned pairs.

Detection and localization errors cannot always be clearly distinguished. When using the cost function c^A fromEquation (18), a co-occurrence of a false positive and a missing detection manifests itself as a large localization error (Figure 4(a)), sometimes even affecting the whole assignment (Figure 5(a)). To mitigate this issue, we can modify the cost function to include gating. Whenever the distance between a detection and a ground-truth point exceeds a certain threshold, the cost is set to ∞, which means that the assignment algorithm is prevented from assigning that pair:

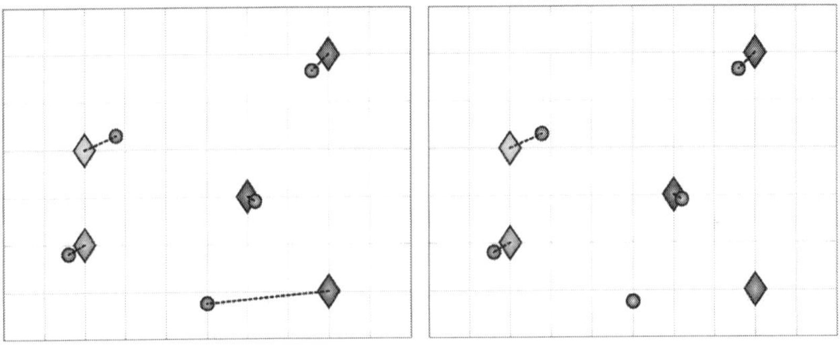

(**a**) Assignment under *Metric A*. (**b**) Assignment under *Metric B*.

Figure 4. An illustration of co-occurring false positive and false negative detection. Since detections are anonymous, such detection errors are indistinguishable from gross localization errors. Evaluation using different cost functions for constructing assignments reflects this error in different ways. Under *Metric A*, the error manifests itself as a large localization error, as shown in (**a**). Under *Metric B*, the error manifests itself as a pair of false positive and false negative detections, as shown in (**b**).

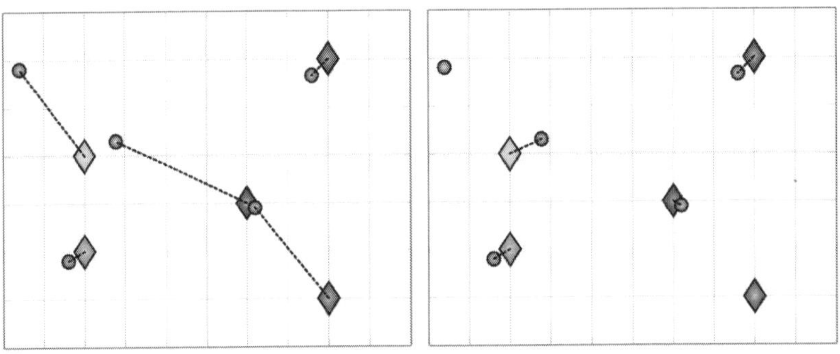

(**a**) Assignment under *Metric A*. (**b**) Assignment under *Metric B*.

Figure 5. An illustration of a situation when co-occurring false positive and false negative detection affect whole assignment under *Metric A* (**a**). In such cases, *Metric B* results in more intuitive assignment, shown in (**b**).

$$c_{ij}^{B} = c^{B}(\mathbf{d}_i, \mathbf{g}_j) = \begin{cases} \|\mathbf{d}_i - \mathbf{g}_j\| & \text{if } \|\mathbf{d}_i - \mathbf{g}_j\| \leq T_d \\ \infty & \text{otherwise} \end{cases} \tag{19}$$

Modified assignments, obtained using the above cost function, which we refer to as *Metric B*, are shown in Figure 4(b) and Figure 5(b). Under *Metric B*, gross localization errors contribute to false positive and false negative statistics instead of localization error statistics.

The result of evaluation using either *Metric A* or *Metric B* includes the false positive and false negative statistics, and the localization error statistics. The latter can be given either in the form of mean error and standard deviation, or in the form of (cumulative) distribution plot. If ground-truth points have identities, the false negative statistics can be computed on per-person basis, whereas for false positives, only overall statistics can be provided, since we cannot tell to which person a phantom detection belongs. It should be noted that differences in update frequencies between systems can also be accounted for via localization error, if evaluation is performed at the frequency of the fastest system and positions from slower systems are held until new ones are obtained.

5.2. Evaluation for Systems that Perform Detection, Localization and Identification

In addition to coordinates on ground plane, systems that perform detection, localization and identification, either in form of tracking or on frame-by-frame basis, also include identity information γ in their detection hypotheses: $\mathbf{d}_i = (x_i^d, y_i^d, \gamma_i^d); i = 1 \ldots D$. For evaluation, identity information must be supplied by ground-truth annotations as well: $\mathbf{g}_j = (x_j^g, y_j^g, \gamma_j^g)$. One way to obtain the mapping is to directly assign closest detections and ground-truth points with same identities, which is formally the same as using the following cost function, which we refer to as *Metric C*:

$$c_{ij}^{C} = c^{C}(\mathbf{d}_i, \mathbf{g}_j) = \begin{cases} \|\mathbf{d}_i - \mathbf{g}_j\| & \text{if } \gamma_i^d = \gamma_j^g \\ \infty & \text{otherwise} \end{cases} \tag{20}$$

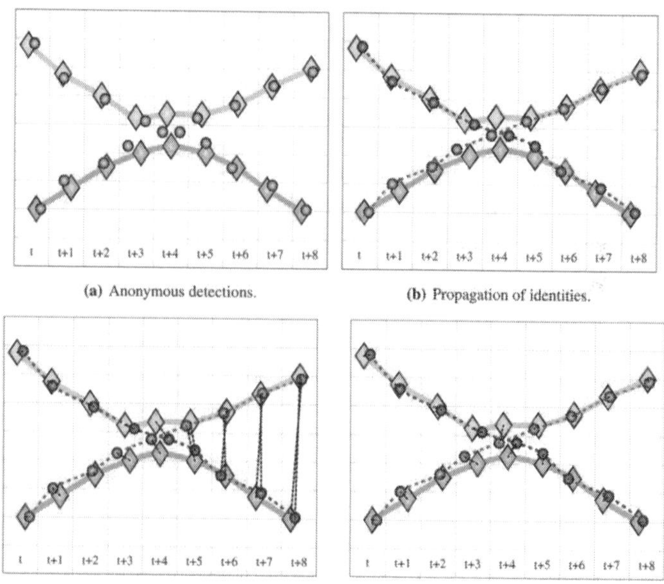

(a) Anonymous detections. (b) Propagation of identities.

(c) Assignment under *Metric C.* (d) Assignment under *Metric B.*

Figure 6. An illustration of a propagated identity switch occurring during identification by tracking. (**a**) shows ground-truth trajectories of two individuals (diamonds) and resulting anonymous detections (gray circles). When individuals come close together, localization becomes difficult. (**b**) shows identification by tracking, *i.e.*, propagation of identities along tracks. Due to poor localization results, identity switch occurs at time instant $t + 4$ and is propagated further on. (**c**) and (**d**) show evaluation under *Metric C* and *Metric B* (cost functions c^C and c^B from Equations (20) and (19)), respectively. Resulting assignments are denoted by black dotted lines. Under *Metric C*, a propagated identity switch directly manifests itself as localization error. Under *Metric B*, identities of assigned pairs are compared after spatially-optimal assignment is obtained, and confusion matrix is constructed for detailed analysis.

In the resulting assignment, spurious multiple detections with same identity contribute to false positive detection counter, and missing detections to missing detection counter; since identity information is available both for detections and ground-truth points, per-person statistics can be obtained. Propagated identity switches manifest themselves as large localization error, as shown in Figure 6(c).

Even more detailed evaluation is possible using *Metric B* (cost function c^B from Equation (19)), under which each detection is assigned to its closest ground-truth point, regardless of their identities (Figure 6(d)). This way, the resulting localization error reflects only system's (anonymous) localization performance. Then, identities of assigned detections and ground-truth points are compared, resulting in a confusion matrix—for an example, see Section 6.4. Unassigned detections contribute to "phantom detections" row and unassigned ground-truth points contribute to "missing detections" column. The rows of confusion matrix sum up to the number of all ground-truth points with corresponding identities, whereas columns sum up to the number of all detections with corresponding identities. Therefore, per-person precision and recall can be obtained by taking diagonal value and dividing it by row or column sum, respectively. The non-diagonal elements show how often a system mistook a given person for someone else.

Note that confusion matrix also allows computation of MOTA metric components. The ratio of misses can be computed as the sum of missing detections column over number of all detections (sum of all rows of confusion matrix). Similarly, ratio of false positives can be computed as the sum of phantom detections row over number of all detections. The ratio of instantaneous identity mismatches cannot be computed, as the proposed methodology has no notion of tracking; however, the ratio of global identity mismatches, proposed to be used instead by [13], can be computed as the sum of all non-diagonal elements over number of all detections.

6. EXPERIMENTAL RESULTS

We validate the proposed tracking-by-identification system on a challenging indoor dataset, which we describe in Section 6.1. First, in Section 6.2, we separately evaluate detection and localization performance of each subsystem. Results of this evaluation have been used for summarized comparison in Table 1, which also served as the baseline for the fusion of both subsystems. This is followed by results for fusing both subsystems with the aim of improving anonymous detection and localization in Section 6.3, while the whole proposed tracking-by-identification system is evaluated in Section 6.4.

6.1. Dataset

To the best of our knowledge, there is no publicly-available dataset comprising video streams from multiple calibrated video cameras and data stream from a radio-based localization system. Therefore we captured and annotated a challenging dataset ourselves. As this is the first dataset of its kind, we make it publicly-available for other researchers to use [5].

We captured the dataset by placing four Ubisense sensors and four Axis P1346 IP cameras into a 8.0 × 7.5 m room (Figure 7), at height 2.2 m.

The views from cameras are shown in Figure 8. The room represents a realistically cluttered indoor environment, which is challenging both for radio-based and camera-based person localization. On one hand, difficulties in accurate and reliable camera-based position estimation arise due to occlusions of individuals, both among themselves and by inanimate objects, such as office furniture. On the other hand, the presence of radio-reflective metallic surfaces, in conjunction with obstacles, leads to multipath-related problems in radio-based localization.

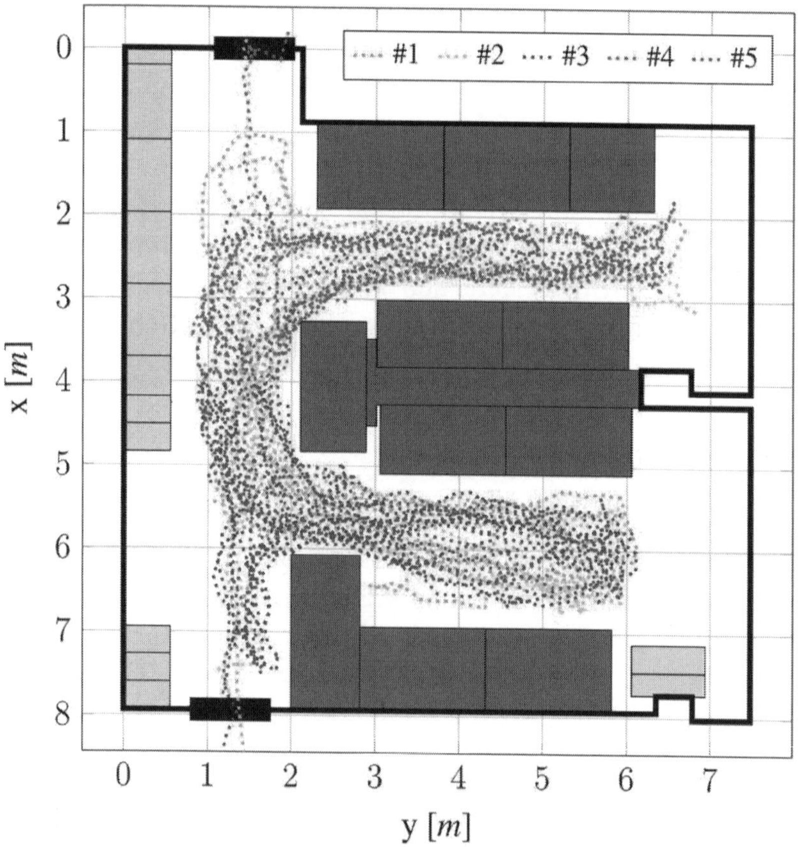

Figure 7. Top view of the room with ground-truth trajectories of the five individuals.

Figure 8. The views from all four cameras. Original images are shown in top row. We use images with lens distortion calibrated and corrected, as shown in the bottom row.

Cameras and radio localization system were time-synchronized using a Network Time Protocol (NTP) server. Video from all four cameras was streamed at resolution 2,048 × 1,536 and 20 frames per second, and stored to hard drive using H.264 video codec. As indicated in Section 3.2, we downsampled the video streams to 512 × 384 before using them with POM for performance reasons. However, capturing the dataset in high definition broadens the possibilities for its further use.

Location events from the radio-based localization system were also stored in a file together with timestamps of their occurrence. The videos were later manually synchronized using timestamps printed on top of the frames, which are also used to associate radio tag location events with individual frames. Ground truth was annotated manually, by clicking on individuals' heads in each view and, using calibration information, reconstructing their 3-D coordinates.

The scenario of the dataset involves five people, equipped with radio tags, walking around the room. At frame #231, individuals begin to enter the room, and by frame #551, all five of them are inside. After walking around for roughly two minutes, they begin to leave at frame #2861. By frame #3211, everyone has left the room and additional lights have been turned on, changing the illumination. Individuals begin to re-enter the room at frame #3481, and by #3721 everyone is inside again. After walking around for 200 seconds, people begin to remove their radio tags at frame #7761 and then proceed to leave the room.

Since the radio signal penetrates through walls, the radio-based system tends to detect tags even before they enter the room, and localization error makes them appear inside the room. During evaluation, this would result in false positive detections. Therefore, to make the comparison fair, we evaluate only on the portions of dataset where all people are present in the room. Specifically, we split the dataset into two non-overlapping parts. The first part encompasses frames 551–2861, which amounts to approximately two minutes, and is used to evaluate detection and localization performance of subsystems. The second part, consisting of frames 3721–7761 (200 s), is used to evaluate both stages of proposed fusion.

6.2. Evaluation of Subsystems' Detection and Localization

To gain insight into strengths and weaknesses of both subsystems, we separately evaluate each of them. At this point, we are interested only in their detection and localization performance. From their nature, we already know that radio tags carry the identity information, which, in itself, is reliable, whereas camera-based detections provide no identity information unless it is manually assigned to the trajectories produced by the tracker. Evaluation and comparison are performed using methodology from Section 5.1, on the first part of the annotated dataset (frames 551–2861).

We evaluate two occupancy map resolutions: 25 cm, which is used by authors of [10], and 10 cm. In both cases, silhouettes are approximated with rectangles that assume a person's width and height to be 50 cm and 175 cm, respectively. Figure 9 shows obtained precision and recall values when assignments are constructed under *Metric A* and *Metric B*. For the latter, we chose the distance threshold that corresponds to the assumed width of a person, T_d = 0.5 m. The curves for camera-based detection are obtained by varying the σ_{pom} parameter, which controls the desired fitting between the input binary images and back-projected synthetic images, and therefore influences the compromise between resulting occupancy map's precision and recall. Table 3 shows precision, recall and mean localization error for several operating points (σ_{pom} values) of camera-based system and a single operating point of radio-based system.

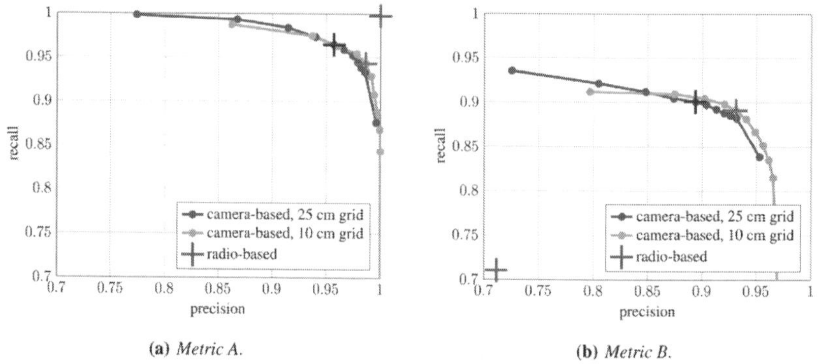

Figure 9. Comparison of camera-based and radio-based detection and localization: precision and recall curves under *Metric A* (**a**) and *Metric B* (**b**). The colored curves represent precision-recall curves for two occupancy map resolutions as σ_{pom} parameter is varied. The crosses on the curves denote the operating point we chose for further experiments, σ_{pom} = 0.005. The red cross denotes the result of radio-based localization system.

Table 3. Comparison of camera-based and radio-based detection and localization: precision, recall and localization error for several operating points (σ_{pom} values) of camera-based system and a single operating point of radio-based system, evaluated under *Metric A* and *Metric B*.

System			Metric A			Metric B		
			precision	recall	localization error mean ± std [m]	precision	recall	localization error mean ± std [m]
radio-based			1.00	1.00	0.44 ± 0.34	0.71	0.71	0.30 ± 0.11
camera-based, at specified σ_{pom} values	25 cm grid	0.003	0.95	0.96	0.22 ± 0.37	0.90	0.90	0.16 ± 0.10
		0.005	0.97	0.94	0.21 ± 0.33	0.92	0.89	0.16 ± 0.10
		0.007	0.98	0.93	0.21 ± 0.31	0.93	0.89	0.16 ± 0.10
		0.009	0.99	0.92	0.20 ± 0.30	0.94	0.88	0.16 ± 0.10
		0.010	0.99	0.92	0.20 ± 0.30	0.94	0.88	0.16 ± 0.10
		0.020	1.00	0.87	0.19 ± 0.29	0.96	0.84	0.16 ± 0.10
	10 cm grid	0.003	0.97	0.95	0.19 ± 0.36	0.92	0.90	0.14 ± 0.10
		0.005	0.99	0.94	0.18 ± 0.32	0.94	0.89	0.13 ± 0.09
		0.007	0.99	0.90	0.16 ± 0.19	0.95	0.86	0.13 ± 0.09
		0.009	1.00	0.86	0.15 ± 0.15	0.96	0.83	0.13 ± 0.09
		0.010	1.00	0.84	0.15 ± 0.15	0.97	0.81	0.13 ± 0.09
		0.020	1.00	0.27	0.13 ± 0.10	0.98	0.27	0.12 ± 0.09

Under *Metric A*, which evaluates detection performance, the radio-based system achieves perfect precision and recall (red cross in Figure 9(a)), since there are practically no false positive and negative detections. However, as indicated by evaluation under *Metric B*, significant portion of these detections are poorly localized, which is reflected in the reduced precision and recall under this metric (red cross in Figure 9(b)). Conversely, it can be seen that false positive and false negative detections are more common in computer-vision-based approach, but at the same time, obtained detections are much better localized. The difference between Figure 9(a) and 9(b) is significantly smaller for computer-vision-based system, while quite obvious for the radio-based one. As expected, occupancy map with higher resolution results in better detection and localization. Based on the results, we chose $\sigma_{pom} = 0.005$ as the operating point for further experiments.

Figure 10 shows cumulative distribution function (CDF) of localization error for radio-based system and camera-based system in the chosen operating point, under *Metric A* and *Metric B*. Again, it can be seen that camera-based detections are much better localized.

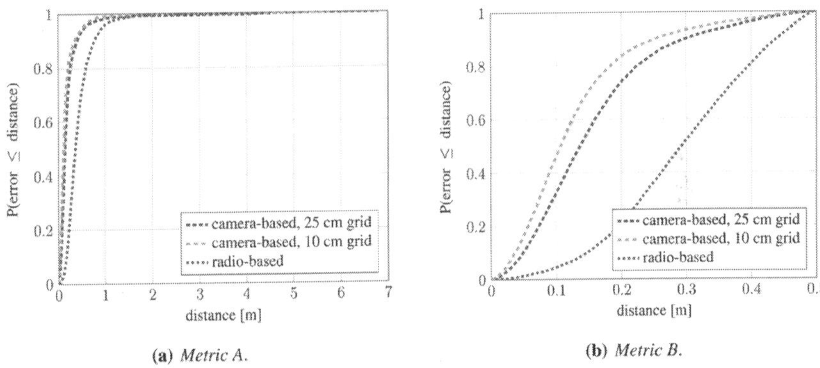

Figure 10. Comparison of camera-based and radio-based detection and localization: cumulative distribution function (CDF) of localization error under *Metric A* (**a**) and *Metric B* (**b**). The steeper the CDF curve and the sooner it reaches 1.0, the better. The operating point for camera-based system is $\sigma_{pom} = 0.005$.

It is worth noting that this is also the case under *Metric B*, which considers only detections within the specified threshold. Therefore, we can conclude that the radio-based system provides very reliable detection, with practically no false positive and negative detections, but with considerable localization error in a cluttered environment. On the other hand, computer-vision-based approach offers better localization, but the detection sometimes suffers from false positives and false negatives. These findings are consistent with those of our previous work [41].

6.3. Improvement of Anonymous Detection and Localization

Here, we evaluate the first stage of fusion, which aims to improve anonymous detection and localization (Section 4.1). We run the original and modified POM algorithm on the second portion of the dataset (frames 3721–7761), using occupancy map resolution of 25 cm. Evaluation is performed using methodology from Section 5.1. Figure 11 shows precision-recall curves as the σ_{pom} parameter is varied. Under *Metric B* (Figure 11(b)), which characterizes system's localization performance, the shift of the data points on the curve indicates improvement in recall and slight improvement in precision. This means that the proposed combination of systems improves localization of anonymous detections, which is also reflected by slight increase in steepness of CDF curves for localization error, shown in Figure 12. An example is shown in Figure 13(a). However, under *Metric A* (Figure 11(a)), which characterizes detection performance, the shift of data points indicates somewhat lowered precision in individual operating points. The reason for this is that the proposed combination of systems sometimes results in two detections in adjacent cells. In cases, such as the one illustrated by Figure 13(b), this results in decreased precision under *Metric A*, but increased recall under *Metric B*. Multiple detections in adjacent cells could be handled by clustering of detections (which was done in [41]), however this would adversely affect situations when people come close together. Instead, we let them to be handled by the next stage of our fusion.

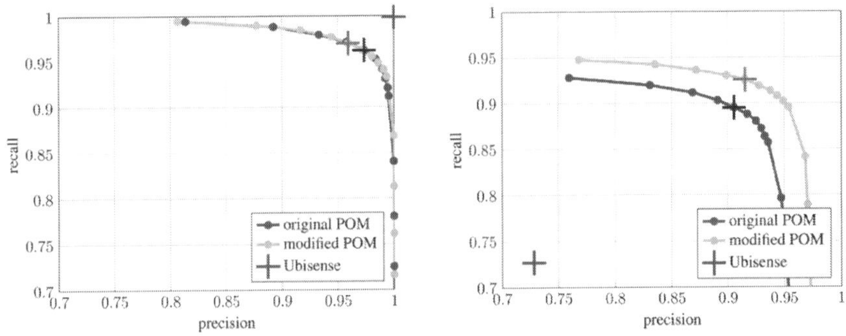

(a) *Metric A.* (b) *Metric B.*

Figure 11. Evaluation of first fusion stage: precision and recall curves under*Metric A* (**a**) and *Metric B* (**b**). The colored curves represent precision-recall curves for original and modified POM as σ_{pom} parameter is varied. In both cases, the occupancy map has resolution of 25 cm. The crosses on the curves denote the operating point σ_{pom} = 0.005. The red cross denotes the result of radio-based localization system.

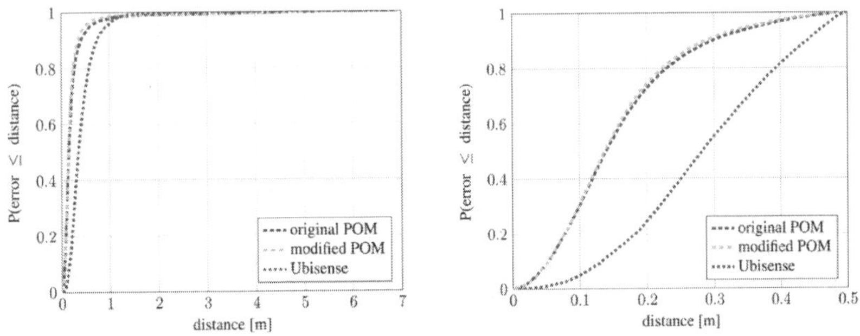

(a) *Metric A.* (b) *Metric B.*

Figure 12. Evaluation of first fusion stage: cumulative distribution function (CDF) of localization error under *Metric A* (**a**) and *Metric B* (**b**). The steeper the CD curve and the sooner it reaches 1.0, the better. Occupancy map resolution is 25 cm and σ_{pom} = 0.005.

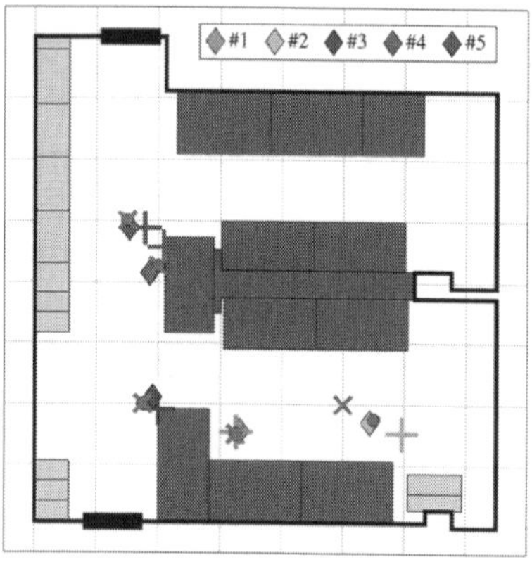

(**a**) Frame #4094

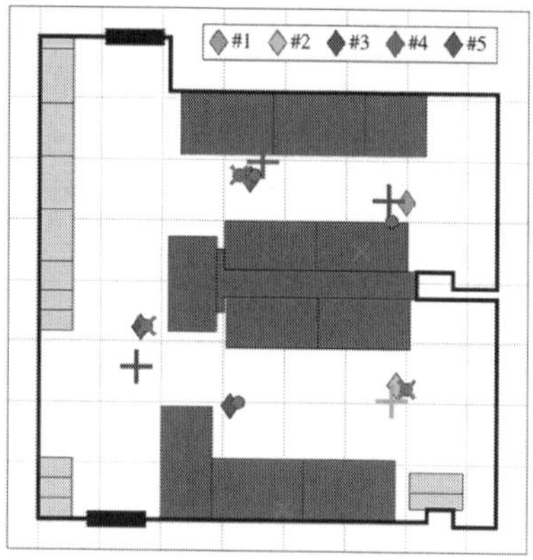

(**b**) Frame #6298

Figure 13. Results of first fusion stage: improved localization of Person #2 (**a**), and improved localization of Persons #1 and #5, with spurious additional detection for Person #4 (**b**). Note the poor localization of radio tag #5 and missing detection of radio tag #1. *Colored diamonds* denote ground-truth points, *colored crosses* denote radio-based detections, *gray X-marks* denote anonymous detections by original POM and *gray circles* denote anonymous detections obtained by modified POM.

6.4. Tracking by Identification

Finally, we evaluate performance of the whole proposed tracking-by-identification system, which consists of KSP tracking step on top of improved anonymous detections that have been augmented with identities from radio tags (Section 4.2). We compare its performance to that of pure radio-based localization and identification, and that of state-of-the-art computer-vision-based identification-by-tracking system, which consists of KSP tracking on top of anonymous POM detections.

For construction of occupancy maps, we use 25 cm grid, and set operating point at σ_{pom} = 0.005. As a result of identification by tracking, when KSP is used on top of anonymous POM detections, the tracker correctly returns five trajectories, to which we assign the identities of the individuals they were initialized on. During tracking by identification, we run KSP tracker separately on top of each sequence of identified detections, which results in five separate identified trajectories. We evaluate these trajectories and the identified detections from the radio-based system using methodology from Section 5.2.

Figure 14 shows CDF of localization error under all three metrics, *Metric A*, *Metric B* and *Metric C*. Evaluating only anonymous detection and localization (*Metric A* and *Metric B*) results in practically identical curves for identification-by-tracking and tracking-by-identification, as shown in Figure 14(a) and 14(b), and is consistent with earlier findings that computer vision offers better localization than radio. However, it can be seen fromFigure 14(c) that identification-by-tracking suffers from propagated identity switches, which manifest themselves as localization error. The radio-based system and the proposed tracking-by-identification system do not have such problems; their localization error CDF curves remain practically unchanged between Figure 14(a) and 14(c).

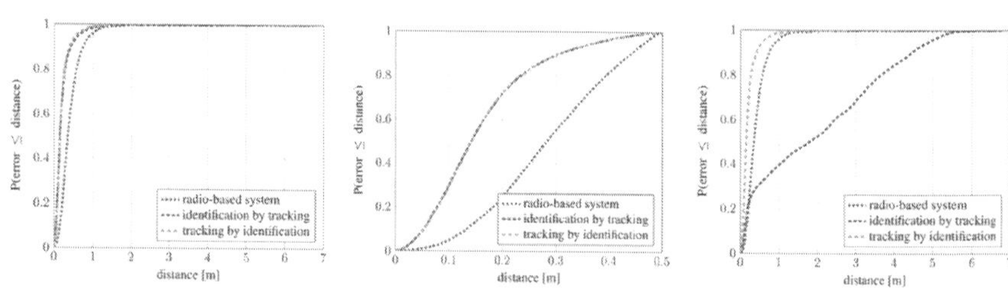

(a) *Metric A.* (b) *Metric B.* (c) *Metric C.*

Figure 14. Evaluation of the proposed tracking-by-identification system: Cumulative Distribution Function (CDF) of localization error under *Metric A*(**a**), *Metric B* (**b**), and *Metric C* (**c**).

Propagated identity switches are also evident from confusion matrices in Table 4. For radio-based localization system (Table 4(a)), the lowered precision and recall are actually the result of poor localization and not identity switches. Most of the errors consist of phantom and missing detections, which are due to enforced threshold T_d = 0.5 m. The rest of non-diagonal elements are from cases when for a person with a given tag, a different tag was localized closer to them than their actual tag was. In case of identification-by-tracking (Table 4(b)), the relatively high values of non-diagonal elements indicate propagated identity switches. There are also occurrences of missing and phantom detections, which are caused by longer periods of missing anonymous detections that serve as input to tracker. These cause the tracker to drift around, causing localization error, which, due to enforced threshold, is captured in missing and phantom detection statistics. Same problems occur with proposed tracking by identification approach (Table 4(c)), as it uses the same tracker. However, significantly lower values of non-diagonal elements indicate that identity switches occur only when people come close, and are not propagated as they disperse again. This confirms that the proposed combination of radio-based and computer-vision-based system successfully prevents propagation of identity switches.

For better illustration, we generated videos of tracking results, which can be found in the paper's supplementary material (http://mvg.fe.uni-lj.si/~rokm/sensors_2012_supplementary/).

Representative frames for radio-based detection, state-of-the-art identification by tracking and proposed tracking by identification are shown in Figure 15.

Table 4. Evaluation of the proposed tracking-by-identification system: comparison with results of radio-based localization and state-of-the-art computer-vision-based identification-by-tracking approach. As described in Section 5.2, we construct confusion matrix using *Metric B* and comparing identities of assigned points. The rows of confusion matrix sum up to number of all ground-truth points with corresponding identities, whereas columns sum up to number of all detections with corresponding identities. Per-person precision and recall are obtained by taking diagonal value and dividing it by row or column sum, respectively.

		DETECTIONS					Missing	Precision	Recall
		#1	#2	#3	#4	#5			
PERSON	#1	**3092**	43	101	0	37	768	0.77	0.77
	#2	61	**3049**	12	0	0	919	0.76	0.75
	#3	15	9	**2048**	0	26	1943	0.51	0.51
	#4	0	0	0	**3071**	8	962	0.76	0.76
	#5	30	8	51	5	**3023**	924	0.75	0.75
Phantom		839	928	1811	965	943		**0.71**	**0.71**

(a) Radio-based system (Ubisense).

		DETECTIONS					Missing	Precision	Recall
		#1	#2	#3	#4	#5			
PERSON	#1	**672**	238	1139	564	899	529	0.17	0.17
	#2	1186	**981**	1049	299	254	272	0.24	0.24
	#3	971	998	**1415**	385	164	108	0.35	0.35
	#4	0	324	0	**1902**	1435	380	0.47	0.47
	#5	924	1338	109	606	**851**	213	0.21	0.21
Phantom		288	162	329	285	438		**0.29**	**0.29**

(b) State-of-the-art *identification by tracking*: tracking on top of anonymous detections.

		DETECTIONS					Missing	Precision	Recall
		#1	#2	#3	#4	#5			
PERSON	#1	**3565**	24	31	2	22	397	0.88	0.88
	#2	76	**3703**	12	0	26	224	0.92	0.92
	#3	77	36	**3661**	0	31	236	0.91	0.91
	#4	14	0	0	**3822**	1	204	0.95	0.95
	#5	24	17	39	7	**3784**	170	0.94	0.94
Phantom		285	261	298	210	177		**0.92**	**0.92**

(c) Proposed *tracking by identification*: tracking on top of identified detections.

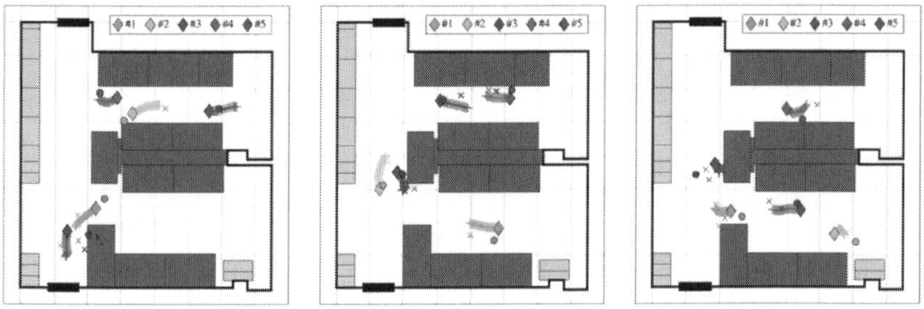

(a) Radio-based system.

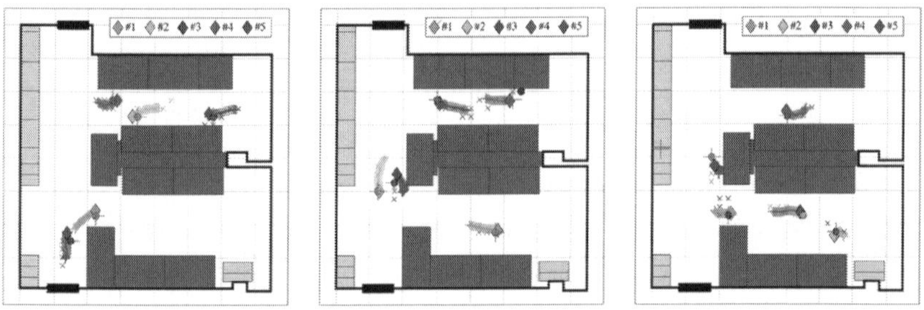

(b) State-of-the-art computer-vision-based identification by tracking. *Gray crosses* denote anonymous detections, the input for the KSP tracker. Note how towards the end of the sequence, most of identities are switched.

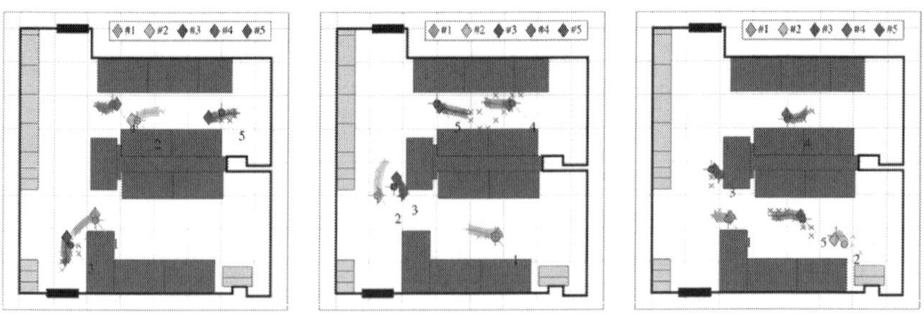

(c) Proposed tracking by identification. *Gray crosses with numbers* denote identified detections, on top of which five KSP instances are run. The proposed approach successfully prevents propagation of identity switches.

Figure 15. Visualization of tracking results for radio-based system (**a**), state-of-the-art computer-vision-based identification by tracking (**b**) and the proposed tracking by identification (**c**). *Colored diamonds* denote ground-truth annotations, while *colored circles* denote identified detections returned by the system. *Colored crosses* and *colored x-signs* are used to visualize 25-frame trails of ground-truth annotations and detections for better impression of their movement. For each system, three frames are shown (from left to right): #3751, #3830 and #7200.

For the sake of completeness, we also performed experiment with 10 cm occupancy map. It should be noted that due to much denser grid (5,396 cells instead of 899), the problem that KSP solves becomes significantly more memory-intensive. For the used test sequence (4,040 frames), the memory consumption rose from 2.7 GB to 16.7 GB. The denser grid yields trajectories with less jitter, and as can be seen from confusion matrices in Table 5, less propagated identity switches in case of identification by tracking. However, they are still present, whereas the proposed tracking by identification successfully prevents them.

Table 5. Comparison of proposed tracking by identification with state-of-the-art identification by tracking, with occupancy map resolution being 10 cm.

		DETECTIONS					Missing	Precision	Recall
		#1	#2	#3	#4	#5			
PERSON	#1	**2192**	1144	13	0	122	570	0.54	0.54
	#2	586	**794**	2451	0	8	202	0.20	0.20
	#3	890	1548	**1502**	0	0	101	0.37	0.37
	#4	11	0	0	**3644**	31	355	0.90	0.90
	#5	15	129	0	6	**3765**	126	0.93	0.93
Phantom		347	426	75	391	115		**0.59**	**0.59**

(a) State-of-the-art *identification by tracking*: tracking on top of anonymous detections.

		DETECTIONS					Missing	Precision	Recall
		#1	#2	#3	#4	#5			
PERSON	#1	**3714**	34	24	0	15	254	0.92	0.92
	#2	96	**3720**	10	0	0	215	0.92	0.92
	#3	26	13	**3879**	0	5	118	0.96	0.96
	#4	2	0	0	**3830**	9	200	0.95	0.95
	#5	4	1	5	8	**3940**	83	0.98	0.98
Phantom		199	273	123	203	72		**0.94**	**0.94**

(b) Proposed *tracking by identification*: tracking on top of identified detections.

7. CONCLUSIONS

We presented a novel person localization system that performs tracking by identification, by combining a commercially available person detection and localization system based on Ultra-Wideband radio technology, and a state-of-the-art computer-vision based system for person detection and tracking with multiple calibrated cameras. The proposed system combines the best of both worlds: good localization offered by computer vision and strong identity information provided by the radio system. Therefore, compared with the radio-based system, the proposed solution offers much better localization, while at the same time addressing the problem of propagated identity switches that are present in the used state-of-the-art computer-vision based system.

Due to use of radio tags, the system is currently suitable for applications where wearing such is permissible; however, we expect that eventual miniaturization of radio tags will allow wider adoption also in various sports applications and that combination of radio-based and computer-vision based localization and identification will become more common due to the complementary nature of both technologies. Furthermore, the presented fusion scheme addresses a conceptual problem of combining a system whose detections are well-localized but not necessarily identified, and a system whose detections are reliably identified, but poorly localized, either because of difficult environment or due to physical limitations of the system. One can envision, for example, combining a computer-vision-based system with a coarse grid of RFID readers located in the floor tiles and passive RFID tags attached to individuals' shoes.

For the purpose of evaluating person detection and localization systems, we introduced a comprehensive metric and evaluation methodology that, using assignments constructed with different cost functions, captures different aspects of a system, namely detection, localization and identification performance. We demonstrated the use of proposed methodology first by comparing detection and localization performance of radio-based and computer-vision-based system, and then by full performance evaluation of both systems and their proposed combination.

Experimental results show the advantage of tracking-by-identification over identification-by-tracking approaches that are commonly found in the field of computer vision. Therefore, our future work will mostly focus on further pursuing this idea, even in purely computer-vision-based approaches, where individuals' identities would be determined from many weakly discriminative visual cues. Such development would on one hand allow completely unobtrusive tracking-by-identification and on the other hand further improve the presented system.

ACKNOWLEDGMENTS

This work was supported by research programs P2-0095 and P2-0098, research project J2-4284 and the research grant 1000-10-310118, all by Slovenian Research Agency.

REFERENCES

1. Hightower, J.; Borriello, G. Location systems for ubiquitous computing. *Computer* **2001**, *34*, 57–66.

2. Yilmaz, A.; Javed, O.; Shah, M. Object tracking: A survey. *ACM Comput. Surv.* **2006**, *38*. Article No. 13.

3. Liu, H.; Darabi, H.; Banerjee, P.; Liu, J. Survey of wireless indoor positioning techniques and systems. *IEEE Trans. Syst. Man Cyber. C Appl. Rev.* **2007**, *37*, 1067–1080.

4. Santiago, C; Sousa, A.; Estriga, M.; Reis, L.; Lames, M. Survey on Team Tracking Techniques Applied to Sports. Proceedings of the 2010 International Conference on Autonomous and Intelligent Systems, Povoa de Varzim, Portugal, 21–23 June 2010; pp. 1–6.

5. MVL Lab5 Dataset. Available online: http://vision.fe.uni-lj.si/research/mvl_lab5/ (accessed on 21 December 2012).

6. Iwase, S.; Saito, H. Parallel Tracking of All Soccer Players by Integrating Detected Positions in Multiple View Images. Proceedings of the 17th International Conference on Pattern Recognition, Cambridge, UK, 23–26 August 2004; Volume 4. pp. 751–754.

7. Xu, M.; Orwell, J.; Jones, G. Tracking Football Players with Multiple Cameras. Proceedings of the 2004 International Conference on Image Processing, Singapore, 24–27 October 2004; Volume 5. pp. 2909–2912.

8. Otsuka, K.; Mukawa, N. Multiview Occlusion Analysis for Tracking Densely Populated Objects Based on 2-D Visual Angles. Proceedings of the 2004 IEEE Computer Society Conference on Computer Vision and Pattern Recognition, Washington, DC, USA, 27 June– 2 July 2004; Volume 1. pp. 90–97.

9. Kristan, M.; Perš, J.; Perše, M.; Kovacic, S. Closed-world tracking of multiple interacting targets for indoor-sports applications. *Comput. Vis. Image Understand* **2009**, *113*, 598–611.

10. Fleuret, F.; Berclaz, J.; Lengagne, R.; Fua, P. Multicamera people tracking with a probabilistic occupancy map. *IEEE Trans. Pattern Anal. Mach. Intell.* **2008**, *30*, 267–282.

11. Khan, S.; Shah, M. Tracking multiple occluding people by localizing on multiple scene planes. *IEEE Trans. Pattern Anal. Mach. Intell.* **2009**, *31*, 505–519.

12. Berclaz, J.; Fleuret, F.; Turetken, E.; Fua, P. Multiple object tracking using K-shortest paths optimization.*IEEE Trans. Pattern Anal. Mach. Intell.* **2011**, *33*, 1806–1819.

13. Ben Shitrit, H.; Berclaz, J.; Fleuret, F; Fua, P. Tracking Multiple People under Global Appearance Constraints. Proceedings of the 2011 IEEE International Conference on Computer Vision, Barcelona, Spain, 6– 13 November 2011; pp. 137–144.

14. Moravec, H.P. Sensor fusion in certainty grids for mobile robots. *AI Magazine* **1988**, *9*, 61–74.

15. Beymer, D. Person Counting Using Stereo. Proceedings of the 2000 Workshop on Human Motion, Austin, TX, USA, 7–8 December 2000; pp. 127–133.

16. Yang, D.; Gonzalez-Banos, H.; Guibas, L. Counting People in Crowds with a Real-Time Network of Simple Image Sensors. Proceedings of the 9th IEEE International Conference on Computer Vision, Nice, France, 14– 17 October 2003; Volume 1. pp. 122–129.

17. Franco, J.S.; Boyer, E. Fusion of Multiview Silhouette Cues Using a Space Occupancy Grid. Proceedings of the 10th IEEE International Conference on Computer Vision, Beijing, China, 17– 20 October 2005; Volume 2. pp. 1747–1753.

18. Delannay, D.; Danhier, N.; De Vleeschouwer, C. Detection and Recognition of Sports (Wo)Men from Multiple Views. Proceedings of the 3rd ACM/IEEE International Conference on Distributed Smart Cameras, Como, Italy, 30 August– 2 October 2009; pp. 1–7.

19. Munoz-Salinas, R. A Bayesian plan-view map based approach for multiple-person detection and tracking.*Pattern Recog.* **2008**, *41*, 3665–3676.

20. Losada, C.; Mazo, M.; Palazuelos, S.; Pizarro, D.; Marrón, M. Multi-camera sensor system for 3D segmentation and localization of multiple mobile robots. *Sensors* **2010**, *10*, 3261–3279.

21. Berclaz, J.; Fleuret, E.; Fua, P. Principled Detection-by-Classification from Multiple Views. Proceedings of the 3rd International Conference on Computer Vision Theory and Applications, Madeira, Portugal, 22–25 January 2008; Volume 2. pp. 375–382.

22. Alahi, A.; Boursier, Y.; Jacques, L.; Vandergheynst, P. Sport Players Detection and Tracking with a Mixed Network of Planar and Omnidirectional Cameras. Proceedings of the 3rd ACM/IEEE International Conference on Distributed Smart Cameras, Como, Italy, 30 August– 2 October 2009; pp. 1–8.

23. Zhang, X.; Rad, A.B.; Wong, Y.K. Sensor fusion of monocular cameras and laser rangefinders for line-based simultaneous localization and mapping (SLAM) tasks in autonomous mobile tobots. *Sensors* **2012**, *12*, 429–452.

24. Hernandez-Aceituno, J.; Acosta, L.; Arnay, R. Fusion of a variable baseline system and a range finder.*Sensors* **2011**, *12*, 278–296.

25. Musleh, B.; García, F.; Otamendi, J.; Armingol, J.M.; De la Escalera, A. Identifying and tracking pedestrians based on sensor fusion and motion stability predictions. *Sensors* **2010**, *10*, 8028–8053.

26. Baranski, P.; Strumillo, P. Enhancing positioning accuracy in urban terrain by fusing data from a GPS receiver, inertial sensors, stereo-camera and digital maps for pedestrian navigation. *Sensors* **2012**, *12*, 6764–6801.

27. Meingast, M.; Kushwaha, M.; Oh, S.; Koutsoukos, X.; Ledeczi, A.; Sastry, S. Fusion-Based Localization for a Heterogeneous Camera Network. Proceedings of the 2nd ACM/IEEE International Conference on Distributed Smart Cameras, Stanford, CA, USA, 7– 11 September 2008; pp. 1–8.

28. Shivappa, S.; Trivedi, M.; Rao, B. Audiovisual information fusion in human-computer interfaces and intelligent environments: A Survey. *Proc. IEEE.* **2010**, *98*, 1692–1715.

29. Zhang, W.; Cheung, S.; Chen, M. Hiding Privacy Information in Video Surveillance System. Proceedings of the 2005 IEEE International Conference on Image Processing, Genoa, Italy, 11– 14 September 2005; Volume 3. pp. 868–71.

30. Kulyukin, V; Gharpure, C; Nicholson, J.; Pavithran, S. RFID in Robot-Assisted Indoor Navigation for the Visually Impaired. Proceedings of the 2004 IEEE /RSJ International Conference on Intelligent Robots and Systems, Edmonton, Canada, 2– 6 August 2004; Volume 2. pp. 1979–1984.

31. Cerrada, C; Salamanca, S.; Perez, E.; Cerrada, J.; Abad, I. Fusion of 3D Vision Techniques and RFID Technology for Object Recognition in Complex Scenes. Proceedings of the 2007 IEEE International Symposium on Intelligent Signal Processing, Guwahati, India, 28– 29 December 2007; pp. 1–6.

32. Jia, S.; Sheng, J.; Chugo, D.; Takase, K. Human Recognition Using RFID Technology and Sterero Vision. Proceedings of the 2007 IEEE International Conference on Robotics and

Biomimetics (ROBIO 2007), Sanya, China, 15– 18 December 2007; pp. 1488–1493.

33. Marchesotti, L.; Singh, R.; Regazzoni, C. Extraction of Aligned Video and Radio Information for Identity and Location Estimation in Surveillance Systems. Proceedings of the 7th International Conference on Information Fusion, Stockholm, Sweden, 28 June–1 July 2004; pp. 316–321.

34. Cattoni, A.; Dore, A.; Regazzoni, C. Video-Radio Fusion Approach for Target Tracking in Smart Spaces. Proceedings of the 10th International Conference on Information Fusion, Quebec, Canada, 9–12 July 2007; pp. 1–7.

35. Anne, M.; Crowley, J.L.; Devin, V.; Privat, G. Localisation Intra-Bâtiment Multi-Technologies: RFID, Wifi et Vision. Proceedings of the 2nd French-Speaking Conference on Mobility and Ubiquity Computing, Paris, French, June 2005; pp. 29–35.

36. Cucchiara, R.; Fornaciari, M.; Haider, R.; Mandreoli, F; Martoglia, R.; Prati, A.; Sassatelli, S. A Reasoning Engine for Intruders' Localization in Wide Open Areas Using a Network of Cameras and RFIDs. Proceedings of the 2011 IEEE Computer Society Conference on Computer Vision and Pattern Recognition Workshops, Colorado Springs, CO, USA, 20– 25 June 2011; pp. 33–40.

37. Yu, X.; Ganz, A. Global Identification of Tracklets in Video Using Long Range Identity Sensors. Proceedings of the 7th IEEE International Conference on Advanced Video and Signal Based Surveillance, Boston, MA, USA, 29 August– 1 September 2010; pp. 361–368.

38. Yu, X.; Ganz, A. A Calibration Free Hybrid RF and Video Surveillance System for Reliable Tracking and Identification. Proceedings of the 2011 IEEE International

Conference on Technologies for Homeland Security, Waltham, UK, 13- 15 November 2011; pp. 242–247.

39. Gezici, S.; Tian, Z.; Giannakis, G.; Kobayashi, H.; Molisch, A.; Poor, H.; Sahinoglu, Z. Localization via ultra-wideband radios: A look at positioning aspects for future sensor networks. *IEEE Signal Process. Mag.* **2005**,*22*, 70–84.

40. Research & Development Packages—Ubisense. Available online: http:// www.ubisense.net/en /rtls-solutions/research-packages.html (accessed on 21 December 2012).

41. Mandeljc, R.; Perš, J.; Kristan, M.; Kovacic, S. Fusion of Non-Visual Modalities into the Probabilistic Occupancy Map Framework for Person Localization. Proceedings of the 5th ACM/IEEE International Conference on Distributed Smart Cameras, Ghent, Belgium, 23- 26 August 2011; pp. 1–6.

42. Dibitonto, M.; Buonaiuto, A.; Marcialis, G.L.; Muntoni, D.; Medaglia, C.M.; Roli, F. Fusion of Radio and Video Localization for People Tracking. Proceedings of the 2nd International Conference on Ambient Intelligence, Amsterdam, The Netherlands, 16–18 November 2011; pp. 258–263.

43. Bernardin, K.; Stiefelhagen, R. Evaluating multiple object tracking performance: The CLEAR MOT metrics.*J. Image Video Process* **2008**, *2008*, 1–10.

44. Kasturi, R.; Goldgof, D.; Soundararajan, P.; Manohar, V; Garofolo, J.; Bowers, R.; Boonstra, M.; Korzhova, V; Zhang, J. Framework for performance evaluation of face, text, and vehicle detection and tracking in video: Data, metrics, and protocol. *IEEE Trans. Pattern Anal. Mach. Intell.* **2009**, *31*, 319–336.

45. Scaramuzza, D.; Martinelli, A.; Siegwart, R. A Toolbox for Easily Calibrating Omnidirectional Cameras. Proceedings of the 2006 IEEE /RSJ International Conference on Intelligent Robots and Systems, Beijing, China, 9– 15 October 2006; pp. 5695–5701.

46. Bouguet, J.Y. Camera Calibration Toolbox for Matlab. Available online: http://www.vision.caltech.edu/bouguetj/calib_doc / (accessed on 21 December 2012).

47. Zivkovic, Z. Improved Adaptive Gaussian Mixture Model for Cackground Subtraction. Proceedings of the 17th International Conference on Pattern Recognition, Cambridge, UK, 23–26 August 2004; Volume 2. pp. 28–31.

48. Zivkovic, Z.; van der Heijden, F. Efficient adaptive density estimation per image pixel for the task of background subtraction. *Pattern Recog. Lett.* **2006**, *27*, 773–780.

49. Kuhn, H.W. The Hungarian method for the assignment problem. *Nov. Res. Logist.* **2005**, *52*, 7–21.

INDEX